RAINBOW

RAINBOW

THE STORMY LIFE OF JUDY GARLAND
by Christopher Finch

Designed by Will Hopkins

Grosset & Dunlap
Publishers New York

For Chloe

CONTENTS

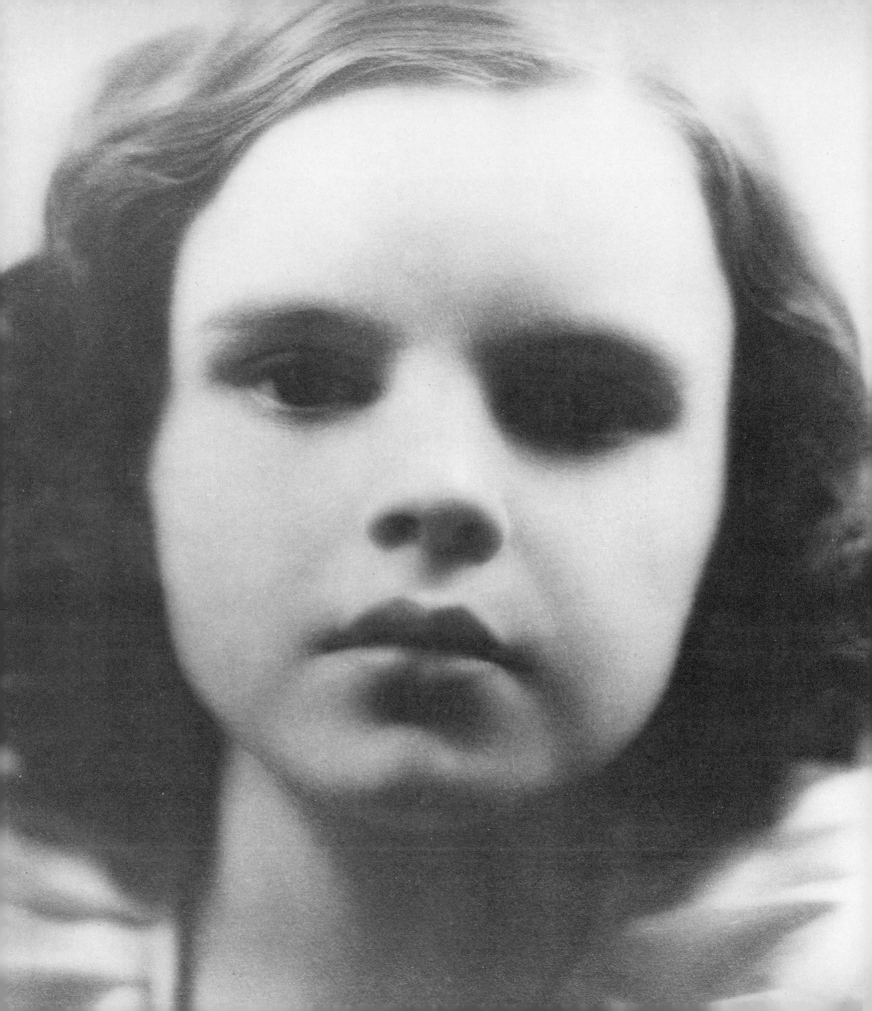

Chapter 1
Debut

Within the emotional deluge of Judy Garland's stage performances, there was one sure moment of calm and equilibrium—the eye of the storm. Wearing her tramp makeup and costume, she would settle cross-legged on the boards and pause before the climax of the show. She had on clown's shoes, baggy pants and an old coat that had once belonged to Wallace Beery (superstitiously, she refused ever to have the coat cleaned). A battered top hat had been thrown aside and she mussed her hair with one hand, clutching a microphone in the other. By this point in the show she was out of breath and sweating. Perspiration streaked the burnt cork smeared on her cheeks and many people chose to believe that she was crying. Yet she was grinning at the same time—one tooth blacked out—and completely composed: a grubby little girl dressed in her father's clothes, counting on her charm to ward off the demons gathering out there in the darkness.

In this moment the tramp disguise became a metaphor for the life she had led and her innocence was redeemed. The years of indignities—whether self-inflicted or otherwise—suddenly coalesced into a sublime dignity that could have been won in no other way.

Judy Garland's life was the basis for every performance she gave—good and bad—but it was Hollywood that provided her with her archetypal images: Dorothy, of course; the tramp, created for *Easter Parade*; the chic, androgynous vamp of her "Get Happy" routine. To understand Judy Garland, one must try to understand Hollywood, and anyone delving into that historical phantasmagoria must sift, like some drunken archeologist, through a glittering garbage heap of myths, half-truths and outright lies. There are facts too, verifiable facts, but the writer must overcome the temptation to ignore them since—in comparison with the gaudiness of the other shards—they sometimes seem bland and commonplace. The ruins are booby-trapped with carefully planted stories, nuggets of misinformation that served

Frances Gumm, Los Angeles, 1932.

some dubious purpose thirty years ago and still lie there, waiting to blow up in the face of the unwary researcher.

Even if he is able to negotiate this minefield, the writer must still be on his guard. Like ancient glass, the anecdotes he pulls from the rubble are apt to have acquired an iridescence that can be attributed to the passage of time. The reminiscences of some survivors are sweetened to the point where they can appeal only to childish palates. Others have recounted their stories with such extreme candor that it becomes difficult to ignore the possibility that some self-serving motive might have deflected memory from its pristine intentions.

As for any story that can be traced back to one of the major studios, it is automatically suspect. Hollywood was in the business of remaking reality. The truth was dispensable.

Stars were dispensable too, as Judy Garland eventually discovered. Hollywood was an arena of power where the strong consumed the weak, usually without malice, seeing themselves as obeying some natural law. Judy Garland had nothing to offer but talent in a society where talent was merely a commodity—a natural resource to be stripped from its clay. She was surrounded by men who had developed the habit of ruthlessness in their dealings with the world at large.

Hollywood destroyed Judy Garland's childhood by trivializing it into oblivion, a process that started the day Metro-Goldwyn-Mayer's publicity department first turned its attention to her. She lacked the stability and security to resist the relentless erosion of fact and, eventually, she came to believe many of the myths invented for her.

When writing about Judy Garland's early life, biographers have—unfortunately—relied heavily on material distributed over the years by M-G-M publicists. This should be taken to include most magazine and newspaper stories written about her during her tenure at Metro, since the information they contain was generally fed, directly or indirectly, from the studio. The other main biographical source has been Judy's own recollections of her childhood, as

20

published in various periodicals. There are occasional moments of honesty in these memoirs, but the overall chain of events she presents does not differ substantially from what will be found in early publicity stories—and this is demonstrably false in many respects. Judy did add one important element, though, when she introduced a villain the studio publicists would not have dared to consider: her own mother.

Judy described her mother as "the real life Wicked Witch of the West"—the archetypal, fire-eating, greedy, ambitious stage matron; a child-devouring monster who was always waiting in the wings.

Before she died, this putative villain offered her own account of Judy's beginnings. By then, she was estranged from her daughter and thoroughly disenchanted with M-G-M, and she wanted to correct some of the misinformation that had been so freely disseminated. She did soften some of the facts, but her version has a realistic basis that is almost totally lacking in Judy's improvisations. The fact that writers and the public have chosen to believe Judy rather than her mother would not matter, perhaps, if it had not also caused innocent people to suffer. But in Hollywood, as in ancient Rome, no public entertainment was considered complete without someone being thrown to the lions.

In 1913 Judy Garland's mother—born Ethel Marion Milne—was employed as house pianist at the Parlor Theater in Superior, Wisconsin. One of the attractions there was a tenor by the name of Frank Avent Gumm. Born in Murfreesboro, Tennessee, he possessed his fair share of southern charm. He had attended Sewanee University and had worked for a while as a court reporter before drifting into show business, very much against the wishes of his family.

At the Parlor Theater Frank and Ethel began to perform duets together, calling themselves Jack and Virginia Lee, Sweet Southern Singers, and on January 11, 1914, they were married. Most accounts of this marriage give the impression that the Gumms immediately settled into a routine of touring the country—or at least the upper Midwest—appearing in bush-league vaudeville houses, grimly hanging on for their big break, settling at last in Grand Rapids, Minnesota, only after they had begun to raise a family. At least one magazine story went so far as to describe their days on the road in detail: the blinking electric sign reflected in a cracked hotel mirror—"Rooms: 50 Cents and Up"—and the miserable supper of cornmeal heated over a dying flame.

The Itasca County *Independent,* one of Grand Rapids' two weekly newspapers, tells us otherwise. On the front page of its edition dated Thursday, March 5, 1914—just a few weeks after the wedding—is a photograph of Frank Gumm and the following news item:

Barlow and Bentz, proprietors of the New Grand Theater, have secured the services of Frank A. Gumm as singer and manager. Mr. Gumm is a native of central Tennessee and is thoroughly acquainted with the show business.

He has just finished an engagement of six months as singer at the Parlor Theater in Superior, Wisc., and for two years previous thereto was manager and singer for the People's Amusement Co., of Portland, Oregon. He possesses an exceptionally pleasing voice and has a large repertoire of the latest song hits.

Mrs. Gumm, who was Miss Ethel Milne of Superior, will take charge of the music at the Grand. Mrs. Gumm is a musician of rare talent and experienced in both vaudeville and motion picture playing. Her method of following the pictures with the piano has been acknowledged everywhere as exceptionally clever and adds great interest to the entertainment at the Grand. Mr. Gumm takes charge today.

Apparently Frank and Ethel decided to take the first offer that would give them some security while allowing them to remain, marginally at least, in "the show business." But the vaudeville career of Jack and Virginia Lee is one myth that should not be blamed on M-G-M since it seems to have been fostered by Frank

Gumm himself—though, needless to say, the blinking sign, the cracked mirror and the tepid cornmeal were later Hollywood glosses.

The village of Grand Rapids stands on the headwaters of the Mississippi River, at the highest point of commercial navigation. Its closest neighbors of any size are the mining towns of the Minnesota Iron Range, but at the time of the Gumms' arrival, Grand Rapids was a center for the logging industry. Timber production had fallen off from the heyday of the 1890s, but there were still log drives on the river. With a population of just under 3,000, Grand Rapids was a tough little town where Slavs, Poles, French Canadians, Swedes, Norwegians and Finns still spoke their native languages. It had a saloon row and a couple of brothels, and—alongside these more traditional forms of entertainment—the movies were beginning to make their mark.

When Frank Gumm took over the management of the New Grand, there was a second movie theater in town—the Gem—but it soon went out of business, partly, we may suppose, because the Gumms provided a better class of live entertainment to supplement the film programs at the New Grand.

Housing was not easy to find and the Gumms stayed, rent free, with the Aiken family—an arrangement that was not unusual at the time. Anyone with musical talent could count on a warm reception in small and relatively isolated communities like Grand Rapids where most entertainment was home grown.

Frank and Ethel seemed to have felt comfortable in Grand Rapids, but they were not looking forward to the Minnesota winter, and toward the end of 1914 they set off for an extended visit to Frank's family in the South. In Chicago, however, Ethel had a bout with "the gripe" and they backtracked to Superior so she could recuperate with her family. By February 22, 1915, they were back in Grand Rapids and a record turnout at the New Grand welcomed them. They stayed at the Aiken home once again, then found a house of their own at what is now the junction of Highway 2 and Second Avenue Northwest, just a few blocks from the theater. Grand Rapids would remain their home for almost a dozen years.

On September 24, 1915, Ethel gave birth to their first child, a daughter who would be christened Mary Jane. On Independence Day, 1917, a second daughter was born. She was given the name Dorothy Virginia, but was called Virginia, a name Ethel was especially partial to.

Three months before Virginia's birth the United States entered the Great War, but Frank Gumm was not conscripted—perhaps because he was the father of two young children, perhaps because of the serious inner ear infection he had suffered from since childhood. Meanwhile, Mr. Barlow had relinquished his interest in the New Grand and Frank had become a full partner with Fred Bentz. He worked the ticket office while Bentz operated the projector. Ethel would generally provide the musical accompaniment for the first show, with Frank taking over at the piano for the second performance. The newspaper advertisements read "Let's go to the Grand Show."

By studying the local news in the *Independent* and the Grand Rapids *Herald-Review,* it's possible to build up a rather clear picture of the Gumms' social life and their position in the community. (Frank supplemented his income from the theater by serving as local editor for the *Independent*.) Certainly they were very active. Frank had been educated at an Episcopal school in Murfreesboro and made himself useful in Episcopal church affairs in Grand Rapids, serving as choirmaster while Ethel played the organ on Sundays. It seems to have been practically impossible to put on a play or a concert or any kind of entertainment without the Gumms. There were many parties and dinners at their home, and they were frequent guests in other households. Both were avid bridge players, and Frank was at one time president of a social organization known as the Pokegama Club, which staged picnics and dances. When a town song was written, it was Frank who was invited to introduce it before a crowd of almost 200 at the Legion Hall:

Grand Rapids, Grand Rapids, where rapid
     waters flow.
Grand Rapids, Grand Rapids, where piney
     breezes blow.
We love your hills and ridges, your river and
     your bridges.
Your Hale, McKinney, Crystal, Forest Lake.
Grand Rapids, Grand Rapids, we love your
     cautious rush.
Grand Rapids, Grand Rapids, your progress
     and your push.
Whate'er you do, we're in it, we're with you to
     the limit.
We're with you for Grand Rapids' sake.

In the fall of 1921 Ethel Gumm found herself pregnant again and the discovery was neither expected nor welcome. The Gumms were on friendly terms with a young man named Marcus Rabwin, the son of a theater owner in the nearby town of Eveleth. They contacted him at the University of Minnesota, where he was studying medicine, to ask if anything could be done to terminate the pregnancy. Rabwin told them he thought they were making a terrible mistake. Apart from the fact that an illegal abortion would be dangerous, he was sure they would regret taking such a drastic step. On consideration, they agreed with him.

On June 10, 1922, the *Independent* noted that Terry's *Uncle Tom's Cabin* tent show

Frances Gumm, age one, in Grand Rapids during the summer of 1923.

would be coming to town—"darky pastimes on the old plantation"—and that the first radio receiver in the vicinity was being erected south of town. It also reported a death from the effects of moonshine.

On this same Saturday morning, at the Itasca Hospital in Grand Rapids, Mrs. Gumm gave birth to her third daughter, Frances Ethel —named for both parents. When Frances Ethel Gumm had become Judy Garland, and was placed under contract by M-G-M, it was decreed that her birth date should be changed to January 10, 1923, so the studio could claim she was twelve years old at the time rather than thirteen. Judy herself tried to persuade Metro publicists that she had been born in Murfreesboro, perhaps because she thought the name sounded romantic, perhaps because she wanted to establish a bond with her father.

Certainly it was not because she had anything against Grand Rapids. She remembered her birthplace as a green, friendly place, and in summer it is intensely green with dense vegetation standing against the water and the sky. Baby Frances was taken home to the Gumms' wood-frame house on a quiet street that ran down to a tranquil lake, and she managed to pass her first two years in relative obscurity, even by local standards. When the weather was good, she liked to play in the sandbox at the side of the house and reportedly greeted people she recognized with noisy enthusiasm. She came to know some of her relatives. John and Eva Milne, her grandparents, visited often, as did Ethel's sister Norma. (Judy Garland's weight problems were not without precedent in the family: Norma once sang in an all-girl group that was called "the beef rack" because of the hefty proportions of its members.) Another sister, Dorothy, had some local reputation as a vocalist and both she and her husband, Harry Glyer, came to Grand Rapids on a number of occasions. There was still another Milne with aspirations as a singer—Jack Milne, who lived in Duluth. Jack's star was on the ascent when he appeared in Grand Rapids in 1923, and he was favorably reviewed by the local press. Soon he would have a radio contract with the Goodrich Tire Company of Duluth, and a new nickname—the Little John McCormack of the Great Northwest. Then there was Fred Milne, who worked for the Great Northern in Hibbing, a little more than thirty miles away, and still another brother, Frank Milne, who visited from St. Paul.

Baby Frances was often taken on trips, especially to Duluth and Superior, where she must have become acquainted with some of her many cousins. Certainly she had every opportunity to become a gregarious child.

The first significant event in the Garland canon occurred on December 26, 1924, when Baby Frances made her theatrical debut at the tender age of two and a half. It was the coldest December anyone could remember; northern Minnesota experienced sub-zero temperatures for fourteen nights in a row. The youngest Gumm's first entrance was made, naturally enough, on the stage of the New Grand, between showings of a Mary Pickford tearjerker entitled *Thru the Back Door.* As Judy Garland recalled the occasion for Joe Hyams in a *McCall's* article dated April 1957, she saw her sisters performing onstage and wanted to get into the act:

My mother told me to sit quietly in a box . . . but she should have known better. The minute my sisters went on, I marched right out onto the stage. Whatever they were singing I've forgotten, but I paid no attention, anyhow, and launched into "Jingle Bells," the only song in my repertoire. I sang five straight choruses before Daddy carried me off the stage. But from then on I was part of the family act.

It should be noted that Judy did not always stick to this version of the story. On other occasions she claimed that her grandmother had impetuously pushed her out onto the stage.

Baby Gumm in her debut costume, early 1925.

23

Judy's grandmother, Eva Milne, was indeed at the New Grand on this occasion, but the debut of Frances Gumm was not as spontaneous as Judy recalled. It had, in fact, been announced in both the *Independent* and the *Herald-Review* several days earlier:

Added attraction for Friday evening: the three Gumm girls will entertain in songs and dances featuring Baby Frances, two years old, Virginia, seven, and Mary Jane, nine. The little girls will appear between the shows at nine o'clock.

Very likely her grandmother did push her out on cue and very possibly Frances did sing "Jingle Bells." But her appearance had been carefully planned and involved more than repeating the choruses of a single song. The *Herald-Review,* dated December 31, 1924, gave this account:

The three daughters of Mr. and Mrs. Frank Gumm delighted a large audience at the New Grand Theater last Friday night with twenty minutes of singing and dancing. Mary Jane and Virginia, the two oldest girls, are becoming accomplished entertainers while the work of Frances, the two-year-old baby, was a genuine surprise. The little girl spoke and sang so as to be heard by everyone in the house and she joined in the dancing both alone and with her older sisters. The audience expressed their appreciation of all three girls by vigorous applause.

How significant was this event? M-G-M publicists and fan magazines, while not always able to agree on the age at which Baby Frances made her debut, were unanimous in treating it as something that would have provided a show-stopping flashback for one of the Garland and Rooney "let's get the kids together and put on a show in the barn and we'll see our names up in lights" epics of the early forties. It was the proper, romantic way to begin a show business career. Judy herself seems to have thought of it as her first step toward a lifelong addiction. In her article, published in *McCall's* in Jan-

uary and February of 1964, she described the roar of the crowd as being "like taking nineteen hundred wake-up pills," and traced the thrill she still felt while facing a live audience back to that first experience on the stage of her father's theater in Grand Rapids.

Those who have chosen to follow Judy Garland in portraying her mother as a monstrous show business junkie have inevitably pointed to this occasion as marking the beginning of Ethel Gumm's campaign to propel her youngest daughter to stardom. It was that night, they argue, that provided Ethel with the first hint that she might someday be able to live out her own fantasies of fame and fortune through Frances. But Frances Gumm's debut probably had less dramatic significance than it has been invested with. At most, it was just one link in a continuum. It is questionable whether Ethel, at this point in her life, entertained any serious ambitions for either herself or her daughter. She was an imaginative woman and, given her tastes and interests, must have wondered occasionally what it would be like to work in big-time vaudeville, even in Hollywood, but it is unreasonable to conclude that this amounted to anything more than daydreaming. It seems highly improbable that even the germ of a concerted plan existed in her mind. The Gumms had an established position in their small town society and they did not attempt to stray beyond its clearly understood limits. They were the closest thing that Grand Rapids had to professional entertainers—and were constantly stressing their professional background— which gave them a specific function within the community.

It was absolutely natural—and not in the least bit sinister—that Baby Frances should be put on stage to participate in the Christmas show. As the *Herald-Review* noted, Mary Jane and Virginia were already seasoned performers. There were families like the Gumms in small towns all over the United States—families who managed to escape notoriety with great ease.

In later years, after her estrangement from Judy, Ethel explained to anyone who would

The Gumm Sisters, 1925.

listen just how ordinary her daughter's life had been before she went to M-G-M. Not many people cared to listen, however, and even fewer were prepared to take her seriously. After her mother's death Virginia carried on the crusade, with much the same results. Yet most of the evidence—from the local papers and from Grand Rapids residents who remember the family—suggests that the Gumms did lead rather a normal existence in Minnesota. Not only were they active in community affairs, but all three girls seem to have been popular and Frank and Ethel developed a number of close friendships there that continued long after they left Minnesota.

Ethel was entirely justified in protesting the highly colored accounts of her family's history that appeared in a variety of periodicals from the late thirties onward. At the same time, it's clear that the Gumms were considered a little different by the townspeople of Grand Rapids. Their lifestyle was looser than their neighbors' and they maintained a permanent open house where both adults and children constantly dropped by. Out-of-town entertainers inevitably gravitated to the Gumms' home. One former neighbor suggests, with a fond touch of envy, that the Gumms lived like gypsies. This informant, who was Virginia's age, recalls that she loved to visit the Gumms and to sleep over, because the atmosphere was so relaxed and different from what she was used to.

To put things in perspective, the Gumms may have been a shade exotic by the standards of Grand Rapids in the 1920s, but the popular notion that Judy Garland was born in a theatrical trunk and nourished on a diet of greasepaint and lukewarm gruel is far from the truth.

Ethel was not the kind of wife who would let herself be tied to the kitchen stove. Apart from her activities at the New Grand and around town, she frequently took trips to other communities—sometimes with Frank and the children, but often with one or more of her many women friends. Usually she was the motive force behind these expeditions and served as the driver, unless Frank was along. She organized many bridge parties at the Gumm

home, some of which were quite elaborate by local standards. During one week in 1925 she held no fewer than four such parties, at each of which a "dainty lunch" was served to sixteen guests. (According to the local papers, all meals were "dainty"— an epithet that evidently covered a multitude of evils—but Virginia recalls that her mother was an excellent cook who took great care with meals and sometimes fabricated complicated decorative settings from whatever flowers were in season.) Though Ethel was a popular hostess, she did provoke a slight undercurrent of hostility in some quarters. In casual reminiscences the words "dominating" and "overbearing" crop up occasionally. A small woman, solidly built and large-busted, but with tiny hands, she had a mind of her own and a nose for hypocrisy. Add to that her penchant for giving her forthright opinion on anyone or anything and it can be taken for granted that she bruised someone's vanity once in a while.

Many years later, while denigrating her mother, Judy Garland would paint a glowing portrait of her father. Her sister Virginia agrees that Frank Gumm was indeed "a wonderful man" and he seems to have been a popular figure wherever he found himself. He was handsome and had an attractive, slightly mischievous smile and an easy laugh. He was generous to a fault—as if he needed to win approval—but if this was a weakness, it did not cost him many friends. There are people in both Minnesota and California who still speak of him in terms approaching reverence. Like Judy, he seems to have had the ability to seduce people into enjoying themselves, into feeling more alive in his presence.

One thing that Judy Garland did not mention in her published descriptions of her father is that apparently he was bisexual. This was something she became conscious of in time and it's something that cannot be ignored in view of its probable effect on her later life. In Grand Rapids, Frank's bisexuality is spoken of as common knowledge, though it was clearly not so when the Gumms lived there. Evidently Frank's homosexual interludes were discreet. People who considered themselves his friends say he never betrayed any hint of homosexuality, yet they admit to having heard the stories and none of them seem disinclined to believe them.

Virginia maintains that she never heard the rumors and suggests they may have been invented by Judy. Judy conjured up many things, but this does not seem to be one of them. If anything, she attempted to suppress the information, and at the end of her life was still hoping to find certain proof that would satisfy her doubts one way or the other. The notion that her father had been bisexual appears to have caused her considerable torment. In any case, it's unlikely that any stories manufactured by Judy would have gained such general currency in Grand Rapids—unless they appeared in print, which they did not. And the word-of-mouth tradition in Minnesota is substantiated by independent, and more specific, stories told elsewhere.

The stage debut of Frances Ethel Gumm did nothing to change the pattern of life in Grand Rapids. The dirt roads that led to the village were dusty in summer and frozen solid in winter. Prohibition being in effect, citizens drank moonshine to keep out the cold. In 1925 the high school basketball team made its way to the state tournament and the Ku Klux Klan staged a spectacular rally at the Itasca County Fairgrounds (northern Minnesota was also a hotbed of socialist activity). The big paper mill on the banks of the Mississippi was becoming the key to the town's prosperity and automobiles were more plentiful. The lakes were full of muskies and walleyes and the forests were alive with game.

In 1925 Baby Frances—either alone or with her sisters—made two appearances at the New Grand, performed a "descriptive song and dance" at the Itasca Dry Goods Company's Annual Spring Style Show and entertained at the Degree of Honor Convention. She made at least one out-of-town appearance, in June, at the Lyceum Theater in Deer River, fifteen miles from home. The sisters were invited to perform at the Kiwanis minstrel show in Hibbing, but they were forced to bow out when Frank became ill and had to travel to Rochester for the removal of a goiter. In September Frances was rushed to a hospital in Duluth, suffering from a severe intestinal disorder and provoking considerable panic in the family. Virginia recalls that her sister almost died— acute acidosis was diagnosed—but her recovery was rapid and she was back in Grand Rapids within a week.

The first part of 1926 saw another out-of-town performance, this time at the Garden Theater in Hibbing. In Grand Rapids Frances and her sisters were seen between acts of the high school play and appeared twice on the boards of the New Grand, performing such routines as "The Kinky Kids Parade," which had all three in blackface and Frances impersonating Al Jolson. In March they entertained and modeled at the Second Annual Style Show of the Itasca Dry Goods Company and Frances' entrance on this occasion drew comment from the *Independent*:

A real "milinary opening" was one of the novel features of the show. A hatbox, slightly larger than usual, was carried out on the runway. In a few moments it became active, the lid opened as if by magic and out came little three year old Frances Ethel Gumm, looked cautiously around and finally crawled out of the box and gave a lively performance of the Charleston. This was the hit of the evening and a round of applause greeted the little dancer as she went through her antics like a seasoned "Follie."

(In judging this review, it should be taken into account that it may have been written by Frank Gumm.)

To this point, the girls' schedule had not been particularly heavy and had not taken them very far from home. Now their travels were about to begin. On June 5, 1926, the following item appeared in the *Independent*:

Mr. and Mrs. Frank Gumm and their three daughters . . . appeared last Friday and Saturday at the Grand Theater, Bemidji. . . . In a letter of recommendation given them from the owners of the theater, the act was described as one of the most pleasant ever presented in Bemidji.

This letter was put to good use almost immediately. Within a matter of days the Gumm family embarked upon its first theatrical tour.

This first tour has been consistently misrepresented. All the early accounts—which presumably relied on information furnished by M-G-M—were based on the assumption that the Gumms had decided to leave Minnesota to find fame and fortune in the Golden West. They further assumed that the Gumms were forced to work their way to California, begging jobs wherever they could—"singing their way, three little Gumms piled with the luggage in the back of the car, their possessions a few dollars, courage and a pocketful o' songs." That was how *Photoplay* celebrated the migration in the early forties. Later Judy herself embroidered the legend for *McCall's*:

. . . we all piled into our old touring car and spent three months on the road, playing one night stands in just about every city between Grand Rapids and Los Angeles. . . . My father had a wonderful voice; but my mother didn't sing well, and she played the piano very badly. It was a lousy act. And we kids . . . were terrible too. We appeared separately. First we'd sit out front and applaud for Mother and Daddy, and then they'd do the same for us when we were on stage. Mother's song, "I've Been Waitin' for a Rainy Day," always made me cry. She was terribly untalented but very touching. I cried and applauded all the way to California.

Judy even suggested that the act was so bad that audiences sometimes pelted them with food: "I'll never forget the time someone hit poor [Mary Jane] in the stomach with a piece of cheese. We didn't have enough sense to pick it up and save it. We could have used it."

A later food-throwing incident apparently served Judy as a model for this anecdote. Certainly the Gumms had no problems with audiences on their 1926 trip. In fact, almost nothing about Judy's account is supported by the other, very substantial evidence. To begin with, the old family touring car did not figure in these adventures since the family traveled by train (and were very satisfied with the service, according to a postcard sent back to Grand Rapids). The Gumms left Minnesota two days before Judy's fourth birthday—not in the summer of 1924 as she chose to imagine—to embark on a rather brief vaudeville tour that was the prelude to a family vacation. Returning to Grand Rapids, Frank Gumm gave the *Independent* a detailed description of the entire trip:

Leaving home Tuesday June 8, we went into Devil's Lake, N.D., where on Wednesday evening we appeared at the Grand Theater under our former stage name, Jack and Virginia Lee, with three little Lees added to the company. From Devil's Lake, we went to Havre, Shelby, Whitefish and Kalispell, Mont., in each of which towns we appeared with success, financially and otherwise. We then played for two days at Cashmere, Wash., and one day at Leavenworth, at the foot of the Cascades, and this concluded our vaudeville tour as we jumped from Leavenworth to Seattle and did not want to work any more as, after we reached the coast, we wanted our vacation and time to see all there was to see. Incidentally, we had earned in the neighborhood of $300 which gave us more pocket money than we had when we left home.

So much for the pathetic caravan wending its desperate way to the Pacific. Why did Judy's inflamed imagination produce these nightmare images of grotesque performances and hostile

Frank Gumm.

28

audiences? Jack and Virginia Lee and their offspring might not have won plaudits at the Palace Theater in New York, but they were certainly professional enough to satisfy audiences in Devil's Lake and Cashmere. Judy was correct in saying that parents and children appeared separately. Frank and Ethel went on first, then Mary Jane and Virginia sang duets, and finally Baby Frances performed an acrobatic dance. (Judy recalled, accurately, having to do "those horrible Egyptian belly rolls.") As for her critical assessment of her mother's abilities, this can only be attributed to malice or insensitivity. Plenty of witnesses attest that, while her gifts may have been relatively limited, Ethel was a competent pianist and possessed an agreeable voice. Interestingly, someone who saw her perform on a number of occasions remarked that her stage presence in some ways anticipated the style of her granddaughter, Liza Minnelli. The most charitable way of accounting for Judy's opinion is to suppose that, looking down from her own pinnacle of talent, she must have lost perspective with regard to her mother's performances.

Virginia, who was almost nine at the time, recalls how the vaudeville segment of their trip was organized: "We'd stop in a town and my daddy would go to the newspaper, or to the theater owner, and offer to play a show that night. That's the way things were done then."

In Seattle the Gumms stayed with former residents of Grand Rapids and spent two days with the Stanley McMahons at their summer place on Puget Sound. Then they traveled by rail to Portland where Frank, who had lived there for two years, was able to show his family the sights. They took a boat to San Francisco, then continued by rail to Los Angeles where they spent ten days as the guests of Frank Rabwin, who had moved to Hollywood to be near his son Marcus, now a resident physician at Los Angeles General Hospital.

While in Los Angeles, the Gumms managed to visit several movie studios, including—nine years before Judy became a contract player there—Metro-Goldwyn-Mayer, then a rela-

Frank with Mary Jane and Virginia.

tively modest cluster of office buildings and glassed-in stages in the still barren wastes of Culver City. They watched several movies being made and met a number of stars, including (according to the list Frank gave the *Independent*) Marion Davies, Conrad Nagel, Monte Blue, John Gilbert, Louise Fazenda:

. . . and last, and to the kiddies' taste BEST, Fred Thompson and "Silver King." Mr. Thompson and his wife Frances Marion, celebrated scenario writer, were particularly nice to us and Fred gave each of the girls his autographed picture taken with "Silver King" which gave them the greatest thrill they had of the whole trip.

Fred Thompson was one of the great Western stars of the day and Virginia recalls very clearly how they came to meet him:

Fred Thompson was our love, and we went to Culver City to try and get into M-G-M. We had already been through Fox and Warner Brothers, but when we got to Culver City, we knew that was where Fred Thompson worked. There was some kind of hangup about getting into M-G-M, but this convertible went by with a man in a stetson hat—and it was Fred Thompson. My daddy ran right out into the middle of the street and stopped him, and said, "My kids have been dying to meet you"—and he got us in the studio.

They also saw Lillian Gish at work on *Annie Laurie* and shook hands with Lon Chaney. Naturally, they also made the already traditional tour of movie stars' homes. Frank wrote, "Gloria Swanson's palatial residence was advertised for sale and open to inspection. We thought of purchasing it but it contained only forty rooms so didn't bother." He was very fond of this joke and used it again when Rudolph Valentino's house came on the market.

The Gumms visited the Hotel Ambassador and were allowed to "rubberneck" at "the famous Cocoanut Grove dancing place" (the house detective was a native of Grand Rapids). Still another former Minnesota family took them to a concert at the Hollywood Bowl and picnics were made for the Gumms at Ocean Park and Venice. On their first Sunday in Los Angeles, armed with a good deal of skepticism, they went to see Aimee Semple McPherson preach and were so impressed they returned the following week. (Many years later Judy hoped to play the evangelist in a movie and even obtained screen rights to a McPherson biography.)

30 *Baby Frances, 1931.*

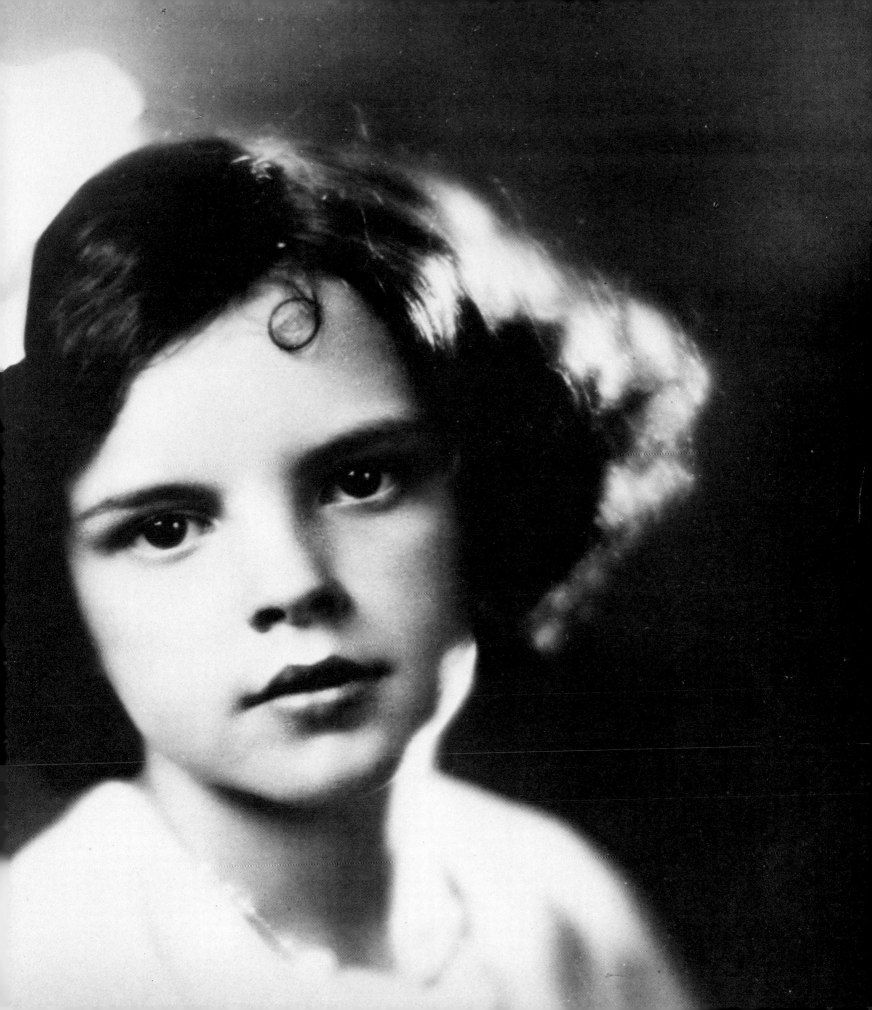

Another high spot of the Gumms' stay was when they went to see the Duncan Sisters in *Topsy and Eva*. Frank described the occasion with enthusiasm:

After the Saturday matinee, the Duncan Sisters presented each child present with a souvenir, a little mirror with their photograph on the back of it. They took a special interest in our baby, had all three of the children sing and dance for them and took our name and address, asking that we keep in touch with them at their permanent address, White Plains, New York, as they might be able to give the baby, anyway, a chance next season. I hope this doesn't sound like bragging, the interest came unsolicited, as no parents were allowed on stage when the souvenirs were presented and the Duncan Sisters kept the baby after all the others had left as they said they noticed her especially and wanted to see more of her. They were not at all aware that we had anything to do with the show business until after they had made their statements regarding the baby's talents.

Following this exciting interlude in Southern California, the family returned to Grand Rapids by way of Salt Lake City, Denver, Omaha and the Twin Cities. Frank confessed to a twinge of regret at leaving California but said they were all glad to be home: "Which after all, is the BEST place."

It's curious that this apparently enjoyable family vacation should have provided the occasion for so many ugly stories. On the other hand, it's easy enough to see why this trip has often been telescoped with the Gumms' eventual migration to California, since the two were separated by less than four months.

The *Independent,* dated October 9, 1926, carried the news that the New Grand Theater had been sold, adding that Fred Bentz would remain in Grand Rapids to operate the filling station he had recently purchased, while Frank Gumm was planning to leave for the West Coast. Frank and Ethel were to visit his family in Alabama, leaving the children in Superior with the Milnes. Then Frank would drive to California to look for work and a home and Ethel would join the children and wait in Superior until he had established a foothold in Los Angeles.

Why the Gumms suddenly decided to uproot themselves is not entirely clear. Some writers have seen this as the first step in Ethel's plan to propel Baby Frances to stardom, but although Ethel had enjoyed her first-hand glimpse of Hollywood glamour, she doesn't seem to have had any such design for her daughter. Years later, in an article for *Modern Screen,* she explained that they went to California "to get away from the coal bills, if you must know, and the storm windows. The whole thing started with Frank saying: 'Let's go to California for a week. . . .' " In her brief description of their vacation she omitted all mention of their theatrical performances and concluded by saying that "what Frank and I really loved was the climate. Roses and balmy skies in the middle of winter. This was the place, we decided, this is it."

Thousands of families moved to California for exactly those reasons. The fact that the Rabwins and other friends had already made the move may also have influenced the Gumms. Perhaps Frank's description of Grand Rapids as "the BEST place" was merely diplomatic. It may be that the move was planned before they returned to Minnesota, but there are people in Grand Rapids who insist that Frank Gumm was asked to leave town because of some homosexual indiscretion and it's possible he had been careless and had allowed some liaison to become too public. If so, many people were still sorry to see the Gumms leave. There was a gala farewell show at the New Grand, and half a dozen going-away parties were thrown for them, including one organized by the Episcopal church and another at the home of the local sheriff.

After the Gumms left Grand Rapids, on October 26, 1926, occasional news of their progress reached their former neighbors. In April, 1927, the following story appeared:

The *Herald-Review* is in receipt of No. 1 of Vol. 1 of the West Hollywood *Journal,* which carries at the masthead, as editor, the name of Frank A. Gumm. In an opening statement, the editor says that the *Journal* is a public servant designed to further the interests of West Hollywood and its citizens, to encourage trading at home and to boost for the district.

When Ethel and the girls first joined Frank in California, they lived briefly in Atwater, a suburb of Glendale wedged between the Verdugo Mountains and the San Rafael Hills. When Frank became editor of the *Journal,* the family moved to West Hollywood, but this proved to be nothing more than a staging post and Frank remained in his new job only a few weeks. Since arriving in Southern California, he had been searching for a movie theater to buy. Those that he looked at in the Los Angeles area were either too expensive or else poor prospects because of the intense competition. His good friend Dr. Marcus Rabwin heard of a theater for sale in Lancaster, and suggested it might be worth investigating.

Seventy miles northeast of Los Angeles, Lancaster is a high desert town, sitting on the edge of the Mohave, and the chief town of the Antelope Valley—a flat, elevated plain, separated from the coastal cities by the barren ridges of the Sierra Pelona and the San Gabriel Mountains (many early Westerns were shot in these arid hills). The San Andreas fault cuts across the landscape within a few miles of Lancaster, and the mountains beyond the rift zone are moving north in relation to the valley. Irrigation makes agriculture possible—alfalfa is the most important crop—but only the best soils are worth farming and even today there are extensive patches of desert land that have never been cultivated. When the Gumms first saw Antelope Valley, very little of it was developed and the landscape must have seemed strange to them—spectacular groves of Joshua trees (giant yuccas) silhouetted against the distant mountain ranges and the harsh desert sky. The valley was sparsely settled (much of it had been homesteaded barely twenty years

earlier) and the population of Lancaster was less than 1,500. The theater that was up for sale was situated on Sierra Highway, which ran parallel to the Southern Pacific Railroad tracks (the first San Francisco–Los Angeles rail link, opened in 1876, was routed through Antelope Valley). The few substantial commercial buildings that existed were concentrated here, on Sierra Highway, and on Lancaster Boulevard, which crossed the highway at right angles, near the train depot. For the rest, the town consisted of a modest grid of residential streets lined with frame houses and Barcelona bungalows.

A five-minute walk from the depot carried you out of town and into a tangle of screwbean mesquite and creosote bushes where you would be more likely to encounter a jackrabbit or a sidewinder than to come across a friendly face. Extremely hot in summer and sometimes very cold in winter, Antelope Valley was hardly the promised land of roses and balmy skies Ethel had envisioned. The antelope themselves had long since vanished; after being hunted by Indians, miners, early settlers and railroad construction gangs, they were finished by the severe winter of 1880, with snow so deep the deer became easy prey for the coyotes.

The main thing the Lancaster Theater had going for it was that it was the only movie theater within a radius of fifty miles. The sole competition was Thursday night films at a church hall in Palmdale, half a dozen miles down the highway, and these were suspended when revivalists visited town. When the Gumms arrived at the theater, they were shocked to find the lessee, Ben Clamen, standing out in front of it with his hat in his hand. As patrons arrived, they threw quarters into it. No tickets were sold. Inside, the theater was shabby and dilapidated.

After the professionalism of his Grand Rapids operation, Frank Gumm was mildly horrified by what he saw in Lancaster, but there was no doubt in his mind that the Lancaster Theater could provide his family with a comfortable living.

Chapter 2
Darling of
Antelope Valley

Although Ethel was a party to the decision to move to Lancaster, she was not particularly enthusiastic about it. Only the proximity of Antelope Valley to Los Angeles made it palatable to her. Frank seems to have been a little less disappointed. He was somehow drawn to small towns. During his childhood, Murfreesboro had had a population of around 5,000 and he seems to have had a good grasp of the psychology of being a big fish in a small pond. In Lancaster, as in Grand Rapids, the local papers make it possible to follow the family's social and professional progress in considerable detail.

The Antelope Valley *Ledger-Gazette,* published in Lancaster, and *The South Antelope Valley Press,* another weekly printed in Palmdale, both provided extensive coverage of local events. Since the movie theater was an important focus of social life in these small communities, the Gumms' arrival was noted with interest. A front-page story in the *Ledger-Ga-*

zette dated May 20, 1927, told the townsfolk that the theater was to be sold to Frank Gumm, and an advertisement in the same issue announced the family's first stage appearance in their new hometown:

Extra Special
Lancaster Theater
Sunday and Monday, May 22–23
Mr. and Mrs. Frank Gumm and daughters
will present a cycle of songs and dances
between shows each evening at nine o'clock
and also at the Sunday matinee.

In a rider to this ad, signed "Respectfully, Frank Gumm," the new proprietor left his prospective customers with the following thought: "Having purchased the theater, I am taking this method of introducing the family to the good people of Lancaster and Antelope Valley."

And the following week, in the same newspaper, the Gumms received their first Lancaster review:

*Chicago, 1934.
The renamed
Frances Garland
poses as Helen
Morgan.*

Frank and Gumm [*sic*] and family . . . made their first acquaintance with their new patrons on Sunday and Monday evenings with an offering of songs and dances in connection with the regular picture program at the theater. Mr. and Mrs. Gumm are accomplished musicians and gave two very pleasing songs while the little daughters completely won the hearts of the audience with their songs and dances.

Frank immediately set about modernizing the theater by installing an Arctic Nu-Air cooling system. He also built a box office and hired a woman to sell tickets. Within a few months he had completely renovated the interior, and had replaced the old seats. When all this was done, he changed the theater's name to the Valley Theater.

Throughout her life Judy Garland retained a benevolent attitude toward Grand Rapids, often speaking of her birthplace with considerable affection, but she habitually heaped abuse on Lancaster and looked back on her days in Antelope Valley with loathing. According to her, the Gumms were despised by the people of Lancaster, who did not want anything to do with show business families. She claimed that she had no friends there, was never invited to parties, was, in fact, ostracized. At Halloween, she insisted, the local children would borrow the Gumms' theatrical costumes, then run off before Judy could join them. On the stage of the Valley Theater, she claimed, the Gumm sisters were pelted with fruit.

A little research in the Lancaster paper tells us that Frances Gumm was invited to plenty of parties and seems to have had dozens of playmates. Commenting on Judy's later claims, Virginia says:

I don't remember anyone being mean to her. Now, when we first moved to Lancaster, the parents were not very nice. They didn't want their kids to play with those show kids. . . . Well, after they got to know my dad, and my mother, that feeling no longer existed.

The neighbors' hostility lasted a few months at the most, and in a piece of accidental symbolism the Gumms spent this time in an isolated house that was actually a couple of blocks outside of town. By early 1928, when they bought a house on Cedar Avenue, a comfortable residential street, they had been accepted by the townspeople. As for the claim that they were pelted with fruit at the Valley Theater, Virginia dismisses it as laughable, explaining, "They loved us in Lancaster."

Most of what Judy said to support her hatred of Lancaster is demonstrably untrue, but the hatred itself was palpably real. Something was wrong and it seems likely that it was during Judy's years in Lancaster that things began to go astray in her world. In most accounts of her life this crucial period is dealt with as a convenient repository for clichés about the agony of growing up gifted but misunderstood. Judy herself propagated this attitude, probably because there were things happening within and around the Gumm family, during these Lancaster years, that she found very disturbing and desperately wanted to forget. Her response was to invent a series of conventional fictions that could serve to explain her unhappiness. Fortunately there is enough verifiable information available to take a close look at the Gumms' life in Lancaster.

By the end of 1927 the Gumms were well on their way to being fully integrated into the fabric of Antelope Valley society. The *Ledger-Gazette* dated December 30 carried the following remarks:

Since Mr. Gumm purchased the theater, the entertainments have been made very much more enjoyable by the ability of Mrs. Gumm at the piano and the occasional specialties by the little daughters of the manager. The theater constitutes one of the finest assets of the community.

This public stamp of approval was borne out by the behavior of the Gumms' new neighbors. As 1927 gave way to 1928, Frank and Ethel were called upon more and more frequently to entertain at Kiwanis functions and

Masonic dinners. St. Paul's Episcopal Church availed itself of their musical talents. The bridge parties and dinners again became a steady feature of their social life, and they participated in local theatricals. One play they were involved with, *First Night*, is of particular interest because in the cast was a man who later figures in the Judy Garland story. The *Ledger-Gazette* was lavish in its praise of this production:

The amateurs of the cast were nicely strengthened by Mr. and Mrs. Frank Gumm who carried the lead characters with professional skill. The trials of courtship and marriage were humorously portrayed by Mrs. Gumm . . . and Mr. Gumm as a suitor. . . . [Another suitor] was well played by William Gilmore.

William Gilmore was an engineer employed by one of the companies that installed and maintained the pumps used to bring up water from the natural springs that flowed through the bedrock beneath Antelope Valley. In time, we shall have to concern ourselves with him more closely, but for the moment he and his wife were just two of the Gumms' many new friends, though Virginia recalls that he had a crush on her mother.

The life that the Gumms were leading in Lancaster was not too different from the life they had known in Grand Rapids. They had a definite position in the community and were considered a touch exotic, but not to an alarming extent. Essentially theirs was a middle-class life, fraying a little at the edges. The girls had more freedom than most children. They were permitted to stay up late, for example, so they could see their father when he got home from the theater after the last show. One schoolmate recalls that they were usually the last to arrive for classes, but this did not seem to harm their academic record—all three were honor students at one time or another.

The Gumms' social activities were not confined to Antelope Valley. They made frequent trips to Los Angeles, both on business and to visit friends, and these same friends often visited them. When radio artists such as the Valry Sisters—the "Belgian Nightingales" of station KELW—visited the town, they were entertained at the Gumms' home. Frank and Ethel had their own moment of glory over the airwaves of KELW, performing as part of a program sponsored by the Lancaster and Palmdale Chambers of Commerce.

As for Frances, she celebrated her sixth birthday with a party for thirty little girls and boys. "Miss Gumm," the *Ledger-Gazette* reported, "was the recipient of a large number of gifts of great variety and usefulness." A couple of weeks later Marcus Rabwin arranged for her to be admitted to Los Angeles General Hospital. Another intestinal disorder had developed into a second acute attack of acidosis. Unable to keep food or liquids down, she had become dehydrated and injections of saline solution were required to restore her to health. This treatment was carried out under the supervision of Dr. Oscar Reiss, a prominent pediatrician of the period.

In 1927 and 1928 Frances made a dozen appearances at her father's theater. Usually, now, she was billed as "Baby Gumm" and her family and friends always called her "Baby" or "Babe." She also entertained at various local events, such as the Antelope Valley Fair, and —more significantly—she and her sisters began to reach a wider audience.

The first break came in August of 1928. Ethel had taken the girls to Santa Monica for a couple of weeks by the ocean. Before returning to Lancaster, she heard of an audition for child performers who were wanted for *The Kiddies Hour,* a radio show broadcast over KFI under the auspices of Kennard Hamilton —better known as Big Brother Ken. Big Brother Ken was a slick operator who had hit on the gimmick of conducting the audition live over the airwaves. Ethel dressed her three girls in matching outfits—one eyewitness recalls white fur jackets, though this seems a little odd for the time of year—then drove them to the department store where the audition was to be held. The Gumm Sisters were just what Big Brother Ken was looking for. On August 17 the *Ledger-Gazette* took note of the girls' radio debut:

Lancaster was again featured in Radioland when the three little Gumm sisters broadcasted over KFI during *The Kiddies Hour*. Local listeners report that their numbers went over very well and that the announcer publicly complimented them very highly. Big Brother Ken was so pleased with the performance that he has asked them to put on the entire hour program next Wednesday beginning at five P.M.

After this the Gumm Sisters made many broadcasts with Big Brother Ken, first on KFI and then KNX. At times they performed on a regular basis, which involved weekly trips to Los Angeles in the family Buick, a tedious drive on poor roads over a 3,000-foot pass. (In the words of one veteran of the trip, "If you hit thirty-five, you talked about it.") In any case, these broadcasts did win the Gumm Sisters the beginning of a following. In September they received a request from the great cowboy star William S. Hart, who asked them to sing "There's a Long, Long Trail a-Winding."

Then, over the Christmas season, the girls made their first appearance on the stage of a major theater—Loew's State in Los Angeles, where they were featured as part of a Meglin Kiddies Review. In theaters that featured stage shows between movie programs, kiddie shows were popular attractions at that time of year and the companies organized by Ethel Meglin were among the most famous in Southern California. (The ads that year spoke of "One Hundred Meglin Wonder Kiddies . . . Kute . . . Klever and Kunning!") Ethel Gumm seems to have made her first contact with Ethel Meglin in 1927, when she tried to open a franchised branch of the Meglin Dance Studio in Lancaster, and the girls had taken part in a Meglin recital a couple of months before the Christmas show. Loew's State was the real thing, however, even meriting a review from the *Los Angeles Times*:

The children perform like tried and true troupers in both solo and chorus numbers. They more than make up for occasional mistakes in the breathless, do or die manner in which they work.

The writer did not single out individual performers for attention, but the word that reached Lancaster was that Baby Gumm's number was received with great enthusiasm.

As the year ended, Lancaster audiences were given a chance to judge the merit of this enthusiasm when Baby Gumm and her sisters repeated their Loew's State routines on the stage of the Valley Theater. In the early weeks of 1929 there were a couple more local performances. Baby Gumm delighted the Kiwanians with her impersonation of Fanny Brice, and she portrayed a character called "Bonnie Bee" in the high school operetta *Cinderella in Flowerland*. Virginia played the title role and Mary Jane was cast as the Prince. Then, on March 1, the following story appeared in the *Ledger-Gazette*:

Mrs. Frank Gumm and daughters leave next week for Los Angeles where they will reside indefinitely in order that the girls may pursue special studies. They will spend their weekends in Lancaster, Mrs. Gumm furnishing the music at the theater. Mr. Gumm will continue to reside at the family home on Cedar Avenue.

These special studies were with Ethel Meglin and, in June, as part of the Meglin troupe, the Gumm Sisters appeared at the Shrine Auditorium in a Milk Fund benefit show. Later that same month, also with the Meglin Kiddies, they made their motion picture debut.

Most film historians have recorded that Judy Garland's first movie was *Every Sunday,* made in 1936 with Deanna Durbin, but, in fact, her first picture was *The Big Revue,* shot seven years earlier. The film is a short and really quite awful. Even given the limitations of early talkie productions, the camera is remarkably static and—for the most part—the children seen on screen are not far short of terrible. The

Gumm Sisters appear in the chorus and also as a trio in a feature entitled "In the Sunny South," which demonstrates that Virginia had a rather pleasant voice and that Mary Jane was awkward but charming. It also gives evidence that their kid sister could outshout either of them and that she already had a remarkable screen presence. She blew a portion of her dance routine, but that was at least partly because she was gazing into the camera lens with such fierce concentration. Her performance is devoid of self-consciousness. Though it does not prefigure the character of her mature talent, this is unmistakably the future Judy Garland and there is no denying that she already had a personality capable of imprinting itself on the viewer's mind.

By Labor Day Ethel and the girls were back in Lancaster, full time. For the time being, "special studies" were over.

These early, modest successes came very easily. Virginia does not remember ever having to work hard for them: "Unfortunately, we did not rehearse very much, because we didn't have to—it came easy for us. We did not spend hours in a grind, learning to do things. We could do them and we just did them. It was fun."

All three sisters were local celebrities, but it was Baby Gumm who was habitually singled out for special praise. In a small community, though, celebrity is usually tempered by familiarity. It's likely that the novelty of being in show business wore off more quickly for her playmates than it did for Baby Gumm herself, and she may have found their relative indifference irritating. Some of her contemporaries describe her as a little spoiled, a little bratty at times (it must be remembered that they are aware of Judy's later hostility toward Lancaster and of her stories that implicate them as her tormentors), but all of them seem to have enjoyed visiting the Gumms' home.

Though Lancaster was proud of the Gumms, the pride may have been mixed with a touch of jealousy. Virginia recalls that, while they had a busy enough social life in Antelope Valley, they made few close friends there. Most of their real friends were children they met while working with the Meglin troupe or at dancing school in Los Angeles. The sisters' lives were still pretty normal, but they had started to read *Variety* and *The Hollywood Reporter*. The gap between them and the other children of Lancaster was beginning to widen.

Ethel must have been delighted with these first successes, and we cannot blame her. Certainly there is no evidence to suggest that she was forcing the situation. It developed, and she went along with it. We have seen how the Gumms had their proper function as entertainers within their own community. The fact that the Gumm Sisters were drawing favorable attention in the big city must have seemed to Ethel a satisfactory extension of this. We could hardly expect her to view it as something ominous, something that threatened the stability of the family unit. If a groundswell of ambition was beginning to develop, it was extremely modest; there were no stars in anybody's eyes. The girls' career was evolving under its own momentum, and it seems likely that no one was looking into the future more than a few weeks at a time.

Some accounts of Judy's life give the impression that it was the Gumm Sisters, driven by their mother, who were the family's chief means of support at this time. This notion is

Frances (front center) with a group of friends in Lancaster.

39

quite absurd. The Valley Theater was a successful enterprise and the Gumms enjoyed a modest prosperity by Lancaster standards. The girls were not, in fact, earning much money—their fees were low and they were not working that frequently. Virginia says that they got to spend whatever they earned on themselves, as foolishly as they liked.

On November 8, 1929, there were two interesting items in the *Ledger-Gazette*. One stated that Frank Gumm had signed a contract with RCA Photophone for the permanent installation of talkie equipment at the Valley Theater. The other noted that his three daughters were in Los Angeles, rehearsing with an organization known as the Hollywood Starlets. Apart from one isolated job sometime later, their association with Ethel Meglin was at an end.

The girls' first engagement with the Starlets was at the opening of a new toy department in a Los Angeles store, and on their weekly radio show with Big Brother Ken they were now billed as the Hollywood Starlets Trio. Virginia explains that, until shortly before this, they had not been a trio in the true sense of the word:

We were the first children's trio ever. There were the grown-up trios, the Brox Sisters and the Boswell Sisters. The Boswell Sisters were the ones that we liked. However, the first tune we did as a trio was "But What Do I Care?"— which was a Brox Sisters song.

We had gone to Los Angeles on an interview at Paramount, with Gus Edwards, and at that time [Mary Jane] and I were doing duets. . . . That's what we'd always done— two-part harmony things—from the the time we were real little, before Judy was born.

So we were doing duets and Judy was doing solos and dancing—acrobatic dancing. . . .

40

And it was Gus Edwards who said to Mama— he didn't want us though—"The girls all seem very musical. Why don't they sing three-part harmony instead of just duets?"

We just never had thought of it. Well, after we left Paramount, we went downtown to the Paramount Theater to see a stage show, and the Brox Sisters were in it. . . . They were doing "What Do I Care?" And when we got in the car to go back to Lancaster, we tried the three-part harmony and we could do it. . . . Mother would say, "Not that note—that note." And after that we had a trio.

Although the emphasis was on singing, there was a certain amount of dancing in the act, with Mary Jane the standout in this area, according to Virginia: "We all took dancing lessons, but she was the best dancer—and really liked it. Judy and I just learned enough to get by. We did a shim-sham routine in the act. . . . We could manage."

In December, 1929, the girls' Meglin movie debut was followed by another talking picture —this time a Vitaphone short entitled *Holiday in Storyland*. The Gumm Sisters had a trio feature, "Where the Butterflies Kiss the Buttercups," and Baby Gumm was given a solo spot, "Blue Butterfly." Later that month they were used in another Vitaphone film, *The Wedding of Jack and Jill,* and then they participated in *Bubbles,* which was shot early the following year. Virginia remembers that they played moonmaidens in one of these pictures, all three of which were shot in two-strip Technicolor and released by First National. Unfortunately, they seem to have been lost, though the negatives may still exist, forgotten in some vault.

After several delays the Valley Theater's sound equipment was inaugurated in February, 1930, and the local tradespeople took out a full-page advertisement in the *Ledger-Gazette* congratulating Frank Gumm on his progressive attitude and thanking him for the confidence he had shown in the community. This can reasonably be taken to represent the highwater mark of respect and popularity achieved by the Gumms in Lancaster.

The stock market had crashed three months

earlier, but we can assume this had very little effect on Frank Gumm's liquidity—in fact, the immediate effect of the crash on the economy of Lancaster seems to have been negligible. As America, and the world, slipped into the Depression, Baby Gumm played Goldilocks in a grammar school operetta and represented her church at the Pro-Cathedral in Los Angeles for the annual mite-box service. Her eighth birthday was celebrated with a swimming party at the high school "plunge" and, for the third year in a row, she was a finalist in the Los Angeles *Express*'s Better Babies Contest, which won her a doll donated by Mary Pickford. The three girls spent part of the summer with Ethel in Ocean Park and fulfilled several engagements with the Hollywood Starlets in San Diego, Coronado and Los Angeles.

Between the summer of 1930 and the summer of 1931 the girls were fairly active in and around Lancaster but made only three out-of-town stage appearances. Then, in July of 1931, the *Ledger-Gazette* reported that their mother had been in Los Angeles "arranging for an eight piece orchestra which she will direct and which will play the score for the juvenile extravaganza *Stars of Tomorrow* which opens at the Wilshire-Ebell Theater on Wilshire Boulevard, July 10. The Gumm Sisters are to be featured in the show . . . which is being staged by Maurice Kusell." Maurice Kusell, who ran a talent school in the city, had had extensive theatrical experience and had staged musical numbers for early sound pictures at several major studios. In view of Judy Garland's published recollections of her mother's haplessness, it's interesting that Kusell remembers her as a competent musician and a gifted vocal coach. He also describes Ethel as a pleasant woman. She was not, he says, obsessed with her daughters' career (Kusell was all too familiar with the stage mother as a species). Ethel felt no need to push the children, he explains, because it was obvious that they had talent—especially Frances—and she was confident this talent would speak for itself.

The Gumm Sisters had three featured spots in *Stars of Tomorrow*. In "Garden of Beautiful

Flowers" they were cast as "gardenettes," and "Puttin' on the Ritz" presented them as "Harlem Crooners." The third spot was titled "Floatin' down the Mississippi." Baby Gumm had a solo number and was teamed with Miss Betty Jean Allen for "a plantation melody."

A number of Lancaster families traveled to Los Angeles to see this extravaganza, which ran for a week. It was also seen by Maurice Kusell's agent, who was impressed by Frances. The outcome was that Frances was signed to a five-year contract covering "stage, screen, radio and television" by the firm of Frank and Dunlap, a prominent Hollywood agency (James Cagney was one of its clients). Frances Gumm was the first child they had ever placed under contract. The only thing they were not happy about was her name and it was decided that she should change it to Frances Gayne. Presumably there was an option clause buried somewhere in this contract, and evidently it was exercised at the first opportunity. After one appearance at the Valley Theater, Frances Gayne reverted to her family name and Frank and Dunlap disappeared from her life. As Maurice Kusell recalls, the timing just wasn't right.

During the second half of 1931 the Gumm Sisters performed at two Kusell recitals and, more significantly, Baby Gumm made a number of solo performances—in Lancaster, Tehachapi, Bakersfield, Coronado and Los Angeles. During the Christmas holidays she was featured in a Kiddie Review at the Warner Brothers' Theater in Hollywood. Then, in January and March of 1932, she made two solo "Star Night" appearances at the Cocoanut Grove. To perform beneath the papier-mâché monkeys that adorned the palm trees in the Grove was considered enormously prestigious—but Judy Garland would forget these bookings along with the rest.

Under the management of Fanchon and Marco, the Gumm Sisters played a number of summer engagements at movie theaters throughout Southern California. The Golden Age of Vaudeville had already been killed by Hollywood, and these bookings were gener-

ally seven-day or split-week dates at theaters that featured live acts between movie shows. The girls would do a twenty-minute routine five times a day—six times a day on weekends. They particularly enjoyed playing theaters near the ocean—such as the Dome in Long Beach, which was at the end of a pier—so they could hurry to the beach between shows. Virginia recalls that they were usually sunburned and peeling, but it didn't show under the stage makeup.

In December Baby Gumm played solo engagements at the Fox-Arlington in Santa Barbara and at the Million Dollar Theater in Los Angeles. By now, her voice was beginning to mature rapidly. She was only ten years old but, to quote Virginia, "She didn't sound like Shirley Temple." By the end of 1932 she had a growing reputation in Southern California. She had appeared in some of the best theaters in the region and was a veteran of dozens of radio shows and at least four films. The big break was still a way off, but there was a definite momentum.

Back in Lancaster, things were changing. The Gumms had been a very close family. Now a series of intermittent separations began. In her *McCall's* memoirs Judy referred to a rift between Frank and Ethel, without specifying what might have caused it. She spoke of trouble within the Gumm household and said that because of this, at one point, Ethel took her to Los Angeles while her sisters remained in Antelope Valley with Frank. Judy remembered that on this occasion she and her mother stayed for some time at an establishment called the Hotel Gates. Unfortunately she gave no further details and it's impossible to tell exactly what period she was referring to. We can say with certainty, however, that by 1933 such separations had become commonplace because of a new development, announced in the *Ledger-Gazette* dated December 31, 1932:

After the first of the year, Mrs. Frank Gumm plans to spend the greater part of her time in Los Angeles where she will be associated with Maurice Kusell, producer.

A city newspaper made the following comment: "An addition to the Kusell faculty is Ethel Gumm, personality and harmony jazz singer. Mrs. Gumm trained the sensational juvenile singing trio, the Gumm Sisters, who have won acclaim as modern harmony singers."

Commenting on Ethel's decision to move to Los Angeles at this time, Virginia says, "My mother never did like Lancaster. She really didn't like the town and she didn't like the people there. . . . She didn't like the kids that we associated with much—and frankly we didn't either." This explanation doesn't take into account the fact that Ethel would be leaving Frank behind to run the Valley Theater.

Some writers have said that the move to Los Angeles was made because of Judy's hay fever, and this may have been a factor. Both Virginia and Marcus Rabwin confirm that Judy did suffer from respiratory problems in Lancaster, though Dr. Rabwin describes her problem as a lung ailment rather than hay fever. It was so bad at times that Ethel would have to wrap her in a blanket and drive up into the mountains with her in the middle of the night. Once she was away from Lancaster, it cleared up within a few months. It's also possible that Ethel took the Kusell job for purely professional or financial reasons. The Valley Theater was no longer doing so well (the Depression was beginning to make itself felt in Lancaster) and Frank was actually forced to reduce prices at the box office. Though the Gumms were far from the bread line—the children's earnings were never co-opted for the family budget—a new source of income was probably welcome.

It seems likely, though, that there was friction within the family and that it contributed to Ethel's decision to shift her base of operations to Los Angeles. It's evident from the local papers that during 1932 the Gumms had been withdrawing from Lancaster social life and one explanation would be a domestic crisis.

Judy claimed many years later that her father resented the way her mother was pushing the girls and that this was a major cause of the hostility between them. To believe this we would have to accept Judy's portrait of Ethel, which is contradicted by other evidence. The record shows that Frank traveled to watch his daughters perform whenever he could and Virginia says he was enormously proud of their success. He would stand in the lobbies of theaters where they were appearing, stopping total strangers to say, "Those were my girls up there. Aren't they wonderful?" Others who knew Frank agree that, far from opposing the girls' career, he was very supportive.

A more likely cause of ill feelings between Frank and Ethel was the continuing aggravation of Frank's bisexuality. As in Grand Rapids, Frank's homosexual tendencies are spoken of as common knowledge in Lancaster and the stories are more specific. He is said to have become involved with a local storekeeper. It is also hinted that he made advances to students at the high school. These rumors may have been behind the Gumms' sudden abandonment of social activities. Whether or not Frank was open with Ethel about his homosexual liaisons, she must have found the situation difficult to live with. The need to shelter her children from the growing insinuations would, in itself, have provided her with ample reason to move to Los Angeles. But she may have moved too late to protect her youngest daughter. One informant reports that other children were beginning to tease Frances Gumm about her father. Even if both tormentors and tormented were ignorant of the full implications, this taunting must have had a terrible impact on the mind of a bright ten-year-old. If this story is true, it explains why Judy felt so alienated from Lancaster in later years. The trauma may have been enough to obliterate several years of happy memories. Later the trite inventions of M-G-M publicists would provide her with a featherbed to fall onto whenever this period was discussed.

As Virginia recollects, she and her younger sister moved to Los Angeles at the beginning of 1933, along with their mother, while Mary Jane stayed on in Lancaster until the spring in order to graduate with her high school class. Eva and Norma Milne came out from Minne-

On the set of a Meglin Kiddies film, 1929. Mothers watch anxiously as their children perform.

sota to help Frank look after the house. Virginia points out that this was far from an absolute separation. Ethel and the children occasionally spent weekends in Lancaster, and Frank often came to visit them in Los Angeles. Maurice Kusell remembers that Frank would stop by at the dance studio almost every week.

During the first half of 1933 Baby Gumm made more solo appearances, and then, early that summer, all three girls became regulars on KFWB's *Junior Hi-Jinx Hour,* where they attracted a good deal of favorable attention. The radio columnist of the Los Angeles *Examiner* remarked of their performances on that show, "Nothing on the air at the moment is so original."

On August 3 the *Ledger-Gazette* announced that the Gumm family had moved to Los Angeles, adding that Frank would still spend some of his time in Lancaster to take care of business at the theater. It was reported that the Gumms had rented a house at 2605 Ivanhoe Drive in the Silver Lake district of Los Angeles.

Los Angeles in 1933 was very different from the city that exists today. Its population was less than one and a half million. The first freeway would not be completed for six years and "Black Wednesday"—the name given to the day of the first great smog—was still a decade away. The automobile was already king, but

43

there was also an efficient mass transit system provided by the Big Red Cars of the Pacific Electric Railway, along with smaller streetcars and buses. The San Fernando Valley was full of working ranches, and orange groves were common within the city limits.

Situated between downtown Los Angeles and Hollywood, the Silver Lake district clung to the hillsides around an artificial reservoir. Palm trees and carefully nurtured gardens blended with architecture which showed a predominant Mediterranean and Mexican influence. Some of the buildings were a little bizarre, including—according to Virginia—2605 Ivanhoe Drive:

It was a wild house—I don't know how we came to rent it. It stood on the side of a hill and it was round. You went over a bridge to get to the front door. The first floor was all living room, and outside there was a terrace you could go out on—you could go all the way around. The house had four floors. The next floor up was the kitchen and the dining room and two bedrooms—and the top floor was bedrooms and a playroom. On the bottom there was a sauna bath and all sorts of things. . . . It had been fixed up as a gymnasium.

Immediately before leaving Lancaster the Gumms had been visited by Jack King and Bob Winkler of the RKO booking office. This led to an appearance at the RKO Hillstreet Theater where, according to King, the girls came to the enthusiastic attention of an M-G-M talent scout named Ben Piazza. It's unlikely Piazza's enthusiasm had any bearing on Judy Garland's eventually being placed under contract by M-G-M—that was still more than two years away—but he does seem to have followed the girls' career for a while, asking for progress reports from the managers of some of the theaters where they were appearing.

A few days after their appearance at the RKO Hillstreet the girls traveled with both parents to San Francisco to fulfil an engagement at the Golden Gate Theater. By the end of August, however, Frank was back in Lancaster, and for the next eighteen months he

lived apart from his family most of the time. He still made regular visits and accompanied the girls on road trips when he could, but for weeks at a time he did not see his wife or daughters. Presumably this is the phase Judy referred to in her *McCall's* memoirs when she said, "As I recall, my parents were separating and getting back together all the time. It was very hard for me to understand those things and, of course, I remember clearly the fear I had of those separations." They seem to have been the only thing from her childhood that she did remember with real clarity.

Frank, too, found these separations painful. In the barber's shop where he went every day to be shaved, he often talked about how lonely and isolated he felt. The house on Cedar Avenue had been sold and he had moved into a one-room shack near the railroad tracks that had no heating, and in cold weather he slept in his overcoat. He maintained his church and Masonic affiliations, but otherwise dropped out of Lancaster social life completely. Why he chose to live so poorly is not entirely clear. Certainly the Depression had affected business at his theater, but not to the extent that he needed to live in a shack without heating.

In Los Angeles his family was living rather more comfortably. Ethel had enrolled Frances and Virginia at Mrs. Lawlor's Academy—a school for show business children—and it was here that Frances met Mickey Rooney. There must have been a shock of recognition on her part, since she had seen him in dozens of Mickey McGuire shorts at her father's theater. Rooney was almost two years older than Frances, but they took a liking to each other. Virginia, meanwhile, struck up a friendship with another young movie actor, Frankie Darro.

After the San Francisco trip the Gumm Sisters were relatively inactive for several months. Then, in February and March of 1934, they made a tour of the Pacific Northwest. Opening in Portland, Oregon, they also played Seattle, Vancouver and several smaller cities. Judy's later descriptions of this trip include an attack on her mother which has been taken as

The Gumm Sisters, Lancaster, 1932.

gospel by most biographers. Judy implied that she was dragged unwillingly to Seattle and Vancouver and that in one of these cities Ethel —annoyed at her daughter's behavior—punished the child by slowly packing her bags and telling her she was leaving. If Judy's version were to be believed, we would have to accept that she was then left alone in a hotel room, thinking that her mother had abandoned her. According to Judy, this form of punishment was used because Ethel took pride in not spanking her daughters.

It may be that Judy did once find herself alone in a hotel room and was terrified by the experience. To suggest this was planned as retribution seems to have no basis in fact.

The only element of truth in this story is that Ethel did take pride in the fact that she never spanked her girls. This was Baby Gumm's only working trip to Seattle and Vancouver, and if Ethel had wanted to terrify her daughter in this way she would have had to do so in concert with the other girls (Virginia doesn't remember any such threats) and Frank, who was also along on the trip—though he immediately returned to Lancaster when they got back to California.

Contrary to Judy's horror stories, Ethel's attitude was rather benign and casual. That the girls didn't worry much about the consequences when they were performing is illustrated by a story Virginia tells:

There are spots where the audience just takes over and you can't do a thing. That happened to us in a little town, right outside Los Angeles. It was a small neighborhood theater and we were booked in for two nights, Saturday and Sunday—matinee and an evening show each day. Well, we got in and we went on for the first matinee show. The audience was just children—terrible children—and there was this terrible smell. The kids had squeezed garlic in the footlights—and it came up. You could hardly breathe. We started to sing, and it didn't matter what we did—they didn't want anything. They were reasonably quiet during the first number, because it was fast. Then the second number we did was

called "Beside an Open Fireplace"—and we had a little bench, and we sat down on the bench and started this number, which was the slow number. . . . All of a sudden, you could see something coming through the spotlights —and it hit my sister [Mary Jane] right in the middle. It was a salami and cheese sandwich. . . . We broke up. We couldn't get through the song.

Between shows, they discovered that there was no lock on the dressing room door, so they took all their belongings with them in the car when they went out to eat:

We went up the road a way and came to a pig stand and ordered something—and we were all pretty down, and Mama said, "Have you ever seen anything like that in your life before?" We all said, "No." And she said, "Let's don't go back." So we never went back. . . . We didn't get paid—but that shows you how much the show must go on. . . . We just went on home.

Apart from giving us the source of Judy's story of having food thrown at them—which she said took place on the family's first trip to California—this incident gives us an interesting glimpse of Ethel's casual attitude. By 1934, however, she was undoubtedly beginning to take her daughters' career more seriously. Up until then, Ethel and the girls had been playing at being in show business; now the game was fast turning into reality. The enrollment of the two younger girls at Mrs. Lawlor's was an admission of this.

In May the Gumm Sisters played the *Movie Star Frolic* at the New Gilmore Stadium, where their act was a solid hit. In June, accompanied by Ethel, they set out on a road trip that would keep them from California for four months. Judy Garland's published recollections of this trip are characteristically sketchy and somber. Virginia remembers that the trip was undertaken "just for a lark," though she recalls her father was opposed to it. When he relented, he gave her mother several hundred dollars' worth of traveler's checks, which Ethel was determined not to use. (This was during the period when Frank was living in a shack in Lancaster.

46

If he was in a position to give this amount of money to his family for what was, in part at least, a pleasure trip, it's hard to understand why he was living so squalidly, unless he was deliberately punishing himself for some reason.) In *Modern Screen* Ethel insisted that the whole thing started out as an innocent joyride —an expedition to the Chicago World's Fair —and that they decided to pay their way to Chicago by taking a few bookings along the way. Frank's only objection, according to Ethel, was to their traveling without a checkbook. But all the evidence suggests that the tour was not arranged as casually as this would seem to suggest. Three months earlier the *Ledger-Gazette* had announced that the Gumm Sisters would be undertaking a major tour that summer, a trip that would carry them to Chicago and New York. Because Frances was too young to appear on the New York stage, that part of the tour never materialized. Ethel and the girls did make it to Chicago, however, and beyond.

On June 17, 1934, there was a farewell party for them at Ivanhoe Drive. The following day Frank saw them off to Denver where they were booked into a nightclub—their first club date except for Baby Gumm's solo spots at the Cocoanut Grove. They arrived to find that this particular club was a gambling spot, and the gambling paraphernalia had been confiscated by the police the previous night. The musicians were glum about the club's prospect of staying open, since without the gaming they were not likely to attract many customers. For want of anything better to do, they began to rehearse the act and finally the owner arrived. To the surprise of everybody he said that the club would stay open and the Gumms found themselves playing for a week to a house that consisted of the owner and his friends. This same man obtained a booking for them in Colorado Springs, then they went on to Chicago, arriving there around the middle of July.

The World's Fair—"A Century of Progress" —was in its second year, and dotted among the futuristic structures that housed the main exhibits were several high-kitsch watering places, one of which went by the name of the Old Mexico Café. It was here that the Gumm Sisters worked, along with a comedian–M.C. and an act that went under the name of Frances and Her Mule (a mother and daughter team, one of whom dressed up in an animal costume). The Gumms had been living high on the hog in Denver and Colorado Springs, and now Ethel asked for a $35 advance. It was the last money they would draw from Old Mexico.

To quote Virginia, "Old Mexico was way out on the island, and it didn't draw flies." Between shows they had a good time exploring the fair—but the management of the café was not providing them with much in the way of financial support. At the end of the first week, Ethel was told that the owners were a little short and was asked to wait a few days for the girls' money. The request was repeated the second week. During the third week they arrived at work one day to find Old Mexico boarded up.

Ethel, who was not a timid person, searched for the manager. He advised her to forget about the money owed them unless she wanted to find herself at the bottom of Lake Michigan.

Ethel Gumm and her daughters, Chicago, 1934.

Chicago, 1934.

dresses in the bathtub. And my big sister said, "What are we going to have for breakfast?" And Mama said, "I don't know. Go and look. See what we have and fix it." So my sister went to the kitchen and she came back and said, "All we have is one egg and a half a loaf of mouldy bread." My mother started to laugh, and she couldn't stop. We thought there was something terribly wrong with her. She'd just been told she was going to be thrown into Lake Michigan, and here she was slaving over these damn costumes—and now all we had was one egg and a half a loaf of mouldy bread. . . .

We had decided we weren't going to touch Daddy's checks, but we'd run out of the money we earned and we sat around saying, "Isn't it awful? What are we going to do?" And I said, "Why don't we cash one of Daddy's checks and go out and eat?" Which we did.

The threat was not intended as a joke and Ethel was shaken.

Since the Gumms still had a little money left, they stayed on in Chicago in a pleasant, inexpensive hotel frequented by show business people. A dance team called Mack, Jack and Al told them about the Friday night tryouts at the Belmont Theater, explaining that these provided a valuable showcase because there was always someone from the William Morris Agency in the audience. The Gumm Sisters performed at the Belmont that Friday and stopped the show. Delighted, Ethel hurried to the William Morris offices the following morning and made her pitch, only to be told that no one from the agency had been in the theater the previous evening.

Back at the hotel, where the Gumms had a small suite, Virginia remembers her mother washing the girls' costumes by hand:

These costumes were double ruffled—God, they were awful—and they were made by a woman named Marviola. They were hell to wash. You couldn't have them cleaned, because they had sequins all over them, but you could wash them. One morning Mama was in the bathroom, washing these terrible

When Judy Garland told this story, she omitted the fact that they had Frank's money to fall back on. In any case, very soon after this incident—Virginia thinks the following day—the Gumm Sisters had a new booking.

It seems that the Oriental Theater, a prestigious downtown house, had booked a fan dancer as part of a bill to be headlined by George Jessel. Fan dancers were in vogue because of the spectacular success Sally Rand was enjoying at the World's Fair, but the young lady engaged by the Oriental was thought by the management to be a touch too raunchy for high-class vaudeville. A replacement was needed in a hurry, and Jack Cathcart, a musician in the pit at the Oriental, mentioned this to a friend who had been in the band at Old Mexico. He recommended the Gumm Sisters and they rushed over to the theater. The date was August 19, 1934. The management did not have time to preview the girls' act. They were sent on cold during the second show.

A moment's silence for the too candid charms of that forgotten fan dancer . . . her misfortune precipitated one of the most celebrated anecdotes in the Garland catalogue of myths. Judy's own version of the story, as reported by Joe Hyams in their 1957 *McCall's* article, has been accepted almost universally:

48

In Chicago we were billed on the marquee of the Oriental Theater as "The Glum Sisters." We protested violently to . . . George Jessel. He told us bluntly that Gumm wasn't any improvement on Glum. "They both rhyme with crumb and bum, and in this business that isn't so smart. . . ."

Mr. Jessel suggested we call ourselves Garland after a friend of his, Robert Garland, who was drama critic of the *New York World-Telegram*.

The provenance of this story can be traced back to Judy's early days at M-G-M, and the interesting thing about it is that it has been montaged together from elements of truth—but these elements have been telescoped and reworked in the interest of slick copy. The Gumms' name was *not* misspelled on the marquee of the Oriental Theater (since they were rushed in at the last moment, not even arriving in time for the first show, their name was probably not even on the marquee that first day). On the other hand, it is true that George Jessel was the person who suggested they change their name to Garland, and this did happen at the Oriental. Virginia remembers clearly how it came about:

We went on for the second show . . . at around two, and they had no idea what we did, or anything. Jessel opened the show, then they had a line of girls, and then we were on—second on the bill, which is lousy. Jessel introduced us as the Gumm Sisters and the audience broke up. We got a big laugh. I think he thought we were a comedy act, because he really punched the name. Well, we came on and we weren't funny—but we stopped the show. It couldn't go on, and we liked that. No encore, but they wouldn't stop applauding—so we kept coming back and coming back. Finally Jessel had to stop it.

He was just horrified because he had introduced us and gotten a laugh, and he said, "You have to change your name." Heck—Gumm wasn't funny to us! We said, "To what?" And he said, "I don't know. I'll do it." Between shows he got a long-distance call from Robert Garland. We were standing in the

wings for the third show and he introduced us as the Garland Sisters. . . . And it didn't get a laugh, so we just kept it.

Coincidentally, one of the hit movies of that summer was *Twentieth Century* in which Carole Lombard played an actress called Mildred Plotka whose name is changed to Lily Garland.

A success at the Oriental, the Gumm Sisters now found themselves represented by William Morris and their new agency immediately set up a tour for them. Although they were now working as the Garland Sisters, the girls had signed with William Morris under their family name and the contracts that went out to theater managers still had the name Gumm on them. Thus, several weeks later, they arrived in Milwaukee, to find "The Glum Sisters" advertised on the marquee of the theater where they were performing. Far from being horrified, they thought this was a wonderful joke and even took a photograph—since lost—to commemorate the occasion.

The act was becoming very polished. Frances did torch songs—such as Helen Morgan's hit "Bill"—wrapped in a shawl and partially hidden by her sisters. The audience would

The marquee of the Paramount Theater in Los Angeles, May, 1935. A Garland family snapshot.

49

hear a mature, powerful voice—it could fill a large theater without the assistance of a microphone—then, at the conclusion of the number, Frances would shed the shawl and reveal herself as a rather diminutive twelve-year-old. If the audience had not already been won over by her voice alone, it was bowled over by this revelation and the act was strong enough to exploit this initial enthusiasm to the hilt. By now, Frances was definitely the star and her sisters were reduced to providing the appropriate background for her.

While at the Oriental, the girls also did two shows a day at a Chicago nightclub. On September 7 they opened for a week at the Michigan Theater in Detroit, and the tour continued with dates in Milwaukee, Kansas City, St. Joseph—where their costumes were stolen—and finally Denver once again.

It was a long tour and, in her *McCall's* memoirs, Judy spoke of how the girls missed their father:

All the time we were away from home, my sisters and I were lonesome for my father, but we didn't dare mention it to Mother. . . .

She described how the four of them arrived back in Los Angeles and recalled that she ran to her father and threw herself into his arms, crying for sheer joy. It was, she said, the only time she behaved this way. During their separations, she claimed, she tried not to think of her father, fearing that thinking of him would lead to yearning for him.

The suggestion that the girls were afraid to mention their loneliness to their mother is implausible, although it's easy to believe that their reunion with their father was an emotional one. It didn't last long. Frank spent the greater part of the winter of 1934–35 at his shack in Lancaster.

Throughout that same period the Garland Sisters worked steadily. They were at Grauman's Chinese Theater in Hollywood, where they were very well received, but they refused to take up their second week's option because the orchestra leader would not allow Ethel to play piano on stage. They were in San Fran-

Onstage at the Paramount, 1935. The only known photograph of the Garland Sisters in live performance.

cisco twice, in Long Beach and at the Orpheum in Los Angeles. They made two appearances as a trio at the Wilshire-Ebell as part of Irving Strouse's Sunday Night Vaudeville Frolics, and Frances also sang there as a solo performer. On December 7, 1934, the girls made their last appearance at the Valley Theater.

By this time Frank was beginning to encounter problems in Lancaster. On March 28, 1935, he announced in the *Ledger-Gazette* that his lease was about to expire and that, unless he could renew it, he would be forced to close the theater for a while. The announcement reads suspiciously like a plea for sympathy; all the circumstantial evidence suggests that the lease was available to anyone *except* Frank Gumm.

The stories told in Lancaster echo those heard in Grand Rapids. If they are to be believed, Frank's homosexuality had finally touched a raw nerve and there were powerful citizens who wanted him out of town. But judging from his appeal in the newspaper, Frank was not counting himself out yet. He still had friends in Lancaster and was looking to them for support. Whatever help may have been offered, it was not enough to turn the tide. On April 4 Ethel visited Frank; there must have been an urgent conference. By April 11 the Valley Theater was under new management.

To Frank Gumm's youngest daughter, her father's troubles must have seemed a blessing in disguise. For a while, at least, the family would be together. Ethel and the girls had left Ivanhoe Drive and were now living on Mariposa Avenue, south of Griffith Park, not far from the 20th Century–Fox studios. Frank joined them there, and within a matter of weeks he had a new theater in Lomita—which was then a rather isolated suburb of Los Angeles—twenty miles from their new home but still within commuting distance. As if making an effort to cut off his past, Frank adopted his daughters' name and became Frank Garland. Two days before Frances' thirteenth birthday the sisters performed for the patrons of Garland's Lomita Theater.

50

Chapter 3
Discovered

The next period of Judy's life is crucial to her story. It has received a great deal of attention from publicists, journalists and biographers, who have made of it a tangle of uncertainties. Most of the eyewitnesses are dead, but it is possible to put together a sequence of events that makes sense in terms of the known facts and probabilities.

In June and July of 1935 the Garland Sisters played an extended season at the Cal-Neva Lodge in Lake Tahoe. The youngest sister was now calling herself Judy Garland, having borrowed her first name from a Hoagy Carmichael song (up to this point she was still being called "Baby" by her family and friends). The two older sisters also had new first names—Mary Jane became Sue or Suzanne, and Virginia Jimmie.

A chance encounter at the Cal-Neva brought Judy Garland a new agent and carried her one step nearer to her film career—and incidentally provided fan magazines and other publications with a splendid opportunity for creative copy.

A typical account of what happened on this occasion appeared in the September, 1940, issue of *Photoplay,* under the byline Dixie Willson:

The season at Tahoe closed . . . the Garlands piled everything into their car and started home. Then discovered that [Jimmie] had left her hat box. Of course it was little sister Judy who went back. The Lodge was deserted except for the manager and a young composer who had dropped in to telephone. A third gentleman was there too, an agent. . . .

"Now there's a kid you should get hold of," remarked the manager to the agent.

This account continues with Judy agreeing to sing but wondering who will accompany her since her mother is out in the car. The composer, naturally, volunteers his services and Judy asks if he knows "Dinah"—which is her favorite song. Does he know "Dinah"! His name is Harry Akst and he wrote the damn thing. All of which leads to the agent arranging for Judy to audition at M-G-M.

Shortly after being signed to an M-G-M contract, Judy Garland arrives at the studio to begin work.

A similar version of this story can be found in an M-G-M publication, *The Lion's Roar,* dated November, 1942. There are some minor discrepancies between the two accounts, however—enough to suggest we should keep an eye open for fiction-mongering. No mention is made of Harry Akst here, and the hatbox has been erased from the story. Instead, it is the Garland Sisters' sheet music that has been left behind:

The manager asked her to sing for an agent who had just come in. . . . After one hasty chorus of "Dinah" she hollered her home telephone number to the interested gentleman and ran out. A week later she received a call, and in a few days signed a contract with Metro-Goldwyn-Mayer.

Other versions, including one written by Hedda Hopper, suggest that another song-writer—Lew Brown, lyricist in the famous De-Sylva, Brown and Henderson partnership—was the man Judy sang for at the Cal-Neva Lodge.

While Virginia does not remember in detail what happened, she is able to set the record straight to some extent. They did return to the Cal-Neva because of a forgotten hatbox—though it did not belong to her but to her big sister: Sue was a hat freak. During their run at Tahoe they had lived in a cabin among the trees behind the lodge. Returning to this cabin, they were intercepted by a man called "Bones" Remer—the bouncer-manager at the Cal-Neva, a massive and formidable character who adored Judy. He asked Ethel if she would bring "Baby" to the lower bar because there were some important people down there. Virginia is not exactly certain who was in the bar, but she believes that both Harry Akst and Lew Brown were present. This would make sense since both of them were employed by Columbia Pictures at the time. She thinks that Al Rosen, soon to be Judy's agent, was also there, but it may be that Akst and Brown introduced him to Judy when they returned to Los Angeles. In any case, Akst did play the piano for Judy and she did sing "Dinah," surrounded by slot machines. Back in Hollywood, Brown probably had Judy tested at Columbia—certainly he was in a position to arrange a screen test since he held an executive post there. Apparently, however, Harry Cohn, the president of Columbia, was not impressed enough to give Judy a contract.

This setback does not seem to have upset anyone. It was not the first time Judy had been tested by a film studio. As early as 1930 she had had a tryout at Paramount as part of her prize in one of the *Express*'s Better Babies contests. It seems that she also auditioned for Universal around 1931, and she definitely tested at 20th Century–Fox a few months before the Cal-Neva incident—Dore Schary, who had heard her at the Paramount, had recommended her to Sol Wurtzel for a part in a film that was then going into production. In each case, it appears that though she was impressive, no one knew what to do with a little girl who sang like a grown woman.

Al Rosen became her representative and began to plan her future as a solo performer. The Garland Sisters were about to dissolve because Susie had fallen in love with one of the musicians at the Cal-Neva Lodge, a young man called Lee Cahn. On August 17, 1935, the three girls took part in a Lewis Lewin short entitled *La Fiesta de Santa Barbara* (a clip from this picture was incorporated into *That's Entertainment*). It was the last time they worked together. On August 14 Sue had flown to Lake Tahoe and the next day she married Lee Cahn. Very soon after this, Judy auditioned at M-G-M.

Most accounts suggest the audition sprang directly from the impromptu session at the Cal-Neva, but this does not seem to be true. According to Marcus Rabwin's recollections, the audition came about as a consequence of a party held at his home. Judy sang there and was heard by Joseph Mankiewicz, then a young writer-producer at M-G-M; Mankiewicz was impressed and recommended Judy to Ida Koverman, Louis B. Mayer's executive assistant and one of the most influential people at Metro.

Whatever the case, after signing Judy, Al Rosen booked her into the Wilshire-Ebell—where she was, by now, something of a house favorite—and Ida Koverman was in the audience. Judy stopped the show and Koverman went backstage to speak with Al Rosen, telling him she wanted Judy to test at the studio. Since, as we have seen, this was not the first nibble from the movie industry, neither Judy, nor Rosen, nor Frank, nor Ethel was particularly excited by the prospect. Koverman's enthusiasm was quite genuine, however, and it appears that she asked Jack Robbins, the music publisher, to listen to Judy (Robbins Music had been bought by M-G-M at the beginning of the sound era).

A few days later a call was placed to Mariposa Avenue requesting that Judy be brought to Culver City for an audition. Ethel was out and Frank took her just as she was, dressed in slacks and sneakers, and she sang for Robbins and Koverman, accompanied by her father. Frank's repertoire was limited, so Koverman sent for Roger Edens—a pianist and vocal arranger in the M-G-M music department—to replace him at the keyboard. Everyone was impressed by Judy's talents and Koverman asked Louis B. Mayer to come down from his office and listen to the girl. She sang for Mayer—"Zing Went the Strings of My Heart"—and they waited for his reaction.

Virginia was not at the audition, but she does remember her father's account—given to her and to Ethel when he and Judy returned from the studio. At the end of Judy's song Mayer had leaned back and said, "Very nice. Thank you very much." At this platitude, Frank got angry and protested, "This is all ridiculous. My child is tired." Then he took Judy home. Mayer, of course, was hardly the kind of man to betray enthusiasm for a performer he was thinking of putting under contract, but some people—notably Hedda Hopper—have suggested that he really wasn't particularly impressed with Judy, but told Ida Koverman that she could go ahead and sign her because she was so taken with the girl. Koverman knew Mayer too well to do anything

of the sort without getting further opinions to back her up. Hedda Hopper said that Koverman took Judy to sing for Jack Cummings—a producer who also happened to be Mayer's nephew—and that he was the one who set contract proceedings in motion. Cummings remembers that Judy did audition for him, and that he was very enthusiastic, but he thinks this probably took place a little later, when she was already under contract.

One of the most persistent myths in the Judy Garland canon is that she was the only star ever signed by Metro-Goldwyn-Mayer without a screen test. This is simply not true. A few days after the initial audition Judy was called from class at Mrs. Lawlor's Academy. She and

Judy at Los Angeles Superior Court for final approval of her M-G-M contract.

her mother went to the studio and were taken to a sound stage where the test was to be shot. The director, interestingly enough, was George Sidney, who worked with Judy again a decade later, under very different circumstances. Roger Edens was on hand to accompany Judy, but she had brought props for a baseball routine that was unfamiliar to him so Ethel played instead. After the test Judy and her mother returned home and nothing was heard from the studio for a couple of weeks. Then they, along with Frank, were invited to Culver City to see the test. The enthusiasm in the screening room told them it was considered highly satisfactory.

Mayer's personal commitment to Judy may have been unsure at this point, but she had cleared the first and most difficult hurdle. It may be that Mayer wished to put Ida Koverman on the spot vis-à-vis her protégée. That was the kind of power game he enjoyed and it was a small risk—$100 a week, with the girl's first option coming up in a few months. On the other hand, Mayer may have realized from the start that Judy had the potential to become a major talent. It's doubtful that he found it necessary to explain his motives to any of his subordinates.

At all events, the wheels had now been set in motion and on October 15, 1935, Judy's contract was approved by the Superior Court and she became an official member of the M-G-M family.

A few days later, on October 26, Judy was a guest on *The Shell Chateau Hour,* broadcast from the studios of KFI and hosted by Wallace Beery. Beery, himself a major M-G-M star, made no mention on the air of her new affiliation but predicted a brilliant future for the youngster. He introduced her as "twelve-year-old" Judy Garland though she was already four months past her thirteenth birthday, and she sang "Broadway Rhythm"—significantly, a song from a current M-G-M release, with words by Arthur Freed, who was to have an important influence on her career.

Air check recordings of this broadcast have survived, and they give us a good idea of what the excitement was about. The singer we hear

With Roger Edens.

At a rehearsal for The Shell Chateau Hour, *with Wallace Beery and Jackie Cooper.*

is unmistakably Judy Garland—perhaps lacking some of the finesse of the mature performer, but none of the energy. The voice has all the power and sparkle and many of the distinctive inflections.

Three weeks later, on Saturday, November 16, Judy was back with Beery on *The Shell Chateau Hour.* This time Beery told his listeners that the little girl had been placed under contract by M-G-M—implying that this had happened since the last broadcast—and Judy sang "Zing Went the Strings of My Heart." The air check of this show has been preserved too, and this time Judy's number is even more remarkable, leaving no doubt that she was already an extraordinarily convincing performer. The first chorus is taken very slowly, then the tempo picks up and she rips into the lyric. The surface is bright and scintillating, but the emotional underpinning is powerful—far more so than one would expect from a thirteen-year-old.

On that particular occasion there was a special reason for her to put a little extra into the song. The previous evening her father had gone to Garland's Lomita Theater as usual, but left after only a short while, complaining of a pain in his ears. He returned to Mariposa Avenue and went to bed. At around four in the morning he woke Ethel. He was now suffering

intense pain, and at about noon on the 16th he was taken to Cedars of Lebanon Hospital where his illness was diagnosed as a virulent type of spinal meningitis. Frank had suffered throughout his life from an infection of the inner ear. It was the kind of ailment that could be treated quite easily today, but at that time the appropriate drugs were not yet in use. Finally, the infection had drained into his body, bringing on the meningitis.

It was realized immediately that Frank had very little chance for survival. One of the doctors at his bedside was Marcus Rabwin, who called the studio to tell Judy that her father would have a radio by his bed that evening to hear her sing. She had not been told how ill her father was, but said later that she sensed there was some urgent motive behind this call. (Curiously, in later years Judy was under the impression that she had been broadcasting with Al Jolson that night rather than with Wallace Beery. Otherwise, though, her recollections of the occasion fit the facts.)

The next day Frank Gumm was dead. The end came at three o'clock in the afternoon. It was Ethel's birthday, as Virginia remembers:

My father had planned a surprise party for her—he hadn't even told us—and all these people they knew came to the door with presents. Some of them were from Grand Rapids. That's the saddest thing I can remember. My mother was lying on the couch, and all these people came to the door and said, "Happy Birthday!"

Years later, when Judy tried to analyze her own reactions to this catastrophe, she characterized it as the most terrible thing that ever happened in her life. There is no reason to suppose that this is anything less than the truth and she often spoke of her shame at being unable to cry at her father's funeral. In *McCall's* 1964 article, she spoke of more than a week passing before she could shed a tear. When the deluge arrived, according to that account, she shut herself in a bathroom and cried for fourteen hours. In the same piece, she made an attempt to sum up her relationship with Frank:

I wasn't close to my father, but I *wanted* to be all my life. . . . And he wanted to be close to me, too, but we never had much time together.

It's hard to know what to make of this—"we never had much time together" is an exaggeration—and to measure the real distance between Frank Gumm's death in 1935 and his daughter's 1964 memoirs, we would have to resort to some Einsteinian concept of relativity. Galaxies of pills had intervened.

Frank died just when the separations were ending, just when the family seemed to be finding a new stability. He died just when Judy was reaching the age where she might have been able to understand the complexity of the situation that had led to the separations. Had Frank lived, she might still have experienced pain in coming to terms with the notion that he was bisexual—but at least she would have had the opportunity to resolve things in her own mind.

When Judy said, "I wasn't close to my father, but I *wanted* to be," she was probably telling the truth. At the time of Frank's death she was still treated as the baby of the family. Even her sisters babied her—especially Suzanne. Sue had always been her father's favorite, and Virginia had been closest to her mother. As the baby, Judy had been lavished with affection by everyone, but at some cost. She was spoiled, perhaps, but treated as somebody apart. The others had formed their alliances and there was no one left in the family for her to establish a special relationship with. She unbalanced the family equation, and her extraordinary gifts isolated her still further. This might not have been noticeable at the time, but it would make itself felt eventually.

Frank Gumm was the only man Judy had known intimately. She had no male siblings to provide her with another masculine image, and Frank's legacy was ambiguous and confusing. Judy must have felt disoriented, and she seems to have dealt with this by trying to blot out the past and start again from scratch. This way of coping did not happen overnight, of course, but it was almost certainly set in motion by her

father's death, which could hardly have occurred at a worse time. She was just beginning her new life at M-G-M, and the aims of the studio and the aims of her subconscious coincided. M-G-M invented a surrogate childhood for her to escape to, thus destroying any hopes she might have had of finding roots and stability. The pills and the morphine and the rest of the junk would eventually finish the job—blurring whatever survived the fictionalizing process—but, to all intents and purposes, the truth was buried the day her father died. Eventually the happy times and all of the successes were obliterated, to be replaced by a catalogue of comic disasters.

Frank Gumm near the end of his life.

Chapter 1
The
Gilded Cage

For half a dozen blocks, from Overland Avenue to Jasmine Drive, Washington Boulevard forms the boundary between Culver City and the Palms District of Los Angeles. On the south side of the boulevard, stretching almost the full six blocks, is an unbroken stuccoed wall, about twenty feet high, decorated with evenly spaced pilasters. Behind this is Lot One of the Metro-Goldwyn-Mayer Studio. Near Jasmine Drive is an imposing gateway flanked by Corinthian columns. This has been chained for almost forty years, but it was through this portal that thirteen-year-old Judy Garland first entered the M-G-M world that would shape her life for the next fifteen years and which would haunt her to the end of her life.

Adjacent to this gateway, almost opposite a church built in the mission style, is a three-story building that once housed the studio's executive offices. When Judy came to Metro, Louis B. Mayer occupied a suite on the third floor of this building and Irving Thalberg, then

head of production, had his offices right below. Thalberg died in 1936, shortly before the executive offices were moved to a new and much larger building nearby. Dubbed the Thalberg Memorial Building, this structure—faced with white marble—is massive and solemn, with a blunt central tower. Totally lacking in architectural distinction, it resembles many municipal buildings of the period—caught in an aesthetic vacuum between the modern and the traditional—and this is perhaps appropriate since M-G-M was, to all intents and purposes, an independent community, with its own police force, its own fire station, an emergency hospital and many of the other services one would expect to find in a decent-sized town. It even had its own oil well.

Once the new executive offices were in use, the East Gate—just a few yards away—became the main entrance to the studio. In M-G-M's heyday the sidewalk outside the Thalberg Building would be lined every afternoon with kids out of school (and not a few

Judy with Jackie Cooper, 1936.

61

adults), hoping to glimpse Gable or Garbo or some other idol through the window of a sleek limousine—many in this eager crowd clasping autograph books and pencils. Today the few limousines that pass through the East Gate provoke little curiosity. Television shows and occasional feature films are still produced on Lot One, but the place seems almost deserted. Metro once had more than 5,000 employees, and on a busy day, with extras and visitors, the number of people on the lot might be considerably in excess of that. The combined populations of Grand Rapids and Lancaster could have been absorbed into the crowd without causing too much of a stir. There was even a mass transit system on the lot for the convenience of players and crew. (The stars, of course, traveled everywhere by limousine—even to the bathroom.)

The streets seem very quiet now, but everything is more or less intact and it's possible to wander among the giant sound stages and make some tenuous contact with the excitement of Metro's past. On the north side of the lot's main street, a couple of hundred yards beyond the East Gate, is the entrance to Stage Five, where many production numbers were staged for the spectacular musicals of the thirties and forties. Almost every scene that demanded a proscenium arch and an orchestra pit was shot here. Stage Five could become, at short notice, the New Amsterdam Theater or a Continental opera house. It has seen more triumphant opening nights than any theater on Broadway. (M-G-M screenplays seldom called for opening night disasters.) Astaire, Kelly, Garland and Rooney, Eleanor Powell, Frank Sinatra and dozens of other stars performed here to the ecstatic applause of elegantly attired dress extras.

A little farther along the main street, on the other side, is Stage Fifteen, said to be the largest sound stage in the world. It was here that M-G-M craftsmen built a full-sized replica of an aircraft carrier for *Thirty Seconds over Tokyo*. Altogether there are more than thirty stages, not to mention dozens of other buildings, and each of them has its phantoms. There are art deco fitting rooms still furnished with

The old main gate at M-G-M as it looked in 1935.

62

the mirrors that reflected Jean Harlow. You can walk along tiers of cubicles that resemble changing rooms at a public bathhouse. In the twenties these were dressing rooms for some of the biggest names in Hollywood. By the time Judy arrived, the stars and featured players were housed in grander dressing rooms which formed a row of boxlike structures that might have been designed for some Bauhaus model city. These are still there, but the mobile dressing rooms—exotic trailers furnished with antique chairs and crystal chandeliers—have long since vanished.

Only Garbo shunned the commissary, which was the social hub of the studio, a world within a world in which rank and taste were expressed in terms of where you sat and whom you sat with. Everyone had his appointed place. If there was a telephone call for Spencer Tracy, there was no need to page him since he always sat at the same table. A bus boy would bring a telephone to the table and plug it into a convenient jack. Since the commissary was generally packed, the certainty of its social conventions was indispensable. Somewhat modified, it still exists today and you may even see a few familiar faces there—actors guesting on *Medical Center,* perhaps—but whatever atmosphere clings to the place belongs entirely to the phantoms.

The real ghost towns, however, are to be seen across Overland Avenue on Lot Two— once one of two busy back lots maintained by M-G-M. Lot Three is already gone, replaced by a housing development, but Lot Two survives—for the time being—a rambling landscape of blitzed nostalgia.

It began life as a hole in the ground that was being offered for very little money. Since the hole was adjacent to his studio, Louis B. Mayer decided to look into the possibility of acquiring it. He had noted that the city of Los Angeles was planning to excavate La Brea Tar Pits, and it occurred to him that the city authorities might need somewhere to dump the material they would be ripping from their site. Discreet inquiries confirmed that this was indeed the case. Mayer bought the hole and the city of Los

Angeles filled it in. Thus M-G-M acquired several acres of valuable property for next to nothing.

Over the years dozens of outdoor sets accumulated on Lot Two, filling every available corner. A counterclockwise tour brings the visitor first to the so-called New York Street (also used to represent London, Chicago, Paris and a dozen other cities). Even in ruins, it is still impressive because of its scale—rows of brownstones, tenements, storefronts, banks and office buildings, all with smashed windows and peeling facades, tarpaper stonework hanging from wooden scaffolds. The school used in *Blackboard Jungle* looks as though it has been subjected to vandalism beyond anything that was called for by the scenario.

A side street, adjacent to the steps on which Van Johnson and Judy Garland played the opening scene of *In the Good Old Summertime,* leads to a totally different world. In a tangle of vegetation stands the house built for *The Philadelphia Story*—still in relatively good condition—and, through an ancient-looking archway, is the street on which parts of *An American in Paris* were shot. A little farther on is a clump of trees where Tarzan barked monosyllables at Jane. The cottage used in *National Velvet* is standing and the bushes Garbo ran through in *Camille* are still there, though sadly unkempt. Beyond them is Esther Williams' swimming pool, and nearby—alongside fragments of a Chinese temple, souvenirs of *The Good Earth*—is the train station used in *Waterloo Bridge.* At its platforms are abandoned railroad cars, their insides spilling out through warped openings where doors have been ripped from their hinges. A smaller depot, a hundred yards away, is notable as the spot where Gene Kelly made his first movie entrance—stepping from a train at the beginning of *For Me and My Gal.*

In Metro's glossy make-believe world people often sailed for the real and imagined delights of Europe, so a New York pier was built on Lot Two, complete with a full-scale replica of the superstructure of an ocean liner.

All of these relics are falling apart, rusting

and rotting and crumbling to dust. Among the saddest sights is Carvel Street, setting for most of the Andy Hardy saga. It would be easy to find symbols here: Polly Benedict's home is boarded up and the Hardy residence is choked with vines. Too easy, perhaps, since these structures were not intended to last, any more than the films they were built for were expected to have a life beyond their initial release. If Louis B. Mayer were alive today, he would certainly be shocked by the persistence of the images he sired. It's ironic that Mayer, a man who was consumed by the need for power, had no concept of the lasting power over the imagination that resided in the talent he controlled.

By all accounts, Louis B. Mayer was himself one of the greatest performers Hollywood has ever seen, able to unbutton his soul on cue, spilling sentiment on problems like honey on blintzes. Faced with a recalcitrant star, he would weep as easily as another man blinks; and if tears did not turn the tide, he could throw a fainting fit as convincing as any in the repertoire of Lillian Gish. (His style owed a great deal to his early association with silent movies.) His secretaries soon learned that these swoons were no cause for great alarm—a little cold water splashed on his face was the only medication called for—but they did work wonders in bringing arguments to an end. No display of emotion was too extreme as he played out scenes that would have been priceless if captured on celluloid.

Nor was his technique limited to the demands of soap opera. He could also play the swashbuckling hero, especially if the honor of American womanhood was slighted in his presence. Hearing Erich von Stroheim remark that all women were whores, Mayer punched him in the nose. Similar evidence of his chivalrous instincts was meted out to Charlie Chaplin and John Gilbert, to mention only some of his more distinguished victims. Unfortunately, his stocky frame did not permit him to bring the acrobatic flourish of a Fairbanks to these assaults.

Mayer was a man obsessed with his own position, hungry for approval and unable to deal calmly with any challenge to his authority. Having spent much of his life crossing swords with such ruthless characters as Lewis J. Selznick, William Fox and Nicholas Schenck, he had good reason to be on his guard; but the challenge did not have to be so formidable in order to unlock his ire.

Jackie Cooper was M-G-M's first child star, and *The Champ,* which teamed him with Wallace Beery, was one of the great successes of 1931. When the time came to cast Jackie in a new picture, his mother was horrified to discover that the studio was planning to use him in something that was little better than a B movie and she announced that she would not let the boy work unless a better role was found for him. Mayer responded by suspending him. Cooper was in the second year of a seven-year contract, so there was no question of his finding work elsewhere. He remained idle for six months until a go-between arranged a conciliatory meeting.

Jackie's mother brought him to the meeting (Mayer considered it desirable to have the trophy on hand) and he recalls sitting in the great man's office, bored, while the adults thrashed out his future. Mayer managed to keep his emotions under control for the duration of this discussion; then, when it was over, he saw everyone to the door. Cooper recalls what happened next:

I was last to leave the office and he stopped me as the others were standing just outside the door. He grabbed me by the shoulder, and turned me around and pointed a finger in my face—as though I was some thirty-year-old delinquent—and said, "It's a Goddamn good thing you showed up for work today, young man! And don't you forget it!" He was dead serious! I busted out crying. But evidently he just couldn't help it.

Jackie Cooper was nine years old at the time.

We should not be misled, however, into reducing Louis B. Mayer to a random catalogue of his personal eccentricities. He was, in his way, a remarkable man. A poor immigrant, he started his working life as a ragpicker in

Canada, graduated to scrap dealing, then gained a foothold in the fledgling motion picture industry by purchasing a small nickelodeon in Massachusetts. Before long he became a film distributor, and a single business coup—acquiring New England distribution rights to *The Birth of a Nation*—made him a wealthy man and enabled him to become a producer. His career closely paralleled the careers of other movie nabobs of his generation. The final successes of these men—Harry Cohn, Carl Laemmle, Jack Warner and the rest—owed their distinctive flavor to the fact that they had stewed for decades in a marinade of mutual suspicion and acrimony.

In 1924 Mayer found himself in control of the newly amalgamated Metro-Goldwyn-Mayer company and, with the invaluable assistance of Irving Thalberg, built it into perhaps the most formidable array of talent ever assembled in Hollywood. Following Thalberg's death, Mayer was in total command of the studio (though constantly harried by Nicholas Schenck, head of the parent organization, Loew's, Inc.). In 1937 Mayer earned—with bonuses—$1,300,000 making him the highest salaried man in America, a distinction he continued to enjoy, and even flaunt, for the next decade.

As Mayer's personal assistant, Ida Koverman—Judy Garland's benefactor—wielded considerable power and influence at the studio and was a formidable woman in her own right. Known to her friends as Kay, she met Mayer and became his right hand as a result of his feverish involvement in Republican politics. Koverman had once been Herbert Hoover's secretary and was well connected within the party organization. A tall, stately woman with a somewhat disconcerting facial resemblance to her employer, she served Mayer for more than two decades for the princely salary of $250 a week—being too proud to ask for an increase which Mayer, it seems, never offered on his own initiative. She lived modestly and drove an old Dodge her boss had given her in a rare moment of generosity, but this austerity did not reflect her importance to the studio. It

was Koverman, for instance, who was Metro's lobbyist in Washington when bills that might affect the industry were before Congress. It was Koverman who codified the star system, authoring such dictums as "A star may drink champagne and nectar, but not beer." And Koverman had a real nose for talent. In championing Judy, she was only maintaining her already impressive track record. It was Koverman who discovered Robert Taylor and Nelson Eddy, and she is the person who has generally been credited with rescuing Clark Gable from early oblivion. Mayer had not been impressed by Gable's screen test, but Koverman—sure that Gable was a winner—had it run for a group of female employees and their reactions changed Mayer's mind.

Ida Koverman's indifference to worldly rewards was not much imitated in the movie colony. While gaunt families migrated to California from the dust bowl and the bread line, Hollywood stars, directors and executives were earning $5,000 a week and more, and for the most part this money was not left to gather cobwebs or interest but was used to fuel a lifestyle that blended nostalgia for ancient luxuries (as imagined by Cecil B. De Mille) with respect for the more pragmatic advances of the twentieth century such as the cocktail shaker and the internal combustion engine. Strangely, the nation did not resent the sight of chauffeur-driven Duesenbergs and Silver Wraiths depositing celebrities with manicured smiles on the sidewalks outside the Pantages Theater. The crowds traced the wandering beams of the klieg lights to their source just to catch a glimpse of these glittering creatures. Hollywood transformed the Depression into a lottery with a long-term contract as the winning ticket.

Curiously, the winners tended to huddle together. Some bought ranches in the San Fernando Valley or farther afield, but most preferred to turn certain privileged areas, such as Beverly Hills, into clannish enclaves. Douglas Fairbanks once went so far as to propose that a wall be built around Beverly Hills, and while this extreme was rejected, the movie colony did manage to insulate itself in what can be thought of as the ultimate suburb—an exotic dormitory area within easy commuting distance of the nation's fantasies. Musical comedy chateaux once besieged by Hedda and Louella, overblown Tudor cottages set amid groves of palm trees, Moorish palaces built to accommodate the Jazz Age still survive and bear witness to the grandiose eclecticism of Hollywood. Audiences all over the world paid tribute to the men and women who built these structures, and they, in return, paid tribute to the world by borrowing idioms from every period and culture imaginable and tossing these appropriated forms against the Santa Monica Mountains to create a unique environment.

Judy Garland was not established immediately in a Beverly Hills mansion. Because Ethel could not bear the associations with Frank's death, the family left its home on Mariposa Avenue and moved into a house on McCadden Place. Although smack in the middle of Hollywood, McCadden Place was respectable rather than glamorous.

Meanwhile, on Lot One, Judy found herself attending classes with a group of youngsters that included her old friend Mickey Rooney, now a rising star. Their schoolhouse was a small Spanish-looking building with a red-tiled roof, surrounded by a picket fence. The studio had a legal obligation to see that young contract players received a certain number of hours' schooling each day, even if they were working on a movie.

For Judy, work was not an immediate problem since the studio did not have any pressing plans for her. At the instigation of Victor Young, orchestra leader on *The Shell Chateau Hour,* Decca Records approached M-G-M to sign Judy to a recording contract. As early as November 27, 1935, just ten days after her father's death (and two days after her reported crying marathon), she was summoned to a recording session Decca had set up primarily for Ginger Rogers. Judy cut two tracks—"No Other One" and "All's Well." These songs were not released and Decca did not call on her again for several months. Meanwhile her schedule at the studio was rather undemanding.

Another young contract player, almost the same age as Judy, was in a similar position and someone at M-G-M decided to see what they could do on screen. The other girl's name was Edna Mae Durbin. Later, of course, she became Deanna Durbin. A screen test was shot using the allegorical theme of Opera versus Jazz. Judy, of course, represented jazz—belting out a song in her usual style—while Deanna, an adolescent diva, trilled away in the upper registers. The test went well enough for the front office to approve the idea of featuring the two girls in a short built around this same jazz versus opera theme. The result was *Every Sunday,* an unpretentious but fascinating little film directed by Felix Feist. The plot, such as it is, exists as an excuse to have Judy and Deanna perform at an open-air band concert; their musical numbers are the *raison d'être* of the picture. *Every Sunday* gives us a marvelous glimpse of Judy's talent in its unrefined state. As on the air checks, we discover a singer whose technique is a little rough but who already knows how to channel all her energy into a performance and who owns a distinctive vocal personality. The real pleasure to be found in this movie, though, is in witnessing the sheer youthfulness of the two girls— each a singular synthesis of prettiness and *gau-*

Clowning with Deanna Durbin on the back lot.

cherie. Deanna's diffidence and Judy's explosive exuberance are touchingly recorded, and what we see is something far removed from the facile charms of most juvenile performers.

When she sang, Judy already had the habit of planting her feet apart and confronting the audience (or camera) directly, as if challenging it. She was tiny and a little plump, with huge eyes and a mouth that stretched into a grin at the slightest provocation. People who knew her then recall her as being like any other thirteen-year-old, yet her precocious talents were very much in evidence. It was not only her voice that was remarkable. She already possessed a highly developed sense of the ridiculous which made itself felt in a number of ways. She was a clever and accurate mimic—no one was safe from her impersonations. You could not afford to be pompous in her company because she would feed your mannerisms back to you, heightened for the sake of effect.

Everything she did tended to be heightened by her imagination. She had a knack of taking incidents from her everyday life—innocent enough events—and twisting them a little to show the inlay of absurdity she seemed to find everywhere. She had a distinctive way of telling a story—altering pitch several times within a sentence—and her sense of timing was immaculate. Needless to say, Hollywood provided her with plenty of material, but her need to destroy her own past may have been the prime impetus behind her anecdotal wit. It's easy enough to imagine how she developed this pattern. Talking about Lancaster, for instance, she might start by saying, "You can't imagine how *awful* the kids were. They hadn't even heard of *Variety*!" After a few dozen retellings, this might evolve into, "You can't imagine how *terrible* the kids were. They hated anyone in show business!" And before you had a chance to question this statement, it would dissolve into that incredible laugh—bursting out unexpectedly, apparently out of control. It was so infectious and unaffected, so self-deprecating, you had to believe whatever she had just told you, however preposterous.

68

She was already a consummate comedienne and couldn't resist trying out her gifts on friends and family. The sheer energy jammed into such a tiny frame was impressive in itself. Often she was so pent up with enthusiasm that she appeared out of breath. George Bassman, a composer and arranger who first encountered Judy during this period, says that when he met her he thought that she actually had some serious respiratory problem. Like others who worked with her then, he recalls her as an energetic little girl in white ankle socks, always accommodating and almost overly anxious to please—willing to do anything that was asked of her.

Before *Every Sunday* was seen by the general public, Judy had made her first feature film—but not for M-G-M. Somehow she came to the attention of 20th Century–Fox where a routine campus football comedy, *Pigskin Parade,* was being cast. The scenario called for a singing kid sister for Stu Erwin, who was set to star as a Texas yokel turned gridiron sensation. Metro was only too happy to loan Judy out for this picture. It would give everyone a chance to see what she could do without M-G-M having to risk a penny, and so she found herself on another back lot, working with Erwin, Patsy Kelly, Jack Haley and—in a small featured role— the young Betty Grable. Judy got to act a little and sang three songs: "It's Love I'm After," "The Texas Tornado" and "The Balboa." When the film was released in October of 1936, reviewers noticed her, but managed to keep ecstasy at bay.

Every Sunday was not shown until later in the year, and by then Deanna Durbin was gone, released by Metro and snapped up by Universal. For almost forty years Hollywood chroniclers have puzzled over this. Why did

Mayer let Deanna go? She was very much his type, with the touch of "class" that came from "operatic" styling. A number of legends have sprung up to explain this mystery. One suggests that it was an error—that it was Judy he meant to cut (both of the girls had contracts that could be terminated almost at will; agents used to joke about "ten-minute options"). According to this version, Mayer sent down his fiat—"Drop the fat one!"—meaning Judy, but someone misunderstood this cryptic command and released Deanna. Others think Deanna was cut in error while Mayer was on a trip to Europe and that he was furious to find her gone when he returned. This story sounds as though it may have originated close to the throne, after Deanna's enormous success at Universal. At least one producer, since deceased, claimed that both girls were to be released, but that he interceded on Judy's behalf.

The truth seems to be that there was an audition to decide which of the two girls the studio would hold on to. Evidently it had been concluded that there was room for one teenage singer on the M-G-M roster, but not two. The audition was held in the offices of Sam Katz, an executive producer who had total responsibility for all musical productions at that time. Katz was presumably acting as Mayer's surrogate. Various members of the music department were present, including George Stoll (one of Metro's top conductors and music supervisors) and Roger Edens. Jack Cummings, then Katz's top lieutenant, was probably there too. Apparently it was unanimously decided that Judy was the girl they would persevere with, and Deanna's contract was allowed to lapse.

This audition may have been tied to a particular movie role since by March, 1936—less than five months after joining Metro, and very soon after the Sam Katz audition—Judy was being seriously considered for a solid role in a major production, *Born to Dance*. Cole Porter, who wrote the music and lyrics for the picture, recorded this in a diary entry dated March 10 and quoted in George Eells' biography of the composer: "We discussed casting, and I heard

to my great joy that the picture will be played by Allan Jones opposite Eleanor Powell, Sid Silvers opposite Una Merkel, Buddy Ebsen opposite Judy Garland, and Frances Langford to play the jilted society girl."

Katz and Cummings were in charge of this production (the casting discussion had taken place in Katz's office). It's interesting to note that Cole Porter—a newcomer to Hollywood and an outsider at the studio—seems to have known exactly who Judy Garland was and to have been content to think she would be performing his songs. Eleanor Powell, Sid Silvers, Una Merkel, Buddy Ebsen and Frances Langford all survived to the final cut of the picture. Allan Jones was replaced somewhere along the way by Jimmy Stewart, and the Judy Garland part was lost entirely. The most likely explanation is that the opportunity to loan her to Fox for *Pigskin Parade* came up and it was decided to give her exposure that way instead. Fox, after all, would have to pay for the privilege.

At Universal, meanwhile, Joe Pasternak was planning a film, *Three Smart Girls,* that called for a "hot" singer in her early teens. Rufus LeMaire, who had just joined the Universal casting department after being at

In the M-G-M schoolhouse, Mickey Rooney passes Judy a note for the benefit of a visiting photographer.

M-G-M, suggested that Pasternak look at the test Judy and Deanna had made. Pasternak took LeMaire's advice and immediately contacted M-G-M to see if Judy was available. He was told she was not, probably because the loan agreement with Fox had already been worked out and the two productions would overlap. Discovering that Deanna had been released, Pasternak signed her for the part and had the screenplay revised to suit her style of singing. *Three Smart Girls* made Deanna Durbin a star overnight and rescued Universal from possible bankruptcy.

So Judy Garland's way separated from Deanna Durbin's, but the seeds of a lasting love-hate relationship had been planted. In later years Judy, unable to resist a chance to play the mimic, would do a cruel imitation of Deanna's singing posture. (She had broken an arm that never healed properly and she held it rather awkwardly). Unlike Judy, Deanna was not a natural show business type and stardom gave her very little pleasure. In 1948 she retired to France.

A few years later Judy, while visiting London, decided to call Deanna at her home near Paris.

"What are you doing?" asked Deanna.

"I'm in England for some concerts," said Judy.

"My God!" Deanna is said to have exclaimed. "Are you still in *that* business?"

In her memoir *Off with Their Heads!* Frances Marion—the same Frances Marion the Gumms met on their first trip to California—recalled that Ida Koverman became very concerned about Mayer's lack of interest in Judy. She remembered a conversation in which Koverman complained that her protégée was not making any progress: " 'Whenever I suggest her name for a small part in a musical, all [Mr. Mayer] says is, "Stop bleating! I'm running this studio, not you!" ' "

The story continues with Ida Koverman planning her assault on Mayer's sensibilities, deciding on a scheme and implementing it:

L. B. Mayer was a sentimentalist: sentimental love stories, mother-love stories,

and sentimental songs moved him to tears. But nothing touched him more deeply than the hauntingly melodic "Eli, Eli," which he had heard for the first time when it was sung by Belle Baker at the Hammerstein Music Hall. And this is what Ida Koverman had Judy Garland learn, and which she sang for the Big Boss one afternoon when he was alone and depressed.

"You'll never leave our studio," said Mayer when she had finished, the sob in his voice matching Judy's. "That is, if you do exactly what I tell you to do, letter for letter."

There would have been no need to teach Judy "Eli, Eli" since she and her sisters had featured the song in their act. But it can be assumed that Miss Marion's memory is accurate when it comes to Ida Koverman's dismay over her employer's lack of interest in Judy. Mayer was the kind of man who had to be nudged once in a while if one hoped to sustain his interest in an unproven talent. At this stage in the game he probably rediscovered Judy once every three months or so—whenever he was reminded of her existence.

Kay Mulvey, then with the M-G-M publicity department, remembers a party at Ida Koverman's home, with Mayer and his top aides present. Judy sang for them and Mayer waxed enthusiastic, telling everyone that a part must be found for the girl. John Green, the arranger and composer who would later work with Judy on a number of occasions, remembers a night at a Hollywood nightspot when again she sang and again Mayer was outspoken in his praise. But despite all this enthusiasm, nothing was happening in Judy's career.

As a consolation prize for not having landed any big parts, the studio sent her to New York for her fourteenth birthday on a working vacation. Ethel went along and they met Nicholas Schenck and some of the more important people in the East Coast office. On June 12 Judy was at a Decca recording session in New York, cutting two songs—"Stompin' at the Savoy" and "Swing Mister Charlie"—with the Bob Crosby Orchestra. Her first M-G-M feature was still months away.

Early in 1936 Jackie Cooper attended a party at Judy's home. He was a few months younger than Judy, but most of the guests were in their late teens or early twenties—friends of Jimmie's—and he was impressed by the way Judy mixed with and was accepted by this older group. Afterward he told his mother he had had a wonderful time and she asked if he would like to see Judy more often. He said that he would, but there was just one problem: Jackie was too young to drive and there was no way he could see Judy without the use of a car. His mother solved this by hiring a young man who worked at a gas station near the studio to drive them. The outcome was a number of dates that involved a good deal of handholding on the back seat. Judy became Cooper's first steady girlfriend.

That summer Cooper's mother rented a house on the beach at Ocean Park, and Judy was a frequent visitor—often sleeping over on weekends. Cooper recalls it as a happy time:

We could walk to the amusement zone and we could walk to the movies. . . . There were the kids, and there was swimming and night swimming. . . . My mother and I would pick Judy up, and she would stay in the guest room. It was terrific.

I assumed by then—and so did she—that we were going very steady. We were writing each other passionate letters. . . . And we tied up an awful lot of telephones.

It was all wonderfully normal. Years later Judy would enjoy telling the story of how Cooper's mother had served spaghetti one night—a problem for Judy since she had never eaten spaghetti before. Rather than embarrass herself, she pretended she wasn't hungry.

Teenage romances have a way of ending quite abruptly and this one was no exception. Significantly, it was Judy who initiated the break, as Cooper remembers very well:

Towards the end of that summer, she suddenly told me that she'd fallen in love with Billy Halop. And I was crushed because— first of all—he was about three years older

With Billy Halop and Bonita Granville.

than me. I think he was a very old eighteen, or something like that. It was very difficult.

I remember for many years looking back at the conversation—I don't think I said six words. But I remember she was very composed, very determined in how she felt— and that's the way it was. . . . She was trying to explain to me that girls were older, anyway, and that I just had to understand that.

Perhaps this should be seen merely as a normal ending to a normal teenage romance. Given the benefit of hindsight, though, it may have been an early example of a behavior pattern that was to become familiar in Judy's adult life—the compulsion to lash out at someone she loved before that person had a chance to hurt her. It may also be that the hothouse atmosphere of the movie world was already beginning to have some effect on Judy's growth —forcing the fragile illusion of sophistication that sometimes passed for maturity in Hollywood.

There was a tendency, in the movie colony, to elevate precocity to the rank of a cardinal virtue, and—since everyone there was assumed to be eternally young—precociousness could easily become a way of life.

71

About this time Judy experienced her first taste of conscious ambition. All her life she had had a tremendous drive to please people—a drive not uncommon in last-born children—but this was not quite the same thing. According to Virginia, the early successes on the stage and in radio had been very much taken for granted by the three girls, especially Judy:

When you start out doing something as a kid, you just accept it—you don't have that kind of driving ambition. However, when she got under contract to Metro and they almost passed her by . . . that made her mad—and I don't blame her. . . . That she resented!

What triggered this resentment was Deanna Durbin's success at Universal. After her second movie there—*One Hundred Men and a Girl*—Deanna was invited to plant her hands and feet in the concrete outside Grauman's Chinese Theater. Judy was incensed and inconsolable. She felt that her career was a failure. After all, it was she—Judy Garland—who had paid the dues! (She thought of her rival as a rank amateur, however talented.) It was Judy Garland who deserved to be the star. Judy became hysterical and Ethel could do nothing with her. In desperation Ethel eventually sent for Ida Koverman, who did manage to calm Judy with assurances that one day she would see her own prints in the concrete outside Grauman's.

Nor was Judy the only person to become incensed at Deanna's success. Louis B. Mayer was furious because he had let her go, and his anger probably worked to Judy's benefit since

it's reported (and the story is completely in character) that he set out to prove he had not made a mistake in hanging on to her. Legend has him saying, "I'll make the fat kid bigger than Durbin."

In legend, it should be noted, Mayer habitually referred to the young Judy Garland as "the fat one" or "the fat kid"—even, on occasion, as "my little hunchback." In his autobiography, *I Remember It Well,* Vincente Minnelli records a story that Judy later told against herself:

She told of the times Mayer would bring visitors to the set. "Do you see this little girl?" he'd ask. "Look what I've made her into. She used to be a hunchback."

The visitors gasped.

"Yes, a hunchback. Isn't that true, Judy?"

Judy would think about it for a while. "Why yes, Mr. Mayer, I suppose it is."

Judy was a little oddly built, short-necked with a high waist and a large rib cage, and there's no denying that she was a trifle pudgy—baby fat is quite evident in both *Every Sunday* and *Pigskin Parade*. Because of this, she was put on a strict diet and sent to exercise classes at the studio gym. The latter were probably no great imposition because she was a good athlete, but the diet was another matter entirely. Orders were given to the commissary staff that Judy should be served only certain prescribed dishes, the most famous of which—Louis B. Mayer's beloved chicken soup—looms so large in the annals of M-G-M that it's practically worthy of a Ph.D. thesis. Most sources state that it was made from a recipe supplied by Mayer himself, and Frances Marion recalls that as early as 1923, before the birth of M-G-M, Mayer was looking forward to the day when he could serve it to his employees: " 'Someday, when I've got a larger studio, I'll have a lunchroom in it and see that everyone working for me has a big bowl of chicken soup full of noodles or matzo balls. . . .'" Be that as it may, in the early 1940s, the M-G-M publicity department attributed the recipe for the commissary's chicken soup to Walter Pidgeon. Pidgeon seems such a sublimely improbable source that one longs to believe the story, but he was not under contract to M-G-M until 1937, and chicken soup was on the menu well before then. This raises all kinds of fascinating, if slightly arcane, questions—all of which can be answered by the notion that someone in the publicity department had a sense of humor.

Beyond this, it's hard to imagine that chicken soup "full of noodles or matzo balls" would be an effective diet food.

Later in life Judy would point to this as the period when her drug problem began. She claimed the studio had forced her to take pills to lose weight, even suggesting that Mayer had hired someone whose secret task it was to grind amphetamines into Judy's food. While avoiding the more melodramatic implications of all this, Virginia confirms that diet pills were prescribed for Judy at this point in her career:

There are times, at a place like Metro, when they don't give a damn about your talent—all they're worrying about is how you look and they make a big thing out of it. That's when Benzedrine and stuff like that first came out, and nobody thought it was bad. It killed your appetite, and that's why you took it. Nobody realized it was *speed!*

The studio doctor gave her Dexedrine, I believe it was, to keep her weight down. Nobody thought it was bad. My mother didn't think it was bad—if she had, she wouldn't have let Judy take it. But nobody knew anything about it then.

Judy did begin to lose weight, but still there was no part for her and she was receiving very little public exposure except for regular spots on Jack Oakie's radio show.

On the lot she spent much of her time rehearsing songs with Roger Edens. Edens was a tall easy-going Southerner, in his early thirties, who had come to M-G-M from New York, where he had been Ethel Merman's rehearsal pianist. From the outset he recognized Judy's exceptional gifts and he developed a profes-

sional intimacy with her which was to last for many years. More than anyone else, he was responsible for refining her talent—it would be difficult to overemphasize his contribution. It was Edens who nurtured the remarkable voice and raw intuition and helped Judy to gain poise and an assured sense of style. She trusted him completely and—from a musical viewpoint—he allowed her to discover herself.

As time went on, Judy's mother came to resent her daughter's close relationship with Edens. Edens had, after all, usurped her role as vocal coach and all the trust that went with that position. At one point Judy refused to wear any item of clothing Ethel had chosen for her and Ethel had to resort to the strategy of having Edens pretend to pick the clothes, since Judy had implicit faith in his taste. In any case, Edens worked with Judy every day. According to Hollywood tradition—the residue of a million press releases—Ida Koverman sat in on one of these sessions and was struck by the idea of having Judy perform at a surprise party that was being planned for Clark Gable. She probably felt that Mayer needed another nudge. Edens wrote a special verse for the Monaco-McCarthy standard, "You Made Me Love You," which was transformed into "Dear Mr. Gable."

At L. B. Mayer's Santa Monica home. Left to right: Betty Jaynes, Jackie Cooper, Judy, Mickey Rooney, June Preisser, Virginia Weidler.

On February 1, 1937, at the height of the celebration of Clark Gable's thirty-sixth birthday, the fourteen-year-old Judy Garland serenaded the man they called "the King" with "Dear Mr. Gable," a musical fan letter. Everyone was enchanted. Carole Lombard teased Gable and Mayer had Judy sit on his lap. He was fond of these "family" events and Judy's performance brought to this one a touch of sentiment that raised it above the average. Again, he insisted that something had to be found for Judy and this time he arranged for the song—and the singer—to be written into a film that was about to go into production, *Broadway Melody of 1938*. That, at least, is the orthodox version of the story.

Jack Cummings, who produced *Broadway Melody of 1938,* recalls that Judy had figured in his casting plans for this picture from the very first production meeting. Since Cummings was very well aware of Judy's talents and had wanted her for *Born to Dance,* there's every reason to believe him. He also remembers that Roger Edens wrote "Dear Mr. Gable" specifically for the film. Certainly Judy performed the song at Gable's party—there are plenty of witnesses to that—but this is not inconsistent with Cummings' recollections. If the number had been written for the upcoming movie, it's very probable that someone (Ida Koverman would be a likely candidate) suggested that Judy sing it at the party.

Responding to the tribute, Gable later presented Judy with a gold charm bracelet that incorporated the seals of Grand Rapids and Murfreesboro, a theatrical trunk, three little girls with pearl heads, a pack of gum bound with a garland of flowers and bearing George Jessel's name, two wedding rings for Sue and Jimmie (Jimmie had recently married Bob Sherwood—like Sue's husband, a musician), a replica of the studio, a microphone, a contract scroll and a gold book that held a tiny portrait of the donor. This last was inscribed "To Judy, my favorite actress, Sincerely, Clark Gable." It would be pleasant to think that Gable planned this gift himself. But how would he know about Murfreesboro—to mention

74 *Publicity photo, circa 1938.*

just one detail? Probably the whole thing was cooked up by the publicity department. The theatrical trunk has the authentic hokey touch and fits in with the scheme to replace Judy's childhood with a more useful myth. The bracelet would come in handy when the time arrived to promote *Broadway Melody of 1938,* since each charm provided a convenient peg on which to hang some interesting or amusing piece of information about Metro's new singing sensation, Judy Garland.

The film itself was a featherbrained vehicle built around Robert Taylor (as a Broadway producer conventionally short of cash) and Eleanor Powell (as the tap-dancing owner of a racehorse). Judy played the daughter of Sophie Tucker, who was cast as the owner of a theatrical boardinghouse, and was given the chance to play a little comedy (which she did with considerable flair) and do a dance number with Buddy Ebsen. The highspot of the movie, however, came when she sang "Dear Mr. Gable" to a photograph of "the King." Audiences loved it. The song was a hit and Roger Edens' lyric gave Judy, for the first time, a definite identity.

Broadway Melody of 1938. *A segment of the finale that was cut from the release print.*

Stardom was a way off yet, but people were beginning to take notice of Judy Garland. The drought was over. For the next dozen years she would be working almost nonstop.

M-G-M did not wait for the reviews to begin planning new vehicles for Judy, meanwhile withdrawing her from outside activities. *The Hollywood Reporter,* dated April 13, 1937, reported that Judy was set for a picture to be titled *Molly, Bless You,* in which she would be featured with Wallace Beery, Sophie Tucker and Reginald Gardiner. No such picture was made, but suddenly Judy's name began to crop up in the trade papers with a frequency that suggests that someone had lit a small fire under the M-G-M publicity department.

On May 26 readers of *The Hollywood Reporter* were informed that Edwin L. Marin had been assigned to direct *The Ugly Duckling,* featuring Judy Garland. This title does not appear in Judy's filmography because it was eventually changed to *Everybody Sing.* On

May 27 it was announced that Judy Garland would be dropping out as vocalist on the Jack Oakie show—apparently because she was now too busy at the studio. The issue dated June 8 reported that Metro had cast Judy, along with Mickey Rooney and Freddie Bartholomew, in *Thoroughbreds Don't Cry*. (Later, Bartholomew would be replaced by another young British actor, Ronald Sinclair.) On June 11 there was another item about *The Ugly Duckling*, and on June 23 followers of the "Rambling Reporter" column learned that Judy Garland was losing popularity with her neighbors because she had been practicing the saxophone, which she was scheduled to play in her next picture. On August 2 it was mentioned that M-G-M was shaping a story—tentatively titled *Listen, Darling*—that would provide Judy Garland with her first starring vehicle. On August 14 *Broadway Melody of 1938* was reviewed:

The sensational work of young Judy Garland causes wonder as to why she has been kept under wraps these many months. She sings two numbers that are show stoppers, and does a dance with Buddy Ebsen. Hers is a

distinctive personality well worth careful promotion.

On August 16 the *Reporter* followed this up by saying, "With the right material, M-G-M could create a great star with Judy Garland." The paper carried an advertisement on August 20 in which Judy publicly thanked Sam Katz, Jack Cummings and Roger Edens. Three days later an item announced that she had gone north for appearances at the San Francisco Paramount in connection with *Broadway Melody*. On August 31 it was reported that the shooting of *Thoroughbreds Don't Cry* would commence the following day, while *The Ugly Duckling* was due to go in front of the cameras later that week. Working on two pictures at once, Judy could hardly complain that she was being overlooked anymore.

Thoroughbreds was the first to be released. Directed by Alfred E. Green, the film used a horseracing background and starred Rooney as a bragging young jockey who accepts a bribe in order to buy his ailing father an iron lung! The screenplay once again placed Judy in a boardinghouse and teamed her with Sophie Tucker. Judy sang only one number, but she was also given some good comedy situations.

The Ugly Duckling—renamed *Everybody Sing*—also allowed her to show off her talents as a comedienne. This picture is a delightful bit of thirties nonsense about a lunatic theatrical family, with Billie Burke as Judy's dotty mother and Fanny Brice as the family's Russian maid. The plot cannot be adequately summarized. Sufficient to say that Judy, after being expelled from school for jazzing up Mendelssohn, walks in on a situation where her mother is preoccupied with her leading man (Reginald Gardiner) while Allan Jones, posing as their cook, is actually preparing to put on a Broadway show. Surrounded by maniacs, Judy manages to display remarkable poise. Her timing is excellent and she works with the adults as an equal.

These are not the kinds of pictures that can

Everybody Sing.
With Fanny Brice.

Thoroughbreds
Don't Cry. *With
Ronald Sinclair.*

usefully be subjected to serious critical analysis, but they are nicely paced and well crafted. They ooze with period charm and are crammed with the offhand virtuosity that could almost be taken for granted from the M-G-M stock company.

Judy had no sooner finished these two pictures than she was into rehearsal for a third, *Listen, Darling*. As announced in *The Hollywood Reporter,* she received star billing in this movie, along with Freddie Bartholomew, while Mary Astor and Walter Pidgeon—two Hollywood veterans—had to be content with featured billing. Miss Astor was not too happy with the parts M-G-M was giving her at this time, but she did enjoy her first encounter with Judy Garland, as she has recorded in *A Life on Film:*

. . . working with Judy was sheer joy. She was young and got the giggles regularly. You just couldn't get annoyed, because she couldn't help it—it was no act. Something would strike her funny, and her face would get red and "There goes Judy!" would be the cry. And we just had to wait until she got over it. She was a kid, a real kid. It didn't take long for her to get over that.

Listen, Darling, directed by Edwin L. Marin, produced by Jack Cummings, is a charming little trifle (just seventy minutes long), a bit sentimental in spots, but easy viewing. The story has Judy and her friend, played by Bartholomew, kidnapping her widowed mother so she won't be able to marry the sourpuss schoolmaster. Along the way they encounter Walter Pidgeon, who proves to be a more satisfactory match.

In this movie Judy's character is softened somewhat from that of her earlier appearances. She has several scenes that depend on her ability to appear moist-eyed, and they are intended to produce a similar reaction in the audience. Fortunately, she also has some good moments of comedy and three songs, including a sparkling "Zing Went the Strings of My Heart" in which, standing squarely in front of

the camera and using her arms for balance, she shows just why Sophie Tucker had predicted she would be the next Red Hot Mama.

Early in 1938 Judy found time to play a few scenes in *Love Finds Andy Hardy*. This was the fourth of the Hardy movies and it might be considered the quintessence of the entire series. Directed by George B. Seitz, the film has Mickey Rooney trying to raise $20 for his first car, while Judy, Ann Rutherford and Metro's newest glamour girl, Lana Turner, wonder which one of them he'll take to the big dance. The rest can safely be left to memory or to the imagination.

Having escaped the realities of small town

Mickey Rooney puts on a show at Judy's Stone Canyon house.

America, Judy found herself, in such films as *Listen, Darling* and *Love Finds Andy Hardy,* presented to the public as the representative of a quaint platonic abstraction of small town America. It must have seemed odd to her. Her innocence was already slipping away, but there were still plenty of remnants from which to sew a semblance of normality. Although most of her schooling took place on the lot, she was enrolled at Bancroft Junior High, from which she graduated in 1937, and then at University High. A classmate at Bancroft recalls that Judy would show up there from time to time and that she and Rooney often came to sock hops and the like, adding that Judy was well liked by most of her contemporaries. (Jason Robards, Jr., was in the same graduating class.)

There seems to be little truth to Judy's later accusation that her teachers informed her she did not belong with normal children—though there may have been an isolated incident. Yet, from this point on, her life was so different from other kids' lives that in a very real sense she did not belong with them. Celebrity is like an open sore that fascinates and repels at the same time. So far, the sore was small, but it was there and it could not be ignored.

In March, 1938, at the end of a promotional tour for *Everybody Sing,* Judy made a brief return to the real small town world. Along with Ethel and an M-G-M entourage, she visited her birthplace, Grand Rapids, where the citizens

Love Finds Andy Hardy. *With Mickey Rooney, Ann Rutherford and Lana Turner.*

found her charming and quite unspoiled by her Hollywood success. She posed with a fifteen-pound bag of Arrowhead Select potatoes and was lunched at the Pokegama Hotel. She visited junior and senior high schools and spoke briefly between shows at the Rialto Theater (which had replaced the New Grand). She attended a party thrown for her by the young people of Grand Rapids at the Cabin City Tavern. (The M-G-M representatives objected to this event but Ethel put her foot down, determined that her former neighbors should not feel slighted.) Apparently a happy homecoming for everyone concerned, but certainly not an *ordinary* homecoming. However sweet, wholesome and unspoiled Judy may have appeared to the people of Itasca County, she was now perceived as a celebrity. A native of Grand Rapids had made a name for herself in Hollywood. It was as if each citizen had suddenly sprung a solid gold fingernail.

Despite a snowstorm, Judy was met by an armada of cars and her picture was splashed across the front pages of the local papers. In commenting that Judy was "unspoiled," the good people of Grand Rapids betray their *surprise*—as if they thought that, in her position, any one of them might well have taken advantage of the opportunity to become spoiled.

An incident more relevant to Judy's new life occurred a few weeks earlier, at the beginning of the promotional tour. She made her New York theatrical debut at Loew's State and, despite Roger Edens' presence at the piano, began very shakily and was obviously quite nervous. For a few minutes it looked as if she might blow the whole thing and the situation was further aggravated when a baby in the audience began to cry. Judy paused for a moment, uncertain of what to do, then she laughed and immediately had everyone in the palm of her hand.

During the last twenty years of her life Judy Garland loved to tell anyone who would listen how her mother had formed a malicious alliance with Louis B. Mayer to pervert Judy's life. All the evidence, however, suggests that far from acting as an arm of the studio, Ethel had little love for Mayer and his sidekicks. Virginia remembers that Ethel was intensely protective of Judy, just as she had been protective of all three girls during their earlier vaudeville days:

She wanted Judy to have what Judy wanted. It wasn't ever a question of, "You do what they say." If Judy complained, Mama complained.

When we were on the road, we never had to deal with agents and club owners, and all those people—we never came up against them because Mama took care of that. . . . If we asked questions, she said, "Don't worry about it."

Once, at the Hippodrome in Los Angeles, the manager bawled us out, and Mama bawled the manager out. "Don't you talk to my girls like that," she said. "If you have anything to say, you say it to me!"

When Judy went to Metro, they barred my mother from the studio for a year. I took Judy in every morning because they wouldn't let Mama on the lot. And the reason was, Judy hated to get up in the morning—at five o'clock—to go to work. My mother went in to fight for her not to have to go in so early, and they had her barred from the lot because they said she was interfering.

All she was trying to do was get Judy a couple of extra hours' sleep in the morning, because she just wasn't used to getting up early. It was okay when she went to school at nine o'clock—but that five o'clock call was pretty rough.

If anything, Ethel was being overprotective of Judy. It was clearly unreasonable of her to suppose that the studio would change its shooting schedules to suit the sleeping habits of one juvenile, however talented. But the story does demonstrate that she was not timid about protecting Judy, nor was she endangering Judy's career by doing so. The worst M-G-M could do would be to drop Judy's contract, and in that case, every other studio in Hollywood would be fighting over her.

Some people have gone so far as to suggest that Ethel offered Judy to Mayer as a sexual plaything in order to advance her daughter's career. It's impossible to determine whether or not this story originated in Judy's head, but it certainly ranks among the most preposterous ever to come out of Hollywood. There is some reason to suppose, however, that Judy was seduced when she was fifteen or sixteen by a man considerably older than herself—a well-known Hollywood figure. This man was dynamic and self-possessed. He was assertive and his conversation was peppered with aphorisms and arcane references that must have sounded wonderfully suggestive to a young girl. He was a Svengali type, by turns sarcastic and encouraging. Judy undoubtedly found his attentions extremely flattering. She was probably an easy conquest.

By now she had come to think of herself as a trifle homely. Not that she was unattractive, but she was "cute" rather than beautiful and the competition on the lot made "cute" seem rather tepid. Virginia is not sure when her sister first became self-conscious about her looks—she does not believe it happened during her first couple of years at Metro—but remembers that Judy did quite suddenly become aware of Lana Turner's presence at the studio: "I remember her saying to Mama one time that she wanted to look like or be like Lana Turner—that she couldn't wait until she was old enough to be called 'bitchy.' My mother was horrified! But Judy said, 'You get more attention. . . .' " Lana was only a couple of years older than Judy, but those two years made all the difference in the world. Judy was still treated as a child, while no one ever mistook Lana for anything but a budding sexpot.

Left to her own devices, Judy would probably have been able to adjust to this. She would have gone through the normal growing pains and she would have found an image that allowed her to live with herself. To the men who ran the studio, however, she already had an effective image and they did not intend to let her change it. She was the girl next door, trapped in eternal puberty. The only direction they were prepared to let her move in was backward, and that is exactly what she was asked to do for her next film.

Chapter 2
Ruby Slippers

Looking back at Judy Garland's career, the quantum leap to lasting stardom is easily isolated. Everyone knows it occurred when she played Dorothy in *The Wizard of Oz*.

The twister that sucks Dorothy's home off the prairie sucks the viewer's mind out of its roots in the world of common sense. Then, when the farmhouse is set down in Munchkinland, the viewer's imagination is released on the threshold of a carefully constructed fantasy and Dorothy steps out of her monochrome Midwest into full Technicolor. Since color was not yet an everyday commodity in the movies, it endowed *The Wizard of Oz* with sensuality —an innocent sensuality reminiscent of childhood treats: eyes and hands set loose in a candy store jam-packed with jawbreakers, jelly beans, bubblegum, gumdrops, candy corn and Tootsie Rolls. Specifically, this is the sensuality of the late thirties tri-pack Technicolor, with its distinctive blush, its noonday warmth, its faint deepening of the spectrum. The color pictures of the period have as singular a palette as that of any Post-Impressionist painter. In *The Wizard of Oz* the artifice is heightened by the fairy-tale sets and backdrops. Everything is painted or dyed, including the flesh of the performers. The yellow brick road owes its particular pigmentation to several layers of house paint, and everywhere the color lies flat on surfaces—a cosmetic skin, like lipstick or rouge.

Probably no other Hollywood live-action film ever sustained an atmosphere of total artifice so convincingly. (The best of Disney's animated features are the only things that compare.) When Dorothy and her friends emerge from the woods on their pilgrimage to seek an audience with the Wizard, there is a long, ravishing pan shot that comes to meet them—a shot that drifts across a meadow of poppies and discovers the four travelers dancing and singing against a background of brightly illuminated trees, before a cut brings us a first, distant view of the Emerald City. This scene is so breathtaking visually that it seems to lend authority and authenticity to the fabulous events it briefly interrupts.

The Wizard of Oz. *With Jack Haley and Ray Bolger.*

Spectacular shots, such as the one described above, are used sparingly; what makes the film so powerful—besides the overall excellence of the performances—is the fact that it is shot in a straightforward way. The dramatic simplicity of most of the setups makes us accept the artifice of *Oz* as perfectly natural, especially since Kansas has already been treated with exactly the same blend of artifice and realism. Mostly, the camera stays relatively close to the characters and their actions occupy our attention fully. Any temptation to overexploit the fantasy of the environment and the situation is scrupulously avoided.

The quality of *Oz* is self-evident. The point here is that it was the perfect vehicle for Judy Garland at that point in her career. Its one hundred minutes were enough to elevate her to the sparsely populated plateau of permanent celebrity, from which there is no safe descent.

The story of the making of *The Wizard of Oz* has been told many times, and still all the facts are not entirely clear. According to most accounts, Mervyn LeRoy went to Mayer with the idea of making a movie based on L. Frank Baum's classic. LeRoy himself recalls that for many years he had lived with the notion of turning *Oz* into a film. Arthur Freed, however, a few years before his death in 1974, gave a slightly different account of the film's genesis:

Before I was a producer, Mr. Mayer had spoken to me about producing pictures, so I bought *The Wizard of Oz* from Sam Goldwyn. He had owned it for years and never made it. I started out being the associate producer of the film, but it was an expensive picture and Mr. Mayer suggested I take Mervyn LeRoy to produce it.

According to LeRoy's recollections, after the project had been set up, Mayer called him into his office and asked him to take Freed on as his assistant. Mayer wanted Freed to become a producer (he did and his elevation had an enormous impact on Judy Garland's career) and thought LeRoy was the right person to teach him the ropes.

84

The fact that *The Wizard of Oz* was budgeted for over $3,000,000—an enormous sum for the period (several times the cost of most feature films)—tends to support LeRoy's version. Arthur Freed had been at M-G-M for several years, beginning his association with Metro's first musical, *Broadway Melody,* in 1929. Teamed with composer Nacio Herb Brown, he had written such standards as "Singing in the Rain," "Temptation" and "You Are My Lucky Star," but up to this point he had been essentially a lyricist, with some executive responsibilities but no real production experience. It's not likely that Mayer ever seriously considered putting him in charge of such an expensive and chancy project as *Oz* at that point in his career.

LeRoy, on the other hand, was very much the golden boy. He had just been brought in from Warner Brothers, where he had a spectacular track record that included such hits as *Little Caesar* and *I Am a Fugitive from a Chain Gang.* Mayer wanted LeRoy to develop major projects. With Thalberg gone, he needed fresh but proven talents to take up the slack. LeRoy came to Metro with a good deal of clout (symbolized by a guarantee of $300,000 a year) and he certainly needed it to persuade Mayer of the merits of spending so much money on a property as inherently risky as *The Wizard of Oz*–especially since Nicholas Schenck, in New York, was resolutely opposed to the project.

Fantasy is always a risk at the box office. *The Wizard of Oz* had been enormously successful as a book, and it had also been a major stage hit, but previous efforts to bring it to the screen had been dismal failures. L. Frank Baum himself had produced, between 1913 and 1915, *The Patchwork Quilt of Oz, The Magic Cloak of Oz* and *The New Wizard of Oz*—the receptions of which encouraged him to abandon the film business. In 1925 a comedian named Larry Semon starred himself in a version of *The Wizard of Oz,* which strayed far from the spirit and content of the original without stumbling into a formula for success. As early as 1910 the Selig Company put out a one-reel version of the story, which soon vanished without a trace. Even the Meglin Kiddies (after the Gumm Sisters had departed their ranks) took a shot at *Oz* without causing any great stir.

Though Mayer was not free of doubts about this project, he gave it his blessing (it seems he was personally very attracted to the story). The rights were obtained for $50,000 from Sam Goldwyn who, curiously, had been considering *Oz* as a vehicle for Eddie Cantor.

It's common knowledge that Judy Garland almost missed the role of Dorothy, but it would be a mistake to assume that she got the part entirely by default. Both LeRoy and Freed wanted Judy from the very beginning. Freed was one of her staunchest supporters, and LeRoy had wanted to work with her ever since seeing *Pigskin Parade*. Mayer, and some of his aides, had another idea. They saw Shirley Temple as the logical choice for Dorothy, and while we should give thanks that nothing came of this, it's easy enough to follow their reasoning. We can date the selection of Dorothy to somewhere in the spring or summer of 1938. Temple was then at the height of her popularity. She had made *Heidi* and *Rebecca of Sunnybrook Farm* and been the top box-office attraction for three years in a row (1938 would make it four). By the time *Oz* reached the production phase, Temple would be just ten years old—about the age Dorothy seems to be in Baum's book. (Her age is never specified, but the illustrations give a clue.)

A persistent legend says that Mayer went so far as to offer 20th Century–Fox a deal that involved the loan of two top Metro stars, Clark Gable and Jean Harlow, in exchange for Temple's services. This fell through, so the story goes, because of Harlow's death. Mervyn LeRoy has no recollection whatsoever of any such proposal, and the fact that Harlow died on June 7, 1937—several months too early to make her a factor in any *Oz* deal—suggests that the story is just another myth. More likely, Metro made a straightforward request to Fox, which was turned down flat. A film like *The Wizard of Oz* would tie up its star for months, and no matter how attractive M-G-M's offer

may have been, there was no real likelihood that Fox would consider giving up the nation's number-one cash draw for that length of time. After all, she was getting older every day. It's easy to see why Shirley Temple was Mayer's first choice for *Oz*, but it's difficult to imagine that he ever entertained any serious hope of getting her for the part.

Whatever the case, Mayer and his aides decided to go along with the producers' original choice and cast Judy in the role of Dorothy. This was not much of a gamble. Judy was by now a known quantity. The press had already slated her for stardom. She had real screen presence and she had proved she could be charming and funny, though she had not had a part that came within a mile and a half of testing her. Most of all, *The Wizard of Oz* was a musical and Judy had a voice that was little short of incredible. There was not a juvenile in Hollywood who could match her uncanny sense of timing or who could lift a lyric out of the ordinary the way she did.

LeRoy says that Mayer never had serious doubts about using Judy in the film. The one reservation that everyone must have had was the possibility that she was too old for the part. By the time the last scenes were shot, she would be approaching her seventeenth birthday. As things turned out, this was an actual advantage. One problem with a fantasy film is that in order to be a commercial success it must appeal to adults as well as to children. And in *The Wizard of Oz* Judy Garland is an adolescent with a grown-up's singing voice *acting* the part of a child. She is close enough to childhood to be completely convincing, but she is role-playing enough to draw adults into the action too.

Fortunately, she was small. Even in the ruby slippers she would barely top five feet and the producers could surround her with tall co-stars so that she would seem even smaller. Physically, she was almost a woman, but they strapped her into a special corset and bound her breasts flat with yards of tape so she would seem to have the body of a child. (Thirty years later, crazy with hatred of M-G-M, she would

85

Preceding pages:
On the set of The
Wizard of Oz with
Mervyn LeRoy,
Victor Fleming
(holding Toto) and
some of the
Munchkins.

claim that these constricting foundations ruined her singing in the movie—ignoring the fact that all her songs were prerecorded.) To further blur the outlines of her figure, the wardrobe department put her in a loose blue-checkered gingham dress. Outfitted this way, she would have been uncomfortable on a cool morning in Kansas, but she would be working on a sealed sound stage under intensely hot lights that almost knocked you sideways when they were turned on.

It's commonly said that the studio fixed Judy's teeth for *The Wizard of Oz,* but in fact, she wore the shell caps she had already worn in some of her previous films and which she continued to wear throughout her career. Occasionally you will see pictures of her without these caps, which could be slipped on and off like thimbles. Some sources have said she was given a nose job at the same time. This story seems to have grown out of an experiment where putty was applied to her nose to see how it would look if it was straighter. (In some scenes of *Broadway Melody of 1938* her nose looks as if it may have been given a false bridge.) LeRoy and Freed did not see this as an improvement. Nor did they like the blond wig that was tried out at one point. Instead, Judy's hair was reddened and a matching fall was added.

In short, a number of adjustments were necessary to transform Judy Garland into Dorothy, but most of them had the solitary purpose of making her look younger. For the rest, the producers were anxious to keep everything they could of the essential Garland quality and character—which was, after all, what had led them to choose her in the first place.

It has sometimes been reported that LeRoy's first choice for the dual role of Professor Marvel and the Wizard was the redoubtable W. C. Fields, but LeRoy denies this, explaining that the man he wanted for the part was Fields' one-time vaudeville sidekick, Ed Wynn. Wynn was not available and the role went to Frank Morgan, a staple of the extraordinary M-G-M stock company.

A member of the Angostura bitters family, Morgan was known to enjoy the comforts of hard liquor and was, along with Errol Flynn, one of the best yachtsmen in the movie colony. His film roles tended toward the comedy end of the spectrum, but he took his profession very seriously and was responsible for the *Encyclopaedia Britannica's* entry on screen acting, into which he inserted the following paragraph:

The screen has continually been providing a broader canvas for itself. It has grown artistically and technically to a point where practically nothing in human imagination is impossible of realization, from the human characteristics with which Walt Disney has endowed his cartoon creations, as in *Snow White,* to the magical effects achieved when humans are placed in the realm of fantasy, as in *The Wizard of Oz.*

One of the chief problems on the film was makeup. In 1933 Paramount had made an all-star version of *Alice in Wonderland,* which was a singular failure largely because the studio had fitted most of the characters with masks and the stars were unrecognizable. The M-G-M makeup department, under Jack Dawn, bent over backwards to avoid falling into the same error. Its solutions to the special problems posed by *Oz* were spectacularly successful. They were not achieved without experimentation, however, and considerable inconvenience to the subjects of these experiments.

Buddy Ebsen, then under contract to the studio, was cast as the tin woodsman. A rubber jaw was fixed to his face and a rubber cone to his head; then his skin was covered with white clown makeup and he was sprayed with aluminum dust. The effect was magnificent, but inhaling the metallic dust inhibited Ebsen's breathing to the extent that he had to be placed in an iron lung and was unable to continue with the role. Jack Haley was called in to replace him and aluminum paste was substituted for the sprayed dust.

Bert Lahr's rubber-faced clowning and his way of translating simple English sentences into convoluted New York patois—so marvelous on the stage—had been a failure on the movie screen until *The Wizard of Oz*. The fantasy of *Oz* was broad enough to accommodate his special talents, and he made the most of the opportunity. Initially, M-G-M wanted his services for just three weeks, at $2,500 a week. He held out for a guarantee of five weeks and eventually worked twenty-six. The picture is inconceivable without his cowardly lion.

If Lahr was the rubber-faced clown, Ray Bolger was the India Rubber man—an infinitely pliable dancer, the ideal choice for the part of Dorothy's third companion, the scarecrow in search of a brain.

The Wizard of Oz assured a measure of popular immortality for performers who would otherwise have been relegated to the pleasant but shadowy afterlife of the movie buffs' sacred grove. This is true to a greater or lesser extent of Morgan, Haley, Lahr and Bolger. It's also true of Clara Blandick and Charley Grapewin (Dorothy's Auntie Em and Uncle Henry) and Margaret Hamilton, the former kindergarten teacher with a profile as sharp as a sickle fresh from the whetstone who made a wonderful Wicked Witch of the West, a Hecate worthy of the nightmares she surely provoked.

As the Good Witch Glinda, Billie Burke is possibly the most inspired piece of casting in the entire movie. It must have been a temptation to slip some young glamour queen into this role. The widow of Florenz Ziegfeld, Burke was still an attractive woman, but she was by then in her fifties and the girlish look she adopted for the role of Glinda seems deliciously eccentric, like a hat that's slipped down over one eye. Her slightly zany smile blends oddly with the trite "goodness" of the dialogue she was given.

The Munchkins, if we take our cue from the screen credits, were played by Singer's Midgets. According to *Notes on a Cowardly Lion,* John Lahr's biography of his father, this is not strictly accurate. Bill Grady, head of casting at Metro (and famous for holding court nightly in Chasen's Restaurant on Beverly Boulevard), had the responsibility for finding 350 midgets. According to Grady's own version, as told to Lahr, he first approached Leo Singer, an entrepreneur who had managed a number of midget acts. Singer said that he could supply 150, but that was his limit. To find the balance, Grady sought out a midget performer who went by the name of Major Doyle. The major told him he could supply all 350 midgets but would have nothing to do with the affair if Singer was involved because Singer was known for exploiting his clientele. Grady called Singer to explain the situation. The promoter was furious, of course, but there was nothing he could do about it— except, apparently, to see that his name was on

the screen credits. Major Doyle, meanwhile, contacted midgets all over the world and had them rendezvous in New York City. On the day the midgets were scheduled to start out for California, a fleet of chartered buses pulled up outside the Times Square Hotel on Forty-third Street. Grady was present to watch his prospective Munchkins pile into the buses. Everything went according to plan until the buses set off. Instead of heading for the Holland Tunnel, they started uptown, along Broadway. Grady jumped into a cab and gave chase. Eventually, the buses pulled up outside an apartment building at Sixty-eighth Street and Central Park West. The major got out of the lead bus and spoke to the doorman.

"Phone upstairs and tell Leo Singer to look out of the window."

A few minutes later Leo Singer did look out of the window of his fifth-floor apartment to see a spectacular display of naked behinds stuck through and against the windows of the bus. This, so we are told, was Singer's only direct contact with the Munchkins—who now turned tail and headed for the Holland Tunnel and points west.

Once in California, the Munchkins were housed in a Culver City hotel where, by all accounts, they staged lavish orgies every night.

Some of the midgets had been prostitutes; few of the others had any problems with inhibitions. Nor did they confine themselves to activities among themselves. Chambermaids at the hotel went in fear of their lives and movie stars found themselves accosted in the M-G-M commissary. Many of the Munchkins showed a great fondness for alcohol—one of their leaders was never seen sober—and quite a few carried knives or other weapons. M-G-M veterans recall them with a mixture of affection and terror.

Mervyn LeRoy had planned to direct the film himself, but Mayer asked him to concentrate on his production chores. George Cukor and Richard Thorpe both worked briefly on the project, then Victor Fleming was assigned to direct the film.

Fleming was tall, rather handsome and unflappable. An accomplished and sometimes sensitive craftsman, he was one of those people (the type abounded in Hollywood at the time) who had drifted into movies by accident, then managed to build a more or less distinguished career upon fortuitous encounters and chance assignments. He had been a racing driver and mechanic, with no particular interest in filmmaking, when he happened upon a car that had broken down on the highway. Stopping to assist, Fleming discovered that the car belonged to Allan Dwan, a prolific director whose career started before World War I. Dwan offered Fleming a job maintaining camera equipment, and before long he graduated to cameraman. In this capacity he worked on a number of Douglas Fairbanks films and the two became friends. Fairbanks suggested that Fleming try his hand at directing, backing up the suggestion with an assignment. Arriving

90

at M-G-M in 1932, Fleming worked his way through a number of routine productions, eventually finding his place in the history books as the director of *Oz*. (Later he was the director of record on *Gone with the Wind*.) He brought to *The Wizard of Oz* great competence and the ability to deal calmly with technical problems and difficult situations. He is said to have worked on the principle that obstacles make for a better picture. With Munchkins, and special effects, and tempers fraying under the lights, he had all the obstacles he could ask for.

For practical reasons, the black and white scenes were shot last. (In early-release prints they were actually printed in sepia tone.) Fleming left the picture to work on *Gone with the Wind* before these scenes were completed, and some of them, including "Over the Rainbow," were shot under the direction of King Vidor.

M-G-M gave Fleming the best crew that could be assembled, headed by Hal Rosson as director of photography. Once married to Jean Harlow, Rosson was one of the top lighting cameramen in the business. He and Fleming had worked together several times and were good friends. Most importantly, Rosson had proved he could work imaginatively with color, having won an Academy Award for his contribution to *The Garden of Allah*.

It's worth mentioning again that color was still a comparative novelty—three-strip Technicolor had been in use for only a half-dozen years. Since M-G-M was not one of Technicolor's most regular customers, the studio did not have a high priority on Technicolor equipment—a fact that affected the shooting schedule and meant that some scenes had to be shot at night, when the cameras were not needed elsewhere.

Victor Fleming had a definite idea of the kind of coat Frank Morgan should wear in the movie. It should be a real Edwardian jacket—not a copy mistreated to seem old—and Western Costume was alerted to search its wardrobes for something matching this description that might fit Morgan. A few jackets were sent over and he tried them on. One was exactly

what Fleming had in mind and it fit perfectly. When the garment was inspected more closely someone discovered a name tag sewn into the lining. The jacket had once belonged to L. Frank Baum. This was taken as a good omen.

When it comes to making a film as elaborate and delicately balanced as *The Wizard of Oz,* however, much more than luck is needed. Everything must be planned down to the last detail, and fantasy creates special kinds of problems. How, for example, do you go about building Munchkinland without lapsing into cuteness or absurdity? Cedric Gibbons, M-G-M's top designer, explained his approach in *Photoplay,* dated August, 1939:

To fashion a "Munchkinland" which a little girl from Kansas might have dreamed, we began with a premise that the smallest things she had ever seen were probably ants. And

how do ants live? Under grass and tree roots. So with toadstools and anthills as our architectural pattern, we made proportionately larger grass and flowers, such as, for instance, hollyhocks twenty feet tall.

Special effects were also a major consideration; some scenes involved elaborate process shots. In many instances the performers were filmed on a partial set and this footage was combined in the laboratory with film made of backgrounds painted on glass—a technique that demanded the most careful color matching imaginable so that no seam between set and background would be apparent.

One of the most spectacular effects in the film occurs near the beginning, when the tornado sweeps down on Dorothy's home. It's been said that Arnold Gillespie, in charge of special effects, created this funnel cloud by filming a silk stocking twisted by the breeze from a fan, then combining this with live-action footage shot on the Kansas set. Apparently, however, there was also a thirty-foot high black burlap tornado that could track on a monorail while being twisted by a larger fan, and stock footage of an actual tornado was used.

This was just one of many challenges presented to the special effects department. How do you make monkey demons fly? How do you make a witch melt? How do you contrive a luminous, floating sphere for Glinda to step down from? The last was achieved with the help of a ballcock from a common household toilet.

In considering the success of *The Wizard of Oz,* the contribution made by the writers cannot be overemphasized. The screenplay—by Noel Langley, Florence Ryerson and Edgar Allan Woolf—is remarkable in that it avoids all the pitfalls inherent in the project. The scenarists were faced with the task of excising much superfluous material from Baum's original story (which tends to be episodic and meandering) without straying from the spirit of the book. The M-G-M writers added a few ideas of their own to give the plot more shape, ending up with a tight, economical script with just the right tone and color. The screenplay

With Bert Lahr, Jack Haley, Ray Bolger and other players.

93

for *The Wizard of Oz* is one of those rare adaptations that is better than the original.

Then there was the dimension of song. To write the musical numbers, Arthur Freed called in Harold Arlen and E. Y. "Yip" Harburg. The songs they contributed to the film include "Over the Rainbow," "We're Off to See the Wizard," "Follow the Yellow Brick Road," "Munchkinland," "If I Only Had a Heart," "Ding Dong the Witch Is Dead" and "The Jitterbug." This last song was cut from the final print and "Over the Rainbow" almost suffered the same fate. Almost everyone in the front office was in favor of taking the song out because they felt it slowed the picture down. LeRoy, Freed and the songwriters fought this idea until Mayer agreed to leave the number in. It won an Academy Award, and it would be superfluous to remark on its importance to Judy Garland's later mystique.

The Wizard of Oz is constructed in such a way as to invite homespun adages and highflown allegories. But allegory does not help us understand why the film works. *Oz* sends out feelers toward the everyday world, but is completely self-contained. We are told next to nothing about what has happened in Dorothy's life before the story begins. Apparently she is an orphan, which gives her a veneer of pathos, but that is all we know. There is no hint that she will ever emerge from the euphoria with which the picture ends (a fact that was to haunt Judy Garland for the rest of her life). The movie takes the form of a dream within a dream. The episodes set in Oz are explicitly explained as Dorothy's dream, and the Kansas sequences that parenthesize these events are our dream, experienced in the darkness of the theater. *Oz* is self-contained in the way that a piece of music is self-contained. It requires no explanation or interpretation.

The Wizard of Oz was promoted as heavily as anything M-G-M had ever produced. Howard Strickling, head of publicity, managed to place several feature stories in national magazines and 550 release prints—a record number —were prepared so that the country could be

saturated with *The Wizard of Oz,* engagements.

For her contribution to the picture, Judy Garland was paid $350 a week and, even at this modest salary, the studio was determined to get its money's worth. On August 7, 1939, Judy, along with Mickey Rooney and Roger Edens, left for the East Coast where a heavy schedule of personal appearances had been set up. Their first stop was in Washington, D.C., where, as *The Hollywood Reporter* described on August 10, they were greeted like visiting royalty:

The personal appearance of Judy and Mick at the Loew's Palace in Washington, in conjunction with *The Wizard of Oz,* set Washington on its heels. It looked as if another King and Queen had arrived, from the number of people who tried to get inside the theater all morning and afternoon. Mick and Judy went on stage for the first show at two to do twelve minutes, and were kept there for forty with the packed house still yelling for more, while better than six thousand people lined up outside trying to get in. Finally, the house manager mounted the stage and informed seat holders that Mick and Judy were finished for that show, and pleaded with the audience to vacate their seats so others could get in for the next performance.

That same day the *Reporter* reviewed the picture itself, noting that it would undoubtedly advance Judy's career: "Judy Garland gives the role lyric charm and a wholly competent performance dramatically, ably justifying her selection for the key role."

The Garland and Rooney duo moved on to New York, where the picture had opened at the Capitol Theater. Their first day there, they attracted 37,000 cash customers and the overflow filled almost all the neighboring Broadway houses. Sixty police officers were needed to control the crowds.

The schedule was exhausting—nine shows a day on the weekend—and at one point Judy collapsed offstage, but recovered in time for her next performance. George Stoll, who had been dispatched by the studio to conduct the orchestra at the Capitol, fell sick during one show and Rooney, to the delight of the audience, leaped into the pit to take over. Gossip columnists claimed that Rooney was slipping off to nightclubs after the last show, but this was hotly denied.

After ten days at the Capitol Rooney returned to California where he was due to start work on a new Andy Hardy picture. Judy stayed on for a while, and was joined by Bert Lahr and Ray Bolger. When she got back to Culver City M-G-M paid her a bonus and tore up her old contract, giving her a new one that included a substantial salary hike. Later she would claim that, even after the success of *The Wizard of Oz,* there was a concerted effort at the studio to persuade her that she was not particularly gifted or valuable. This is patently absurd. Mayer and his associates may not always have acted in Judy's best interest, but there was no way they could have gotten away with deprecating her talent, even if they had wanted to. *Oz* had created a public demand for Judy that Metro was only too happy to cater to. A rash of Judy Garland stories began to appear in the fan magazines and elsewhere. It was at this time that the fictionalized information about her childhood began to receive wide circulation. Her current lifestyle was also embellished with fanciful detail.

Most of these stories had as their authority the official studio biography—a twenty-two-page mimeographed document put out under the aegis of Howard Strickling. This provided anyone writing a profile of Judy with a measured blend of the trivial and the preposterous, offering such tidbits as the following:

Item: Judy's mother is teaching her to play the piano with the aid of a book titled *Chopin in the Home. Item:* Judy has just started a fund for a hospital dedicated to the poor. *Item:* Just before starting *Oz,* Judy purchased a new home, with a tennis court and a swimming pool that looks like a miniature lake. *Item:* In this home, she has her own suite of three rooms. The main room is done in chartreuse and brown.

Other details of Judy's decor were also given—books, desk, radio, victrola and so on:

Item: She takes care of her own clothes and her own suite of rooms. Fleming and Leona, the household servants, enjoy waiting on their young mistress, but that's taboo in the Garland home. *Item:* In the evenings, Jackie Cooper, Leonard Sues, Bob Stack, Rita Quigly, Bonita Granville, Patty McCarthy, and other friends drop over. Judy's mother is always ready to feed the gang. *Item:* When Judy feels sorry for herself, she plays sad music and cries to herself. Then she plays her favorite game of "Pretend"—imagining herself a great opera singer, a glamorous beauty, or a brilliant lawyer. *Item:* She still says her prayers at the

Judy at the roller-skating rink with Robert Stack.

95

foot of the bed. *Item:* She believes she has the cutest dog in Hollywood, a St. Bernard named Sergei who knocks you down just wagging his tail.

Judy did, indeed, have her own suite of rooms at the new house, and she did often entertain "the gang" there. The house was rather grander than any she had lived in previously, but her home life was still fairly normal and she was even expected to share in the housework. Not that she was always willing, as Virginia remembers: "In the kitchen, one day, my mother told her to wipe the dishes, or clear off the table, or something, and Judy said, 'I don't have to. I'm in the top ten!' " She meant in the top ten box-office attractions, a level she reached with *The Wizard of Oz*. The remark was taken as a joke—Judy herself was quick to see the humor of it—but she must have begun to revolt against this domestic setup, if only in her head.

Judy had turned seventeen at the time *Oz* appeared, and was striving for a measure of independence, not only from Ethel but also from the studio, as *The Hollywood Reporter* remarked on August 3, shortly before her trip east:

The Mickey Rooney exploits probably will be shaved to a conventional mode of life, since the studio is putting him under the thumb, but good. They're also keeping a close watch on Judy, now that she's having dates and driving her own bus.

Dates in the fall of 1939 included Peter Lind Hayes, Walter Doniger (an M-G-M writer), Mervyn LeRoy's assistant Barron Polan, and a University of Southern California student named Clark Liddell. When Judy was spotted at Victor Hugo's restaurant with Jackie Cooper, *The Hollywood Reporter* decided that they were a couple to watch. Had anyone taken this advice literally, they would have found the couple's movements distinctly intriguing.

In the fall of 1939 Cooper encountered Judy at a party and noticed that she seemed depressed. To his surprise, she asked him to come

to her house after the party. His mother was expecting him at home, but he told Judy that he'd keep the appointment. To do so, he had to sneak out of his own house and coast his car down the hill before starting the motor and driving to Stone Canyon. Judy was waiting for him in her suite and they talked for several hours—mostly Hollywood gossip about who was seeing whom. There was no question of renewing their romance, and Cooper remembers that she seemed too adult and remote to arouse his interest. (He was going steady with Bonita Granville at the time.) It was more a case of Judy needing a confidant and turning to someone she knew and trusted.

Shortly after that night Judy again ran into Cooper and asked him if he would be free the following evening. He said that he was and she asked him to pick her up and drive her to someone's house for dinner—adding that he, too, was invited. Only after he agreed to this plan did she tell him that the person they would be dining with was none other than Artie Shaw. On Judy's recent trip to New York she had been seen with Shaw on several occasions, to the considerable annoyance of Betty Grable who was madly in love with the band leader. (Grable was appearing on Broadway, enjoying her first major success in *Dubarry Was a Lady*.) When Shaw had brought his band out to California he and Judy had renewed their acquaintanceship. But Ethel strongly disapproved of Shaw and was making it difficult for Judy to see him, so Judy needed Jackie Cooper to divert suspicion. Since Cooper was a fan of Shaw's, he was quite happy to accommodate Judy and repeated the favor on a number of occasions. After the first time, however, he did not stay for dinner, since there was enough open intimacy between Judy and Shaw to make him feel uncomfortable. He would drop her off at Shaw's rented house on Summit Ridge Drive, then pick her up as late as he could manage—sometimes having to repeat the stratagem of sneaking out and coasting his car down the hill.

While Shaw was evidently amused by Judy, he thought of her as "a moonstruck little girl"

—according to Phil Silvers in his autobiography, *The Laugh's on Me*—and was unhappy at being separated from Betty Grable. He could not understand why she stayed in New York when he was making enough money to support both of them in style. Silvers suggested that he write to her and explain exactly where he stood. He did so, but before Betty Grable's reply arrived, the situation became more complicated. Shaw had a recording session at M-G-M and, accompanied by Phil Silvers, visited the set of *Two Girls on Broadway* where they ran into Lana Turner who, says Silvers, made for Shaw "like a bee making for the honey." Shaw had met Lana before and was not unduly impressed by her, but they made a date for that evening. Shaw asked Silvers to tag along, "because she might bring me down." To Silvers' horror, Lana suggested that they eat at Victor Hugo's, which featured the music of Guy Lombardo—hardly Artie Shaw's taste. As Silvers tells it, there was nothing to suggest this would be an evening to remember:

On the way home, Artie ran through the routine I'd heard so often:

"I want a girl that will be satisfied with me alone on a desert island. . . ." The girl would agree, "Yes, just two people who need each other." And then they would roll into bed for a pleasant jam session. Next day, all the philosophic rationalization would be forgotten. Artie was always brutally honest: He really did mean what he said. Every time.

Lana crossed him up. "That's exactly what I want. A man who has the brains to be satisfied with me only."

He was vehement. "Look, I'm sick of this Hollywood crap. I want to break out."

"Me too. Anywhere you say."

Artie couldn't back out. He turned around, drove out to Paul Mantz's plane rental service and chartered a plane to Las Vegas. To get married. I felt this was reaching too far for a joke, but Artie was flying against the petty restraints of slave society. He gave me the keys to drive his car home.

When Silvers reached Shaw's house, he dis-covered a letter from Betty Grable. She had quit her role in *Dubarry Was a Lady* and was coming out to Hollywood to be with her beloved Artie.

Judy Garland and Mickey Rooney had befriended Silvers when he first arrived in Hollywood, and he was aware of Judy's crush on Shaw. He knew that she would take the news of the elopement badly, and could not bring himself to break it to her. She would read it in the papers, the same as everyone else. To get away from the whole mess, he played a round of golf with Jack Albertson. At the eighth green, he was paged by a caddy. Judy was in the clubhouse:

Judy used to have freckles: now they stood out like black polka dots. She had been crying . . . and she was in humiliating pain. "How *could* they? I confided in her!" To add to her wretchedness, she had to drive to school at Metro this morning. By state law she was still a child.

I rode to school with her . . . and my words came burbling out—anything to comfort her. "You're the luckiest girl in the world. . . . It was just hero worship. . . ."

Her eyes were blinded with tears. . . . I'd seen movies in which a hysterical woman is smacked back into good sense. But I'd never hit a woman. Goading myself, I delivered a soft-edged rap to the cheek.

It worked. Instantly she became Judy Garland, movie star. Slapped by a bit player. . . . She really told me off.

Betty Grable's reaction was different. She yelled a lot and called Shaw an Academy Award–winning son of a bitch, but left little doubt that she would recover from the experience. Unfortunately, Judy lacked Betty Grable's resilience.

Lana Turner's marriage to Artie Shaw lasted a little over four months. At the divorce proceedings Lana's witness was Betty Asher, an M-G-M publicist who would soon become Judy Garland's closest friend. Shaw has said that Betty Asher came to visit him before the hearing and stayed for three days.

Chapter 3
Beyond
the
Emerald City

There is one item of real interest in the studio's 1940 biography of Judy Garland. Toward the end of this document we are suddenly informed that Judy is "thrilled" with her two new brothers, "Bill and Jack Gilmore . . . and with her new sister, Ruth. . . ."

Ethel had remarried. Judy's new sister and brothers were, however, far from strangers to the Garland household. It will be recalled that in March of 1928 the Antelope Valley *Ledger-Gazette* reviewed a play titled *First Night* in which Ethel starred as a woman with two suitors. One suitor was played by Frank Gumm, the other by William Gilmore. Other newspaper stories from that period tell us that Gilmore's wife had something of a reputation as an amateur vocalist, and was often accompanied by Ethel Gumm. Living only a couple of blocks apart, the Gumms and the Gilmores —both parents and children—came to know each other quite well. Ruth was almost exactly Judy's age, and the two boys were a little older.

Early in the thirties the Gilmores moved to Los Angeles, and then to Fullerton, in Orange County, but they remained in touch with the Gumms and continued to see them from time to time. Maurice Kusell recalls that the Gilmores would occasionally visit Ethel at his studio. At about the time of their move from Lancaster Mrs. Gilmore suffered a stroke and spent the remaining years of her life confined to a wheelchair. Gilmore had always had something of a crush on Ethel, and when his wife died, he began to court her—a fact that was noted with mixed feelings by Ethel's three daughters, as Virginia explains:

We all disapproved of Mr. Gilmore— including my mother, before long. That's sort of sad. He'd had this crush on her and Mama more or less brushed him off, but—you go through a period when you get older, you know. He was a great big guy, and he was rather attractive. . . . He started courting my mother, which none of us really liked—but it

M-G-M publicity picture, circa 1939.

was good for her. He took her out. They'd play cards.

But I couldn't understand my mother marrying him, because he was a dodo! He was a big square! I learned later, from a friend of my mother's, that she agreed to marry Bill, then had second thoughts about it and wrote him a letter saying she had changed her mind —and he said he never got the letter!

He came to the house to fetch her to go and get married. She said, "Didn't you get my letter?" And he said, "What letter? I don't know what you're talking about."

She didn't have the guts to tell him she'd changed her mind, so she went ahead and got married.

Well, it didn't last long because they'd been married about two weeks when Bill said, "From now on I'll handle all the money that comes in." Mother said, "The hell you will!" And that was the end of that. . . . They were married about a year.

Later, Mama found the letter with some of his stuff.

Ethel had married Gilmore in Yuma, Arizona, on November 17, 1939, the fourth anniversary of Frank's death. The marriage lasted a little longer than Virginia remembers, but it was not a success. Judy actively disliked Gilmore, and the marriage may have contributed to the deterioration of her relationship with her mother. Did she resent this man usurping

(Below) With Ethel and William Gilmore. Mother's night at the Beverly Hills Hotel. (Opposite page) Judy in the kitchen of her new Stone Canyon house, 1939.

her father's bed? Virginia thinks that "Judy was so wrapped up in her own self, I think my mother could have married Gargantua and it wouldn't have registered. Judy was going through the big love affair with Artie Shaw, and all those things."

In the normal course of events, children slip away as they grow older. For Ethel, things had happened rather suddenly. In a span of four years two daughters had married and the third had become a star. Add to this the shattering loss of Frank, no matter how difficult their relationship may have been, and the extent of the adjustment she had had to make can be guessed at. She must have felt very isolated at times and it's not surprising to discover that she and the mothers of some other Hollywood stars socialized together and even organized themselves into a kind of charity group—Motion Picture Mothers, Inc.—which was described in *Photoplay* by Marie Brown, mother of clean-cut Tom Brown:

Only yesterday they were babies—just little boys and girls who depended upon Mother for everything. Today they are successful men and women in pictures and Mother, who has devoted half her life to caring for them, finds her hands very empty and her heart very full. . . .

An invitation to tea brought twenty mothers. Before the pot was empty, we had become Motion Picture Mothers, Inc. . . .

That was on June 14, 1939. Today we have more than one hundred mothers. . . . We want to inspire mothers the world over to lead useful lives of their own after they have finished living the lives of their children.

Included in this article is a brief account of the Motion Picture Mothers' charities and their funding. Members paid dues of one dollar a month, plus fifty cents for lunch. The money was used to feed, clothe and shelter people in need, including retired former stars. In helping families overcome disaster, Motion Picture Mothers made sure that the victims' cupboards were stocked with luxuries as well as staples, and helped pay for utilities ("What picture

Christmas in Stone Canyon, 1939. Left to right: Sue, Judaline (Virginia's daughter), Gilmore, Ethel, Rooney and Judy.

Foster, were planning to kidnap Judy Garland. Wilson, who had devised the scheme, panicked at the last minute and telephoned the police to tip them off that an attempt would be made that evening to snatch Judy from her home at 1231 Stone Canyon Drive. The police immediately called the house and found Judy there with a group of friends. (Her mother and stepfather were out.) They barricaded themselves in and waited, in the dark, for something to happen. Meanwhile, Wilson and Foster were tracked down to a Santa Monica hotel and arrested.

Wilson, a nineteen-year-old transient from New York, explained that he had planned the kidnap because he was in love with his intended victim. Ransom was not a motive: "I guess I fell in love with Judy by seeing her in pictures. . . . Every time she wiggles that little pug nose of hers, I fall more in love with her. She is my dream girl."

The kidnap plan had been vague and imperfectly conceived, to say the least. The kidnappers had not even bothered to ascertain that Judy would be at home that night. Wilson's primary goal seems to have been an opportunity to make a public declaration of his love for Judy Garland. Whether or not Judy was impressed by this is not recorded.

person can exist without a telephone?"). Along with Ethel and Mrs. Brown, the group included Mrs. Nellie Panky (mother of Mickey Rooney); Mrs. Lela Rogers (the legendarily awesome mother of Ginger); Mrs. Tyrone Power, Sr.; Mrs. Mimi Shirley (mother of Anne); Mrs. C. J. Romero; Mrs. Ruth Brugh (mother of Robert Taylor); Annette Y. de Lake (mother of Ann Sothern); Anna Le Sueur (mother of Joan Crawford); and Alice Cooper (mother of Gary).

Judy, meanwhile, was firmly trapped in the dimension of stardom where bizarre happenings come to seem like everyday events. A curious incident occurred on March 7, 1940. According to contemporary newspaper reports, two young men, Robert Wilson and Frank

So far as Judy's career is concerned, we must backtrack a few months. In the late spring and early summer of 1939, with *The Wizard of Oz* completed but not yet released, the studio had teamed her with Rooney for a bit of hokum called *Babes in Arms*. The director was the redoubtable Busby Berkeley, who recalled the assignment in a 1963 interview with Dave Martin, published in *The Genius of Busby Berkeley*:

It was Judy's and Mickey's first starring picture. I didn't know it until months later, but all the producers and directors at the M-G-M lot had turned thumbs down on doing the script. They didn't think it would be a very good film. Louis B. Mayer gave it to me to see if I would like it after everyone else had rejected it, and I liked it. I did turn out a hell of a picture, because L. B. Mayer made them stars from that time on. . . .

Berkeley was a newcomer to M-G-M—this was his first picture there—and he can be forgiven if he got things a little confused. Rooney had been a major box-office attraction for three years and, as we have seen, Judy was well on her way. Also, while other directors may have turned the script down, it had not been passed over by any producers. It was, in fact, the property Arthur Freed selected to launch his producing career. He bought *Babes in Arms,* originally a Rodgers and Hart Broadway show, with Mayer's blessing, and was given a $600,000 budget to work with (modest compared to that for *Oz,* but still way above average for the period).

The plot concerns a colony of ex-vaudeville performers living, with their children, in a small Long Island town. When money is short, the old-timers revive their acts and take them on tour, but refuse to take the youngsters along—to the intense annoyance of Mickey Moran (Rooney) and Patsy Barton (Judy). Mickey decides to write a show to demonstrate what the kids can do. Patsy will be his star. All, needless to say, ends happily—but not without some close scrapes involving mean Martha Steele (Margaret Hamilton), who wants to have the show children committed to a home, and Baby Rosalie (June Preisser), an overgrown Shirley Temple type who temporarily usurps Patsy's position in Mickey's favor and in the show.

Judy's best moment is when she sings "I Cried for You" to a photo of Rooney in a scene reminiscent of "Dear Mr. Gable." As with the earlier song, a recitative was added:

I know I'm no glamour girl, like Baby—like her. . . . You can't eat glamour for breakfast. Anyway, I might be pretty good-looking myself, when I grow out of this ugly duckling stage. . . . And you're no Clark Gable yourself. . . . Time is a great healer. . . .

Seeing this film today, one notices immedi-

ately how sure and controlled Judy's performance is—and how poignant—and it's hard to understand why she was subordinated so completely to Rooney, who seems by comparison an overstimulated robot bouncing nervously about the screen. Evidently his nervous energy matched something that was abroad in America at that time.

Released in October, 1939, *Babes in Arms* was the prototype of a whole series of pictures that teamed Garland and Rooney in stories built around the staging of backyard musicals. Busby Berkeley would be involved with all of them, sometimes building upon the brilliance of the techniques he had developed at Warner Brothers in the early thirties, sometimes lapsing into self-parody. Arthur Freed would be involved with all of them too. His career as a producer was successfully launched, and within five years the Freed unit would become the single most powerful influence on the Hollywood musical. Judy Garland's fate would be linked to his for another decade.

The work load was becoming heavy now. In 1940 three Garland films were released. In *Andy Hardy Meets Debutante* Judy again played Betsy Booth and got to lecture Rooney on the morals and manners of high society. (After seeing the first Hardy picture, Mayer

Judy with her first car.

103

had made one simple comment: "Don't make them any better." That his dictum was still being taken very seriously is clearly demonstrated by this particular movie.)

Strike Up the Band, the second of the Freed-Berkeley pictures, saw Judy cast as the vocalist in a high school band led, of course, by Rooney. Judy's touching version of "Our Love Affair" is perhaps the best thing in the movie. In *Little Nellie Kelly,* produced by Freed and directed by Norman Taurog, Judy played the dual role of an Irish mother and her immigrant daughter. She makes the most of her only Hollywood death scene, then is reincarnated as the sweetheart of the New York Police Department; but neither Judy nor co-star George Murphy can overcome the sluggishness of the plot and the picture comes to life only during the musical numbers.

With June Preisser. A wardrobe test for Babes in Arms. *Neither costume is seen in the finished movie.*

While these films were in production, Judy was a weekly regular on Bob Hope's radio show and was also pursuing a lively social life. Her routine was demanding, and it seems to have been about this time that she first began to rely upon what she liked to refer to as "bolts and jolts"—amphetamines and barbiturates—to help her get through the day. After she left Metro, Judy would accuse the men who ran the studio of having forced these drugs on her: "They'd give us pep-up pills to keep us on our feet long after we were exhausted. Then they'd take us to the studio hospital and knock us cold with sleeping pills. . . ."

Most people who were there at the time—including some who do not mourn the passing of the Mayer dynasty—find it difficult to accept Judy's version. The studio doctor did prescribe amphetamines as diet pills, and he may have prescribed sleeping pills too from time to time. But there was no real need for a performer to go to the doctor for these "bolts and jolts" because they were readily available on a far more informal basis. Some M-G-M hairdressers and makeup girls were walking pharmacies, ready to satisfy a performer's every need, and the distribution of pills at the studio was not particularly clandestine. Many drugs now considered dangerous were then available without prescription, and prescriptions were easily obtained for the rest. Few were aware of any dangerous side effects from these pills, and not much thought was given to the possibility that some of them might be habit-forming. Many people on the lot used them once in a while. They were taken for granted.

Judy seems to have had the kind of metabolism that welcomes foreign agents and transforms them into hungers that can never be satisfied. She was almost certainly exaggerating, however, when she claimed later on that she was addicted by the time she was sixteen. She may have become a habitual user at that age, but true addiction did not come until several years later.

She sometimes justified her use of pills on the grounds of insomnia. As a child, she had become accustomed to the theater routine of staying up late and sleeping late and she had considerable difficulty adjusting to the Hollywood schedule of early morning calls. (And chronic insomnia seems to have run in her family. One of the reasons Ethel was so sympathetic about Judy's problem in making the early call at the studio was that she too had always had serious difficulty sleeping, and Virginia suffers from insomnia to this day.) Judy would come home from a date at midnight, before a five o'clock morning call, and she would sit up reading or listening to records rather than going to bed until, at last, she gulped down a couple of sleeping pills and managed to snatch two or three hours rest. The following day she would be hard put to get through her work at the studio without swallowing a couple of uppers to keep her going—which only aggravated her insomnia. But she was young and very strong, so the effects on her health were not immediately evident. Before too long, however, she would have built up a real physical dependence on the drugs.

Probably, though, we should rid ourselves once and for all of the lurid images that have been painted for us of evil men standing over poor Judy Garland, forcing pills down her throat. This does not mean her employers were entirely free of guilt. It was they, after all, who worked her to the point of exhaustion and who actively promoted the policy of exposing the fabric of her young life to the corrosive action of concentrated publicity. It was they who had consented to the replacement of facts with polished but unsatisfactory fictions, thus totally disorienting her.

In a very real sense, Judy's life was a losing battle with this process of fictionalization, and it's tempting to interpret her use of drugs as a desperate effort to neutralize the lies. (To what extent did the lies haunt her insomnia?) One can speculate that the lies opened up mental, emotional and spiritual vacuums—and as each vacuum formed, some chemical hunger arrived to colonize it.

Ironically, one of the first films Judy made after the Artie Shaw fiasco was *Ziegfeld Girl*,

Shooting pool with Mickey Rooney and his stand-in, Dick Paxton.

in which her co-stars included two other participants in that unhappy sequence of events, Lana Turner and Jackie Cooper—the latter playing Lana's brother and Judy's boyfriend. Directed by Robert Z. Leonard, the film is overlong but stands up very well as a piece of vintage Metro kitsch. It chronicles the careers of three Ziegfeld girls—Judy, Lana and Hedy Lamarr—who start out together but follow different paths. Judy received top billing as the girl who makes good, but the picture belongs to Lana in the meatier role of the glamour girl who goes wrong. It was this movie that cinched Lana's stardom.

To all outward appearances, Judy Garland and Lana Turner were friends again. Glancing through the gossip columns of the period, we find that they double-dated on a fairly regular basis.

Meanwhile, the M-G-M production line did not let up. *Life Begins for Andy Hardy* came next, then *Babes on Broadway*. Directed, as always, by George B. Seitz, the Hardy film has Andy checking out the attractions of New York—which proved to verge on the carnal and even got the movie into a spot of trouble with the National Legion of Decency. Betsy, alias Judy Garland, manages to salvage him for the monotonously faithful Polly Benedict who, in the person of Ann Rutherford, has been waiting patiently on the Carvel set.

Babes on Broadway was produced by the Freed unit with Busby Berkeley at the helm. The essentials of the plot are covered by the

105

title. Mickey Rooney writes a musical and, with the help of Judy and a platoon of young friends, he takes it to Broadway—though not without experiencing the vicissitudes that commonly attend these ventures. The first meeting of the Garland and Rooney characters leads to a delightful and informal version of "How About You?" and there is a crisp "Hoe Down" routine to which Berkeley brought all of his old wit and camera intelligence, using only the simplest of props. The film demonstrates that Judy's confidence and skill had developed to the point where she knew exactly how to neutralize Rooney's overflow of energy. She never became the kind of actress who would deliberately steal scenes, but from this point in her career on, it becomes difficult to focus on anyone else when she is on screen.

The pace of *Babes on Broadway* is so breathless that, for once, one actually has a sense of the amount of work that goes into the making of a movie. The fan magazines were constantly informing their readers, in sanctimonious tones, that being a star was a job like any other and that it involved a great deal of sweat and sheer physical expenditure. They might have added that being a star was often about as exciting as working on a General Motors production line.

A visitor to the *Babes on Broadway* set (and Berkeley did not welcome visitors) would have found the director dressed in white slacks and white sweatshirt, his perennial uniform, and carrying on like a Marine Corps gym instructor—which is what he physically resembled. Nor was his manner misplaced, since a Berkeley musical number demanded athletic prowess and military precision. Many things had to be coordinated—camera movements had to be choreographed and rehearsed every bit as carefully as the movements of the dancers. One shot in this movie involved no less than thirty-eight camera moves, and each of these moves depended upon several men working together in perfect union. Thus while one man adjusted the focus of the camera, another controlled the vertical movements of the boom and a third its lateral movements, while still others pushed

With Busby Berkeley and (right) a production still from Ziegfeld Girl.

*Preceding pages:
Setting up the
finale of* Babes on
Broadway. *Busby
Berkeley, on the
camera crane, con-
sults with Arthur
Freed, seen at left
in the dark jacket.*

*Off camera, Judy
sneaks a bite.*

the entire rig—which was on rollers—forward, backward, or from side to side, guided by taped marks on the floor, following an elaborate sequence which might have to be gone through dozens of times before everything was just right. During some of these run-throughs Berkeley would ride alongside the operator on the camera crane; on others he would go over the number with the dancers, who had been rehearsing it for several weeks, though not on the actual set. During breaks he could be found waving his arms at the ceiling ninety feet above, discussing lighting changes with Lester White, his director of photography.

A spying system had been set up at the studio and candid reports were called in from each set at frequent intervals to keep Mayer

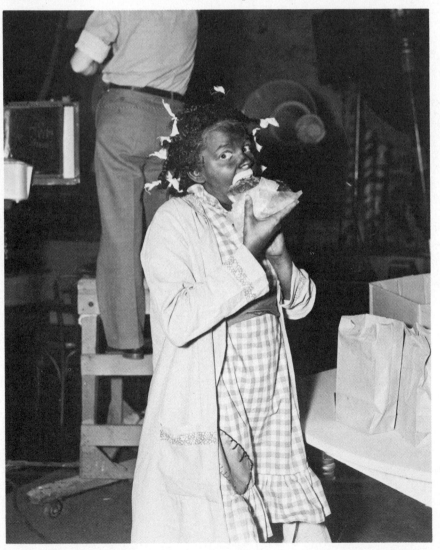

and his aides abreast of a director's progress on an hourly basis. To stay on the right side of the executives in the Thalberg Building (by now nicknamed the Iron Lung because of its formidable air-conditioning system) it was advisable for a director to get a couple of scenes in the can before lunch every day. Berkeley, however, did not work that way. His method was to rehearse an elaborate sequence over and over again, then shoot it in one or two takes. He might take all day over a single setup—which caused a great deal of nail-biting—but he brought his pictures in on time.

His method was efficient, but it was also tedious. Sometimes the principals were needed for run-throughs—and Berkeley was not the type who spared people because they were stars—but they might also find themselves spending hours on end in their trailers, waiting for a call. They alternated between exhaustion and boredom.

Different stars had different ways of dealing with the monotony. Lana Turner listened to phonograph records all day, and even had a girl assigned to her whose job it was to turn the discs over. Rooney made frequent calls to his bookie—a habit Louis B. Mayer, one of the foremost owners and breeders on the West Coast, found positively endearing. Judy had no single obsession and amused herself as best she could.

One activity she enjoyed, but which she was very self-conscious about, was writing. She had written poetry ever since she was a child, an activity that had been discovered by the cast of *The Wizard of Oz* so that, when the picture was finished, Ray Bolger presented her with a fine edition of Edgar Allan Poe's *The Raven.* Eventually she had several copies of her verses bound and presented them to friends and members of her family. One she gave to her mother, with fervent professions of love and affection. By the time of *Babes on Broadway,* however, she had turned her attention to fiction and one of her stories—*Love's New Sweet Song*—was adapted for "The Silver Theater," a popular radio dramatic series of the day, with Judy playing the lead.

One thing that made life more bearable on the set for Judy was the fact that she was adored by the crews. It was a popular notion at M-G-M that to establish yourself you had to get along with the workers—the grips, the carpenters and the sound men—and it was not uncommon to find starlets memorizing the first names of obscure camera operators and desperately waving to junior propmen earning $35 a week. Judy had the great advantage of having been at Metro from the age of thirteen. The crews treated her as family, and their affection helped her later on, when her problems finally surfaced. The men knew they could kid Judy without her taking offense, and she would return the compliment. She might pose as the star for the world at large, but she never tried to pull anything like that on them. Despite everything that was tugging her away from normality, the guys on the crew knew she was always ready to join them for a game of cards, pool or softball.

It's often been said that Judy found it difficult to work with Berkeley, but the reports seem exaggerated—at least as far as this early period is concerned. Not that their relationship was entirely congenial. Berkeley's system of intensive, repeated rehearsals was not ideal for Judy, who responded most happily to more spontaneous situations. She was not lazy, but repetition was tedious for her. Although her concentration span appeared to be short, and she was easily distracted, she had a remarkable memory and almost freaky powers of retention. She had only to walk through a routine a couple of times to have it down pat.

When Berkeley first worked with her, he was driven half-crazy by her apparent inability to listen to anything he was saying. He was partial to giving elaborate instructions and was very put out when Judy stared off into space while he was talking to her. He would then become incensed and scream that she hadn't listened to a thing he had said, whereupon Judy would repeat his instructions, word for word, unable to figure out what had provoked his outburst.

Remarkable as her abilities were, however,

Babes on Broadway.

they did not exempt her from the sheer grind of moviemaking and the fatigue that went with it. Within a couple of years conditions would change for the better, but at that time (1941) contract players were asked to work till all hours of the night. And besides their regular studio routine, they had to make personal appearances, do guest spots on radio shows, and put up with interviews and photographic sessions. If a performer had an hour to spare, he might find himself learning a new song to be sung at some charity benefit or being fitted with a costume to wear at the Hollywood Boulevard Christmas Parade. A movie star had to be tough and resilient.

One day, while she was still pining over Artie Shaw, Judy was scheduled to rehearse for a radio broadcast. She was depressed and at one point shut herself in her dressing room, apparently with the intent of shedding a few tears over her shattered love life. Her misery was interrupted by a knock on the door and she opened it to discover David Rose, Tony Martin's musical director, standing there with a smile on his face and a chocolate cake in his hand. Judy

and Rose were only casual acquaintances, but he knew she adored chocolate cake and correctly calculated that this would cheer her up. This incident blossomed into a romance that led, eventually, to marriage.

The romance began in 1940 and soon found its way into the gossip columns. Not long after, Lana Turner began to date Rose's boss, Tony Martin, and the two couples were often seen as a foursome at fashionable restaurants along the Strip and at Billy Berg's nightclub in the San Fernando Valley, a popular spot that featured live entertainment of the caliber of Billie Holiday.

On May 29, 1941, the following item appeared in *The Hollywood Reporter:* "While the John Paynes were celebrating his birthday at Ciro's last night, Judy Garland and Dave Rose squatted at their table to officially announce their engagement and a September wedding." On July 22 the same paper reported that Judy would be going dateless for the next two weeks while David Rose took a vacation. On July 28, however, Judy and her fiancé rushed to Las Vegas and were married immediately, to the chagrin of *The Hollywood Reporter,* which noted the following day: "In another Nevada spot, Judy Garland became Mrs. David Rose, thereby twisting the tails of the newshounds here who were assured the deal wouldn't come off till September. But happiness to both of them—they're great kids."

The elopement style of the wedding was probably designed to confound the studio rather than the press. Louis B. Mayer, and those who did his bidding, did not approve of the match. They did not approve of marriage for Judy under any circumstances. How could they continue to star her as an adolescent, barely out of ankle socks, if the public knew she was a married woman? Characteristically, they ignored the fact that marriage had never interfered with Mary Pickford's acceptability as an ingenue.

In any case, if wedlock was inevitable, David Rose was certainly not the studio's first choice. He had recently cut loose from his first wife, Martha Raye, and that tainted him. Worse still, he was not a major celebrity. Pick-

ford had had the prescience to marry Douglas Fairbanks. All that David Rose had going for him was that he'd had the sense to be born in England, which suggested a touch of class, and his collection of trains. The match was not made in any heaven known to Louis B. Mayer.

Ethel was suspicious of musicians. The marriages of her two older daughters had not worked out well and she was fond of saying, "I wish you girls would find someone who digs a slide rule instead of a slide trombone." But she had no intention of allowing M-G-M to dictate to Judy in this manner. She backed Judy's decision and, with Gilmore, accompanied the couple to Nevada for the ceremony. A mother's sanction did little to alleviate the annoyance in Culver City, however, where people found ways of snubbing Judy's husband and undermining the marriage.

In retrospect, Judy's first marriage amounts to a relatively unremarkable interlude in her life. It cannot have appeared so at the time, of course, but it came before the deluge and its significance was diminished by everything that followed. The marriage did not last long, and it's very much to David Rose's credit that he did nothing to capitalize on it—did not try to turn the failure into a feast.

Writing in *Photoplay* several years later, Elsa Maxwell gave her recollections of the ill-fated marriage:

I don't know what [David] did or didn't do that was wrong. But I do know that Judy at this time was completely unfitted to be a wife. . . .

One time, I remember, dinner guests arrived at Judy's house to find David out and her having dinner in bed. She had invited the guests, then forgotten them. Other times, because she never did keep the engagement book necessary in a family with two careers, she and Dave would discover they had accepted dinner dates or asked separate groups of friends over for the same evening. The servants, who had seen her as Dorothy in *The Wizard of Oz,* called her Judy. And if she went into the kitchen and said, "We'll have clams and a roast, a mixed green salad . . . ," her cook was not impressed at all.

Judy was discovering that marriage was not

(Left) Judy with David Rose, 1941 and (above) with Rose, in uniform, 1942.

the same as playing house. Ethel tried to help out by assuming the role of chatelaine and attempted to run the household on Judy's behalf. This was probably resented by the servants, and possibly by Judy too.

She had fallen in love with David Rose because he was kind and considerate and gentle, and he was able to make her laugh. She had married him because it seemed the right thing to do—and perhaps because she had wanted to spite the studio—but she was plainly not ready for all the consequences. Not long after the wedding Judy confided to a friend that she was pregnant and that she was worried because she thought that having a child at that time would disrupt her career. No child was born.

Although the marriage was brief, the end was not really sudden. There was no ugly crack-up for the press to zero in on. Soon after the United States' entry into the war, David Rose went into the service. This permitted the couple to drift apart without attracting too much attention from the columnists. They were not divorced until June of 1945, but, to all intents and purposes, their marriage was over years before that.

Accompanied by David Rose, Judy entertains the troops at Jefferson Barracks, St. Louis.

Judy Garland was nineteen years old when *For Me and My Gal* went into production. Amazingly, it was her fifteenth feature film—but it was the first in which she was assigned a leading man who looked and behaved like an adult, and it was the first in which she was allowed to have a romance that added up to more than puppy love.

The new leading man was Gene Kelly, fresh from his Broadway success in *Pal Joey*. Arthur Freed had seen Kelly in this Rodgers and Hart show and suggested to Mayer that he follow suit on his next visit to New York. Mayer took Freed's advice and was impressed enough to ask Kelly to call on him. When Kelly did so, he was flattered by Mayer's enthusiasm but warned him that he could not come out to the Coast for a screen test until the run of the show was over. He did not want to test on the East Coast because the tests made in New York were reputed to be sloppily produced. Mayer told him no test was necessary, but a couple of months later he sent a message to the New York office that said, "Test Kelly." Infuriated that Mayer had gone back on his word, Kelly sent him an angry letter—couched in language Mayer could not fail to understand—accusing him of lying and breach of trust. Kelly did not expect to be dealing with M-G-M again.

In the meantime, Kelly had met David Selznick. The two became friends and Kelly signed a contract with the Selznick organization. Selznick saw no harm in letting Kelly make an occasional musical as a change of pace, but he thought of him as a dramatic actor and planned to use him as the priest in *The Keys of the Kingdom*. This did not pan out, however (Gregory Peck was given the part), and Selznick, who was Mayer's son-in-law, loaned Kelly to the Freed unit for *For Me and My Gal*. Since this picture proved to be a considerable box-office success, Mayer managed to overlook his earlier contretemps with Kelly and bought his contract. Mayer was nothing if not pragmatic, but it seems likely he also had a grudging respect for Kelly because the actor had stood up to him.

Before Kelly came into the picture, George Murphy had been slated to star opposite Judy. Now he was shunted to the far less desirable role of the boy who loses her. Murphy had been the choice of Busby Berkeley, who was to direct, and at first Berkeley resented Kelly as an interloper. But halfway through the shooting schedule the two men became firm friends. Still, Kelly was an outsider—this was his first film and he knew nothing about the special acting techniques the camera demands. Judy, he recalls, was a tremendous help, teaching him dozens of little tricks, such as bobbing down before sitting to make sure your head stays in frame as the camera moves in. She also advised him to tone down some of his stage-actor's gestures, which would look exaggerated when they were blown up on a movie screen.

He had only met her once before—she had visited him backstage in New York—but was grateful for her kindness and charmed by her manner. They quickly became good friends.

Judy, for her part, must have been delighted to work with Kelly. His controlled masculinity was a sharp contrast to the frenetic exuberance of Mickey Rooney's screen presence, and it brought out the best in her. Kelly's distinctive throaty singing voice (which he refers to as his Irish whiskey tenor) blended well with hers. And he was a superlative dancer.

Kelly remembers that he was self-conscious about having to record songs with Judy, and Judy is said to have been very nervous about dancing with Kelly. Not having received much training, her dance technique was necessarily limited, but Kelly found her able to pick up simple tap routines, popular dances and musical comedy numbers as quickly as most professional dancers, and her natural flair allowed her to perform as well as anyone within her technical limitations.

For Me and My Gal was another lightweight vehicle, this time about vaudeville performers who are caught up in the Great War while striving to make the big time. Judy plays Jo Hayden, a young singer who throws her lot in with a cocky song-and-dance man named Harry Palmer (Kelly), knowing he is conceited and opportunistic, but sure she can tame him. When Palmer dodges induction into the army so they can play the Palace, Jo—whose brother has been killed at the front—walks out in disgust. Harry redeems himself by saving a company of soldiers from enemy ambush. The picture ends with both of them onstage at the Palace, backed by a regiment of uniformed men. The film makes use of many old vaudeville songs, but by far the most interesting and charming musical number is "For Me and My Gal"—performed by Garland and Kelly in an empty restaurant. The most surprising sequence is a battlefield montage plucked wholesale from *The Big Parade*.

For Me and My Gal reflected the patriotic mood of the country and did excellent business. Kelly, unused to Hollywood publicity, was surprised at the success and shocked at the

(Above) A publicity picture for For Me and My Gal. *(Opposite page) With George Murphy and Gene Kelly.*

116

amount of attention he received. For Judy, the film was important because it was the first hint that the studio might let her grow up.

Judy Garland's next films—*Presenting Lily Mars* and *Girl Crazy*—are interesting both intrinsically and because they hint at things to come. *Presenting Lily Mars* was produced by Joe Pasternak, who had come over from Universal to organize a second musical unit at Metro. Norman Taurog was the director, and the film allowed Judy to continue the process of growing up on screen, this time without a featherbed of nostalgia. Based on a Booth Tarkington novel, the picture has Judy as a small town girl who comes to New York to make her name on the stage and concentrates her efforts on a handsome Broadway producer, played by Van Heflin.

In *For Me and My Gal* Judy's weight had fallen down to ninety-five pounds and she looked almost emaciated. She was still extremely slim for the new picture, but not to the

point of gauntness. For once, every effort was made to have her look glamourous. When a cult began to crystallize around Judy Garland, *Presenting Lily Mars* became a prime object of veneration.

Girl Crazy was the last picture to be built around Garland and Rooney—and arguably the best. It was produced by Freed and Berkeley was set to direct again; but after spending three weeks on a single number (which now appears as the finale), Berkeley, usually so efficient, was taken off the film and replaced by Norman Taurog. It's often been suggested that Berkeley left the picture because of hostility between him and Judy, but it seems that there were other reasons—quite unrelated to any friction between director and star. It's also been hinted that Judy's first serious outbursts of temperament occurred during the filming of *Girl Crazy*—that she vanished for several days at one point—but Taurog says he had no trouble with her. When working with him, she chose to play the child star, always calling him Uncle Norman.

The picture was set in an all-male desert college where Rooney, an aspiring playboy, has been sent for the good of his manhood. Judy, cast as the granddaughter of the dean, naturally catches his eye.

Locations were shot near Palm Springs, with big cutouts of saguaro cactuses dotted around to make the landscape look like Arizona. The heat was intense, regularly topping 120° F., and to make things worse, the location was near a military airfield and low-flying planes created artificial dust storms that sometimes took hours to settle. The production delays were innumerable.

The plot of *Girl Crazy* is none too distinguished, but the film has the incomparable advantage of words and music by the Gershwins. Judy was in full bloom and eclipsed her co-star completely. After Berkeley's departure, a young man named Chuck Walters (who had danced with Judy in the finale of *Lily Mars*) was called in to work on the musical numbers and a couple of these—"Bidin' My Time" and "But Not for Me"—are among the best things Judy ever did on film.

This picture can conveniently be tagged as marking the end of the first phase of Judy Garland's career at M-G-M. From now on, things would be very different.

It was about this time that a serious rift opened between Judy and her mother. It's impossible to point to any one event or series of events that precipitated it, but it may be more than coincidental that Judy was now in analysis. In their book *The M-G-M Stock Company,* James Robert Parish and Ronald L. Bowers give an account of the circumstances surrounding Judy's first encounter with the analyst's couch:

That same year [1942] Joseph L. Mankiewicz, then a scripter under M-G-M contract, noticed the beginnings of Judy's emotional problems. He wanted her to see psychologist Karl Menninger but could not arrange it secretly. So he talked her into seeing another noted psychologist, Dr. Ernest Simmel. Judy's mother discovered her clandestine visits and reported them to Mayer. Mankiewicz recalled that Mayer was in a rage to think that professional help was better than the attention he and Judy's mother were capable of giving. As a result of this confrontation, Mankiewicz left M-G-M and Judy stopped psychiatric visits.

This account seems to be a mixture of fact and fiction. The date is correct and it was Mankiewicz who suggested that Judy see an analyst. (Far from being a mere "scripter," however, he had already produced a number of important pictures, including *The Philadelphia Story* and *Woman of the Year.*) Mayer may have been in the dark about Judy's visits to the psychiatrist, but Ethel certainly was not. Judy appears to have made no attempt to hide them from her family, and Virginia actually drove Judy to the doctor's office on several occasions.

As we have seen in the case of Artie Shaw, Judy was prone to falling blindly in love. She had also had a manic crush on Tyrone Power, and Joseph Mankiewicz was the current object of her passion. So far as she was concerned, whatever he said was law.

Virginia recalls that she, Judy and Mankiewicz were sitting in a restaurant one day when Judy began to tell a story about going up in a parachute ride with Mickey Rooney and the two of them getting stuck. The details of this incident were drawn more from Judy's imagination than from her memory and Mankiewicz told her she was a pathological liar and recommended that she see a psychiatrist. Virginia was shocked, since she didn't view her sister's skill at telling a story as having anything to do with lying:

I don't call elaboration lying. If you have a funny situation and you tell it exactly as it happened, your story can fall on its can. But if you embellish it a bit, which Judy did—well, you were rolling on the floor by the time she got through describing something—even something that wasn't terribly funny to begin with. If that's being a liar, all comics are liars.

In any case, Judy began to see an analyst. Virginia recalls that Judy liked to mimic the doctor's German accent and evidently did not take her visits too seriously—at least, not at the beginning:

I took Judy to the psychiatrist several times. She'd been going to him for two or three months, and the first time I took her I asked, "Why do you do this?"—because it seemed to make her unhappy. She said, "Well, Joe thinks I ought to do it." You couldn't tell her that what Joe said was wrong without getting your head chopped off. I asked, "What in the world do you talk about for an hour?" And she said, "I make up things . . . I make up stories to see how bad I can make him feel. . . ."
So, I dropped her off and waited for her, and when she came out I asked, "Did you make up a lot of stuff?" She said, "I sure did!"
Well, you can only do that for so long before the psychiatrist eventually gets to you—and all of a sudden you're telling him everything.

Virginia believes that it was as a consequence of these visits to the analyst that Judy turned against her mother. It's highly unlikely that the doctor told her that she should break with her family, but he may have suggested that she attempt to be a little more independ-

With Van Heflin. A publicity shot for Presenting Lily Mars.

ent and reevaluate her relationship with her mother. If Judy was beginning to believe the stories concocted for her by the publicity department, such a reevaluation might well have begun to turn her against Ethel. And the possibility that these sessions stirred up doubts about Frank's sexual orientation must be considered. She may have started to think about those childhood separations from her father, and she may have decided to blame Ethel for them.

In a recent article for *Parade* magazine Lloyd Shearer reports that Judy once asked him, "Did you ever hear anything about my father being a homosexual? I never heard anything about it except one time from my mother, and I don't believe it. I think she said it to sort of alibi her thing with Will Gilmore."

The implication is that Ethel had an affair with Gilmore while Frank was still alive. There is no evidence for this and it seems more likely that Judy invented this story in an attempt to neutralize her own confusion regarding her father. It's hard to believe, too, that she first heard of Frank's homosexuality from Ethel. The Lancaster evidence indicates otherwise.

The rift was not immediate or complete, but increasingly Judy found herself at odds with her mother. Ethel, for her part, resented the influence that Judy's friends at the studio had over her life. Ethel thought that many of Judy's M-G-M friends were phonies, and—given her life with Frank—she may have been disturbed by Judy's camaraderie with the considerable homosexual contingent in the Freed unit. Ethel, who was not the sort to keep her thoughts to herself, may have passed on to Judy a few home truths that her daughter found difficult to swallow. In any case, their relationship began to deteriorate. Judy and her mother would never be close again.

Whatever the reason for this breakdown in communications, Ethel blamed it on Dr. Simmel's influence. She took her grudge to Mayer who apparently intervened on her behalf, ordering Judy to terminate her visits to the doctor.

Before too long, Mayer would find himself paying for her to renew these visits.

In costume for Little Nellie Kelly.

Chapter 1
Playing
the Game

As long as the studio bosses controlled the movie industry, Hollywood stories that reached the newsstands were, for the most part, fiction, with just enough fact included to anchor them loosely in the realm of possibility. With a few exceptions, the journalists who concocted them were like pastry cooks with an aversion to red meat. Conveyed through their pens, Hollywood was a very genteel world. There were, of course, one or two columnists who suggested—largely by means of innuendo—that fornication and insobriety were not entirely unknown in the foothills of the Santa Monica Mountains, and, from time to time, a scandal of some sort (a juicy divorce, an unexplained death) splashed onto the front pages. Anyone close enough to the source to receive word-of-mouth gossip could have had little doubt that there were goings-on in the movie colony that would have sent some of the more squeamish fans into a state of catatonia.

One of the most important functions of stu-

dio publicity departments was to suppress, or at least minimize, scandals. This was one of the few areas in which rival studios voluntarily collaborated. If a star's thirst for amusement stretched to terrorizing a small town with a loaded .45—and such whims were not unheard of—the troubleshooters from the studio could usually persuade the local authorities that such high spirits did not constitute an indictable offense, and that the whole affair was too trivial to interest the busy gentlemen of the press. Many police benevolent funds benefited from these incidents. When a scandal did find its way into the headlines, there were often grounds for suspecting that the central figure was a scapegoat. A typical instance of this was the Robert Mitchum marijuana bust in 1948, when he was found guilty of possession and sentenced to a brief jail term. Tipped off that narcotic agents had their eyes on a number of Hollywood celebrities—including Judy Garland—a consortium of film industry figures decided to sacrifice Mitchum on the theory that

On the cliffs at Carmel, circa 1944.

125

this would draw the heat away from the others. Mitchum's career was just beginning to take off but he had been labeled a troublemaker and was considered expendable. It was taken for granted that this would finish his career—and it probably would have except for Howard Hughes, who chose to ignore the whole thing and buy Mitchum's contract for RKO.

Though the facts of a scandal could usually be suppressed, nothing could stop the rumors that erupted like shock waves through the studios and the service industries. They spread through dimly lit nightclubs and bars; they were passed on by hairdressers, interior decorators, tennis pros, prostitutes and masseurs, eventually reaching even the quiet men who scooped dead leaves out of Bel Air swimming pools. The humblest of these creatures was still an insider who understood the code of this privileged world, so the edifice of pretense survived this leakage for decades.

Certainly there were people in Hollywood who led blameless and reasonably normal lives, or who satisfied themselves with harmless eccentricities, but it's safe to say that Hollywood witnessed more excesses than were common for a community of its size. This was a society in which everything was done with flamboyance. The stars were strange blends of the ordinary and the extraordinary. To succeed, they needed the common touch—a talent for cliché—plus a flair for self-projection that sometimes amounted to full-blown exhibitionism. Many stars discovered their gifts almost by accident, but, at the same time, they were often driven people who were intensely ambitious. At the extreme limits of ambition there are only two possibilities—absolute success and absolute failure—and failure at that level is practically coincidental with death. It is because of this ethos that so many stars followed trajectories that were virtually suicidal. So if Judy Garland sometimes appeared to be bent on self-destruction, it must be remembered that she was one of those who were locked into the pattern of absolute success or absolute failure.

That kind of polarity makes for behavior

patterns that cannot be judged by ordinary standards. Norma Shearer, considered to be a rather grand and proper lady, was known to entertain party guests by standing on her head. This demonstration of prowess, while certainly innocent enough, can be taken as symbolic of the attitude that prevailed in Hollywood: if the stunt doesn't work, you fall on your face. Actors—many of them—were constantly testing themselves, their friends, their rivals, their employers, their subordinates, almost everyone they happened to come into contact with. This was also true of other people in the industry—producers or directors, anyone playing for high stakes—but the stars had to deal with the added dimension of quasi-divinity, which was conferred on them by their public and upheld by publicists and fan magazines.

The phenomenon of stardom can be seen as a reversion to popular religion in which the stars were aspects of the godhead walking among us in mortal form. The canons of the religion were codified (by the Hays office) from the unspoken ideals of American wholesomeness (shot through with a suspicion of violence and naughtiness). As in other primitive religions, the Hollywood gods were apt to end up as human sacrifices. Stardom being a democratic religion, public condemnation at the box office was a usual prerequisite to the formal sentencing which would be announced by the priesthood in the form of a press release indicating that so-and-so's contract had been terminated. This sentence was in some ways less humane than the old forms of human sacrifice, since after the star died, his or her mortal shell was left to get by as best it could, a faint trace of celebrity clinging to it, but sucked dry of the last vestige of deity. The clever ones at least salvaged material comfort out of the experience. Beverly Hills is full of millionaire has-beens.

A few stars clung to their divinity to the very end, resisting every challenge with each last hardening artery. Some, refusing the ritual verdict, engineered successful comebacks, while still others were reincarnated on *The Late Late Show*. Always, however, the struggle to stay

126

alive became more difficult every day. Time and the makeup artist were involved in a running battle, with the odds rigged in favor of time. One crow's-foot too many, or a single surplus ounce of flesh, and it could be all over. Only the greatest stars established sufficient credit with their audiences to purchase forgiveness for the sin of aging. And only an uncommonly well integrated personality could acquire that kind of divinity without losing all sense of perspective.

These were working gods and goddesses, though; their day-to-day routine was, for the most part, regulated, repetitious and boring. All the trappings of luxury—the limousines, the mobile dressing rooms with their Oriental rugs and ormolu mirrors—could not erase the drudgery required of a star. Thus it's hardly surprising that during their leisure hours actors sometimes behaved like cowhands hitting Dodge City after a long cattle drive. Add to this the special dispensation they were given by virtue of their quasi-divinity, and their knowledge that this could be withdrawn without notice, and it's easy to understand why stars sometimes behaved strangely by ordinary standards. Ordinary standards were the standards of the spectator; the star was the antithesis of the spectator. He was forced to live in the present and to squeeze the most from his privileged position while he could. Small wonder he sometimes came a little unhinged.

It was exactly this that made Hollywood so fascinating. We were transfixed by the men who went berserk in the Garden of Earthly Delights, and by the women who tried to model their lives on the lyrics of popular songs. Given the bizarre blend of poetry and avarice generated by the movie industry, given the climate of hard work and adulation, they were as proper to Southern California as zebras are to Africa.

The mind craves absurdity and Hollywood provided it, both in the calculated madness of some of its best films and in the freewheeling lunacy that came to seem characteristic of its social life.

Actors, taken as a group, probably have as firm a grip on reality as accountants, but their horizons are broader and their craft lends itself to richer involvements. Above all, an actor's instinct for role-playing enables him to explore many facets of reality. (When an actor turns director or producer, he at least knows how to look the part.) His particular expertise determines that he will gain a certain knowledge of the world; yet this same expertise, if unmodified by other instincts, can very easily detach him from the nonperformer's perspective on everyday realities. The gifted actor is not necessarily the owner of an exceptional intellect, but he somehow manages to stay downwind of whatever ideas are cooking at the time. He picks up the latest notion and, naturally enough, acts on it. In short, he is ideally equipped to make a perfect fool of himself.

The actor's special task is to explore the borderland between illusion and reality, and to bring too many preconceptions to this activity would inhibit it. There is not much to be gained by exploring that which is already known. The actor acts—and that is all we can reasonably demand of him. Given a good script, the talented actor can walk on water. Left to his own devices, he is apt to sink like a stone.

The problem that an actor always faces is that he cannot leave his work at his place of business, however much he might want to, and if he is also a star, his situation can become grotesque. There are actors and stars who have the security to handle this problem—they are able, in effect, to act their way out of it. They have learned to distinguish between the nature of stage or screen roles and the character of the roles demanded of them by family, friends, business contacts and casual acquaintances. But the actor who has experienced no security other than that he finds in performing may have great difficulty negotiating the transition from illusion to reality. He is always looking for scenarios he can slot himself into. Being a movie actor or a movie star adds a further complication. Film dislocates reality more effectively than any other medium, and many screen personalities, catching the scent of that, seem to have asked themselves: If anything is possible on film, then why not in real life?

The Hollywood actor on the town, in search of a scenario, had thousands to choose from. The last one he was likely to pick would be the pap the gossip sheets were printing about him. Some stars made unfortunate choices and have the dislocated lives to prove it. But no one who has ever enjoyed a Hollywood movie can afford to feel morally aloof, because whatever the virtues or failings of the stars, they were pushed into a world of extremes and—while we must allow for a zooful of exploiters—it took an avid public to put and keep them there. Once someone became a Hollywood star, there was nowhere to escape to—nowhere else he really belonged. He might travel to New York, to London, to Rome, but Hollywood always went with him.

Judy Garland was precisely the kind of star who knew no security other than that which she found in her performances. She had not been thrust bodily into show business, as she claimed, but she had been encouraged to perform almost from the day she was born. Most people are stricken with terror when asked to stand up and entertain an audience; Judy experienced her greatest fears during those intervals that could not be bridged by performances. Everyone who knew her likes to recall how eager she was to sing—whether professionally or for charity; whether at parties, in her own home or simply riding in the back of a car. The generosity with which she squandered her gifts is spoken of with awe. Yet—without wishing to belittle this—it would be absurd to expect anything less. At a party she would stand in front of the band and sing her heart out because, for her, this was the most natural way of relating to people. It established her identity. When she was singing, she *was* Judy Garland.

Even when she was not singing, dancing or speaking lines, she was still performing—mimicking some absent friend, telling a raunchy story, camping her way through an interview, playing games. She was, for instance, a stellar performer on the charades circuit that was so central to the Hollywood social scene during

her years at M-G-M. "The Game," as it was called there, flourished in the climate provided by the movie colony. Each of the several important houses where it was played featured its own variation. At Gene Kelly's home, for example, where Judy was a regular, a very physical version was played—with participants dashing from room to room. Although extremely quick and intelligent, Judy was not well read and was short on formal education. She compensated for these disadvantages with her remarkable intuition and acting ability. If she did not understand a word or phrase, she would mime it phonetically and still get the meaning across with uncanny speed. The sheer will to communicate—so obvious when she faced a movie camera—made her a formidable player.

Hollywood's cultural climate was almost frighteningly ideal for Judy Garland. Her wit and intelligence were committed to entertainment and nothing else. And of all the Hollywood hothouses she could have gravitated to, the Freed unit provided the environment in which she might best be expected to thrive. The men and women who surrounded her there were clever, charming, sardonic—devoted to surface sparkle and apt to mock anyone who didn't share their outlook. In the M-G-M commissary they had their own table, from which they aimed humorous barbs at the rest of the world. Throughout the forties and well into the fifties this table attracted most of the sharpest wits around the studio. If Oscar Levant (who had been the object of one of Judy's infatuations) was working on the lot, this is where you could count on finding him. The cream of the music department would be there —men like Conrad Salinger, John Green, Saul Chaplin, Lennie Hayton, George Bassman and Roger Edens. There would be lyricists and composers too—Johnny Mercer, Hugh Martin, Ralph Blane, Harry Warren and Mack Gordon, whoever happened to be working on a current picture—not to mention screenwriters such as Fred Finklehoffe and choreographers like Robert Alton. The stars who chose to sit at the Freed unit table included Gene Kelly,

Frank Sinatra, Peter Lawford, Liz Taylor (usually with her pet chipmunk perched on her shoulder) and Judy.

To outsiders, the Freed unit appeared wrapped in an atmosphere of cynicism and "in" jokes. Within the group, though, there was a tendency to cultivate occasional displays of suffering as the proper accompaniment to all artistic activity. (The debris of several nineteenth-century cultural movements seems to have found its final resting place in Culver City.) A definite style—sometimes languid and sometimes hysterical, but always mannered—took root in the Freed unit. Some raised suffering to a form of elitism. Judy, who was not unaware of the humor in this, would mimic her friends' more excessive mannerisms. Under pressure, however, she began to fall back on these same mannerisms herself.

It has already been noted that the Freed unit included a sizable gay contingent. Freed himself was very much a ladies' man—a prolific propositioner of girls seeking work at the studio—but he liked to joke about his team being known as "the fairy unit." The many gifted homosexuals who worked on his films were to a considerable extent responsible for the mood and spirit of the musicals he produced, and for the social ambiance that surrounded their making. Judy was totally at home with this group, sharing both its sensibility and its sense of humor.

From the early forties on, Judy Garland became one of those Hollywood stars—Joan Crawford, Bette Davis and Marlene Dietrich were others—who seemed to act as magnets for homosexuals. The gay world at that time was very different from what it is today. The great majority of homosexuals were still in the closet, and Hollywood was the best of all possible closets—so extensive it was practically a parallel universe. And to people who looked to the movie world as an alternate way of life, Judy seemed to be the essence of Hollywood. As she cut herself loose from her past, she seemed to have no need for anything beyond Hollywood's invisible boundaries. And she welcomed people from the gay world because they offered support and sympathy, buttressing the palace of artifice she had built around herself. They accepted her as a performer and did not ask her to be anything else. There is also the possibility that she was drawn to homosexuals because she subconsciously felt they could provide a psychic link to her dead father.

It seems likely that Judy herself had at least one homosexual liaison, with Betty Asher— the M-G-M publicist already mentioned in connection with Lana Turner's divorce from Artie Shaw. Betty Asher appears to have been a studio spy, but one who was not averse to mixing pleasure with business. She had kept an eye on Lana for some time before her assignment was switched to Judy.

Betty Asher was a very smooth operator. Possessing a decidedly worldly manner—the very kind of brittle sophistication that impressed Judy—she eased herself into favor and quickly became Judy's constant companion and confidante. Tom Drake, who would soon be playing opposite Judy in one of her biggest hits, remembers that everyone at the studio was fascinated by the relationship:

Betty Asher was close to Judy, close to Lana, close to everybody! But no one could ever figure out how deep the friendship went— and one reason was that Betty was very close to one of the top executives at the studio, and of course that man was interested in the welfare of Turner and Garland. But Betty Asher got closer to those people than anybody else could ever have gotten.

One evening we worked till about twelve-thirty—and by the time we got our makeup off and had a couple of drinks with the sound man or someone, it was maybe two. I had parked across from the administration building, so Betty and I got in my car and started talking. We were just going to have a cigarette and wrap the evening up with a couple more lines of dialogue—but we actually stayed there till sunrise.

It was kind of dark in the car. You could see an expression in the eyes, perhaps, but not much more. All you really had to go by was the voice and, I swear to God, if I'd wanted to kid myself I wouldn't have known if I was with Betty, with Judy, or with Lana Turner. I couldn't get over it.

Everyone gave Lilian Burns [the studio's speech coach] credit for Lana Turner's manner.... But all three girls sounded the same. They used the same kind of dialogue, the same kind of expressions.

Even before Judy married David Rose she often stayed at Betty Asher's apartment and the two of them rented a house at Malibu together in the summer of 1941, just a few weeks before the wedding. After the breakup with David Rose, Judy and Betty Asher became tighter than ever, and it was during this later period that their relationship may have become, in part, sexual. If so, it was just a passing experiment and the two young women may have been pushed into it by a male friend of Judy's who was amused by the possibilities.

Despite whatever instructions Betty Asher had received from the studio, she seemed to have had a knack for leading Judy into trouble and is cited by many people as having been a negative influence. She encouraged Judy—who, up to this point, had very little taste for hard liquor—to drink on the job. When another woman from the publicity department objected to this, she received a shot of Scotch in the face for her trouble (followed, the next day, by a letter of apology from Judy). We should not forget that Betty Asher was acting as Judy's personal publicist, and was therefore responsible for disseminating the false infor-fation that was doing so much damage to her charge's psyche. How much, then, did she contribute to the myths? At the very least, she seems to have reinforced Judy's belief in them, and hence her growing alienation from her mother. After trusting her completely for several years, Judy eventually discovered her publicist's apparent duplicity and denounced her as a spy. Betty Asher later committed suicide.

The fact that Judy may have had a sexual relationship with Betty Asher is interesting only insofar as it tells us that she was open to that possibility. Certainly she did not take all homosexual activity for granted, as is made clear by her reaction to another incident. An M-G-M scriptwriter took her to Palm Springs for the weekend. All went well until she walked in on him unexpectedly and found him in the arms of another man. Judy was shattered.

This was not the only time she ran into such a situation, and she seems to have become hardened to it with repetition, but in the early forties it did not take much to turn her back into the little girl from Grand Rapids. Throughout her adult life she had an overwhelming desire to establish a viable relationship with someone of the opposite sex. Much of her energy was expended in that cause and many of her disappointments were rooted in it. The irony is that while she wanted to build her life on heterosexual relationships, she actually felt more at home in the gay world. There was a fundamental inconsistency in her perception of gender relationships, an inconsistency that led her to become involved with homosexual or bisexual men who shared her sensibility but who were unable to provide the sexual and emotional counterweight she demanded.

It was a problem that all the little pills with the picturesque nicknames—bluejays, red-birds, yellowjackets—could do nothing to solve.

After *Girl Crazy* Judy's next film appearance was a guest spot in *Thousands Cheer,* a Pasternak extravaganza built around Gene Kelly and Kathryn Grayson. She followed this modest outing with one of the most important pictures of her career.

Meet Me in St. Louis is among the greatest of M-G-M musicals, and one of the least typical. Emphasizing naturalism rather than artifice, it is a delicate period piece that reproduces beautifully the atmosphere of Midwestern bourgeois comfort a couple of years after the turn of the century. Based on *The New Yorker*

Meet Me in St. Louis. *With Lucille Bremer.*

memoirs of Sally Benson, the film is the essence of simplicity—a modest chain of related incidents broken up with musical interludes. Originally, the studio had wanted to use the title and setting as a pretext for an adventure story that would involve the heroine, Esther Smith, in a vapid blackmail plot. Arthur Freed and director Vincente Minnelli had a very different concept in mind and eventually they prevailed. A new screenplay was written, by Fred Finklehoffe and Irving Brecher, which counterpointed two simple stories—Esther's romance with the boy next door and the Smith family's reactions to the possibility of leaving St. Louis—the whole thing climaxing at the opening of the St. Louis World's Fair, the Universal Exposition of 1904.

This was the picture that deservedly established Vincente Minnelli's reputation. Although he was just thirty when *St. Louis* went into production, Minnelli had been around show business for a long time. His father was owner and musical director of the Minnelli Brothers' Tent Theater, which for many years had toured the Plains states every summer, bringing the staples of melodrama to people not unlike Esther Smith and her friends. His mother was the company's leading lady, and young Vincente was pressed into service as a juvenile in various productions. While still in his teens, he was running the costume department for the Balaban and Katz organization, which owned a number of theaters in Chicago that featured elaborate stage shows along with movie programs (the Katz in the partnership was the same Sam Katz who preceded Minnelli to M-G-M). Amalgamation with the Paramount-Publix chain brought Minnelli to New York, where before long he was mounting shows at the then still new Radio City Music Hall. It was only a matter of time before his talents took him to Broadway.

His growing reputation resulted in an early trip to Hollywood, under the auspices of Paramount Pictures, but it was a souring experience and he gladly returned to New York. When "Yip" Harburg introduced him to Arthur Freed and Freed invited him to come to Metro, Minnelli was very wary. Freed, always sensitive to the needs of individual talents, suggested that Minnelli spend some time at the studio without any specific assignment. In his autobiography, Minnelli reported Freed's offer as follows:

You won't have a title, but you'll learn the business. You'll be working with me. Other producers will be able to call on you for your services. You can read scripts and make suggestions . . . direct musical numbers . . . work in the cutting room. . . . If you see that you don't have a future in pictures, then come back to New York.

Minnelli spent a year feeling his way—and watching various directors at work—before getting his first directorial assignment, the all-black musical *Cabin in the Sky*. Next he took on a Red Skelton film, *I Dood It*. Then came his big opportunity.

Minnelli hardly knew Judy Garland and his first professional contacts with her were not encouraging. The people around Judy had tried to convince her that it would be a serious mistake to become involved in *St. Louis*. Their reasoning—and it did have some logic—was that now that the studio had finally begun to let her grow up in roles like Lily Mars, Esther Smith would be a step backward. It was true that the Esther of the screenplay was a seventeen-year-old girl, a high school junior involved in an apparently banal situation. Directed by one of the studio's stock directors, the film would probably have amounted to nothing—and Minnelli was not yet a proven quantity.

Judy evidently felt she could face him down so she went to him with the views that had been thrust on her. "It's not very good, is it?" she asked. Politely but firmly, Minnelli disagreed, so Judy took her complaints to Mayer, who told Arthur Freed that for once he thought Judy was right. But Freed backed Minnelli. (Freed endeared himself to his subordinates by carefully leaving them to their own devices once an assignment had been agreed on, and by defending them against interference from

Meet Me in St. Louis: *left to right, Margaret O'Brien, Lucille Bremer, Joan Carroll, and Judy.*

133

the front office.) Freed had one of the best track records at the studio and Mayer agreed to let him have his way. Judy, reluctantly, went along with the decision.

With screenplay and star settled, the next thing to deal with was the look of the production—the visual details had to be just right or the whole thing would fail. In New York Minnelli had been in the habit of supervising everything himself, from the first sketch to the last lighting cue. At Metro he sometimes found himself at odds with the art department, which had its own way of doing things. On *St. Louis,* however, he worked with a sympathetic art director, Preston Ames, and with Lemuel Ayres, a recent arrival from the New York theater world where he had been a leading set decorator. Costumes would be important too, and here Minnelli was fortunate in having the services of Irene Sharaff, another Broadway import.

An entire new street was built on Lot Three, a handsome thoroughfare with sloping lawns and substantial American gothic villas—all porches, gables, bays and gingerbread trimmings. It cost $100,000 in 1943, and there were those who looked upon it as a white elephant. In fact, it proved to be one of the studio's most durable assets. Dozens of films were shot on the St. Louis Street, including

many produced by other studios, which paid good money for the privilege.

The main interior set, the Smiths' home at 5135 Kensington Avenue, was also an elaborate proposition. Apart from the entire question of accurate period detail, Minnelli did not want to work with a conventional set. Instead of building a series of separate sets, one for each room, with breakaway walls to facilitate camera movements, he decided that he wanted to film on a continuous set—one that would be constructed like the floor of a real house, with interconnecting rooms. This would present certain problems, but it would also offer some advantages and would contribute to the efficacy of one of the movie's key scenes.

All these efforts would have added up to nothing without a strong company to complement the star, especially since *St. Louis* was to be essentially an ensemble piece. Lucille Bremer, Joan Carroll and Margaret O'Brien were cast as the three other Smith sisters, while Mary Astor and Leon Ames were set to play their parents. Harry Davenport was Grandpa and Marjorie Main was given the pivotal role of Katie, the live-in help. Tom Drake was chosen to play John Truett, the boy next door.

As shooting got underway, Judy did not exactly throw herself into her part. Used to flippant, wisecracking dialogue, she was obviously uncomfortable with this low-keyed script and responded by mocking it with her delivery. She was aware that something was wrong and complained to Freed that she had no idea what Minnelli wanted from her. Freed told her to trust the director, and things got a little better, but the atmosphere on the set remained polite rather than warm. Minnelli's work pattern was similar to that of Berkeley, whose methods he had studied closely during his apprentice year. He liked to rehearse a scene over and over till he was satisfied with every detail; then he would shoot it in as few takes as possible— often only one was necessary. Judy took note of this, and Minnelli's mannerisms, and developed a little comedy routine with which she entertained the crew while the director was off the set. She would play two parts—Minnelli

and a veteran bit-part actor who for decades has earned a comfortable living by speaking one line in every movie made on the lot. On this particular morning the actor arrives for work primed for his big moment, which consists of looking up at the sky and remarking, "I think it might rain." He is anticipating another routine paycheck, but has not reckoned with Minnelli. The director runs him through his spot once and suggests that he might consider the possibility of pausing between raising his eyes and speaking his line. Surprised, the actor agrees to try this. Minnelli likes that better, but thinks it might be stronger if the actor were to make an effort to sound a trifle put out at the prospect of rain. They rehearse again. Fine, but perhaps a suggestion of a sneer next time. That's good, but maybe once more with a hint of resignation as the line is spoken. The director likes this too, but wonders now how the *actor* feels he should play the line. . . . This process would continue indefinitely until the skit ended with the bit player reduced to a state of blathering imbecility—unable to remember his own name, let alone the line he is supposed to deliver.

Throughout the early stages of shooting Judy indulged in occasional absenteeism and frequent on-set delays, the former sometimes putting Tom Drake in a somewhat embarrassing situation:

Judy and I dated quite a few times towards the beginning of the picture. On two or three occasions I took Judy home at about one o'clock in the morning and she said, "I just can't go to work tomorrow. I'm too exhausted."

I'd leave with this knowledge and yet I'd have to get up and get to the studio at six-thirty and play absolutely dumb. After the set was all lit up, Judy would send word that she would be two hours late—and everyone would stall for a couple of hours. Then, finally, word would come that she wouldn't be in at all.

Because of her insomnia, she was genuinely exhausted much of the time and there were occasional tearful outbursts which, inevitably, were interpreted as temperament. At other times she would retire to her trailer for prolonged periods, holding up proceedings for no apparent reason. Eventually, as she recalled in *A Life on Film,* Mary Astor decided to confront Judy with this:

I walked into her portable dressing room one tense morning, and she greeted me with her usual cheery, "Hi, Mom!" I sat down on the couch while she went on primping, and said, "Judy, what the hell's happened to you? You were a trouper—once." She stared at me. I went on, "You have kept the entire company out there waiting for two hours. Waiting for you to favor us with your presence. You know we're stuck—there's nothing we can do without you at the moment."

She giggled and said, "Yeah, that's what everybody's been telling me."

That bugged me and I said, "Well, then, either get the hell out on the set or *I'm* going home."

She grabbed me by the hand and her face crumpled up. "I don't *sleep,* Mom!"

And I said, "Well, go to bed earlier then—like we all have to do. . . ."

Miss Astor later blamed herself for being hard on Judy, feeling that if she had been aware of the extent of Judy's problems she might have chosen to restrain herself.

As the shooting of *St. Louis* progressed, Judy's interest in the project increased and her behavior improved. After her shaky start with Minnelli, she began to understand his approach and to treat him with respect. Once the ice was broken, in fact, they got along extremely well. Minnelli explained his ideas to her, quietly and patiently, and Judy began to take a real interest in Esther Smith. Soon Judy and her director started to see each other socially. At first this was rather casual, the two of them accompanying mutual friends Don Loper and Ruth Brady on double dates. Later they began to show up at parties together and would immediately vanish into some quiet corner where they might be glimpsed caught up in some earnest private dialogue. John Green, who was often to be found at the piano on these occa-

sions, recalls that Minnelli would materialize at his side from time to time to request sentimental songs.

Nobody took it too seriously. After all, they were an oddly matched couple—Judy intuitive and extroverted, Minnelli cultured and introspective. Most observers were surprised when, shortly after the shooting of *Meet Me in St. Louis* was completed, Judy Garland and Vincente Minnelli were living together.

Meet Me in St. Louis works so well as a whole that it seems almost inappropriate to select highlights. Ralph Blane and Hugh Martin wrote excellent songs for the movie, and at least three of Judy's numbers are among the best things she ever did on film. "The Boy Next Door" is a Garland classic, staged simply by Minnelli and photographed sensitively by George Folsey (whose color work added greatly to the texture and warmth of the entire picture). "The Trolley Song"—its onomatopoeic rhythms heightened by a spectacular Conrad Salinger orchestration—is quite different in

Preceding pages: With Arthur Freed, left, and Vincente Minnelli.

Meet Me in St. Louis. *With Margaret O'Brien.*

spirit. The director has filled the screen with nervous movement which reflects Esther's mood as she waits anxiously to see if John Truett will arrive in time to join the expedition to the fairgrounds. "Have Yourself a Merry Little Christmas" is straightforward enough on the surface but is built on complex emotional dynamics—the cheerful banality of the lyrics being played off against the melancholy of the occasion.

The entire Halloween sequence, a tour de force for Minnelli, Folsey and Margaret O'Brien, is a memorable evocation of childhood terrors. Superficially, this episode has very little to do with anything else in the movie and the studio seriously considered dropping it; but when the film was run without this segment it seemed flat and Freed had it reinstated. Looking at the picture today, we can see the Halloween sequence is central to the whole thing. The experiences of "Tootie" (Margaret O'Brien) on that October evening symbolize what anchors the Smith family in their Midwestern suburban world. Minnelli uses the bizarre images of Halloween to underline the normality of the family's life.

Perhaps the most effective dramatic scene involving Judy is the one in which, after a party at the Smiths' home, Esther tries to detain John Truett and hits on the stratagem of asking him to help her extinguish the lights. In a series of carefully orchestrated boom moves, the camera follows them through the house without a cut, thus prolonging the tension of the situation (we can see now why Minnelli had insisted on a continuous set for the interior of the Smiths' home). Folsey had so many lighting changes to make in this one shot that he ran out of dimmers and had to improvise by placing venetian blinds in front of some of his sources. All this was done to create a feeling of suspense that built up to nothing more explosive than the possibility of a first kiss, but the suspense is as real as in anything by Hitchcock.

In *Meet Me in St. Louis* Minnelli made a new kind of musical—about as far removed from the sources of the movie musical as could be imagined. He may have learned something from Busby Berkeley's methods, but the set pieces here (Chuck Walters was the dance director) are light-years from the aeriel geometrics of *Forty-second Street* and *Footlight Parade*. In Minnelli's world you do not find cameras tracking through tunnels of wrinkled tights. These masters of the musical film have only two things in common: a predilection for elaborate boom shots and a sure feeling for the orchestration of movement on screen. So far as dramatic sense and pictorial sensibility are concerned, they could hardly be further apart.

Judy never looked better on film than she did in *Meet Me in St. Louis*. The Sharaff clothes were extremely flattering, and for the first time Judy's makeup was done by Dottie Ponedel, who had a touch of inventiveness that marked her off from the general run of makeup artists. It was she who refined Marlene Dietrich's look a decade earlier at Paramount. From *St. Louis* on, Judy would allow no one else to handle her makeup. The later Garland look, with the carefully delineated lips and the arched eyebrows, can be attributed to this woman. The changes were very small—the makeup base was altered and the hairline tweezed a little—but they were instrumental in transforming Judy from an ingenue into something a little more worldly.

Dottie Ponedel had a humorous and offhand approach to her work that Judy found irresistible. According to Minnelli, if there was no water handy, Dottie would simply dip her brush into a mug of cold coffee. For the next dozen years or so she was one of Judy's most constant companions.

Meanwhile, during the summer of 1944, there was a brief hiatus in the Garland-Minnelli romance. Judy walked out on the affair for a final fling with an old lover. Minnelli did not have much time to brood over her desertion since as soon as he finished cutting *Meet Me in St. Louis,* he began work on a $3,000,000 extravaganza to be titled *Ziegfeld Follies*. This was a project that Arthur Freed had been nursing for some time and the idea was to

With Minnelli on the set of Ziegfeld Follies.

create the kind of show Florenz Ziegfeld might have put on had he been able to reach down from heaven and employ the M-G-M stock company. The picture would eventually consist of fourteen segments—a filmed revue—featuring stars such as Fred Astaire, Lucille Ball, Lucille Bremer, Fanny Brice, Kathryn Grayson, Lena Horne, Gene Kelly and Esther Williams. At different stages in the preparation of this movie various spots were proposed for Judy. At first it was she rather than Gene Kelly who was penciled in to perform "The Babbitt and the Bromide" with Fred Astaire. Another idea was to reunite her with Mickey Rooney in a number titled "I Love You More in Technicolor Than I Did in Black and White." In the meantime, Roger Edens and actress-writer-singer Kay Thompson, an old friend of Minnelli's, had been working on a routine intended for Greer Garson—a spoof on that actress's haughty image which they called "The Great Lady Has an Interview." It soon became clear that a real singer would be needed to do justice to this idea and Kay Thompson suggested Judy. This was mildly revolutionary since, even

though the studio was allowing her to grow up a little, Judy's image was still one hundred percent wholesome and Madame Crematon, the "Great Lady" of this sketch, was about as wholesome as a slug of absinthe. Edens and Thompson knew that Judy could handle the routine, but they must have wondered how her public would react to this new image.

Minnelli himself was a little worried about working with Judy so soon after their breakup. This proved to be no problem, however: the Madame Crematon skit was shot without difficulties, and when the film eventually appeared, Judy received generally good reviews. Bosley Crowther remarked in *The New York Times* that she displayed signs of a talent "approaching that of Beatrice Lillie or Gertrude Lawrence." These were not names that had been mentioned before when attempting to fix Judy's position in the entertainment spectrum. Hard-core Garland aficionados swooned over Madame Crematon. This was the Judy they had hoped for, the Judy of their most cherished dreams—a camp madonna.

Looked at today, the piece seems clever, witty and elegant in an old-fashioned sort of way, but also slight. The direction is crisp and Judy's performance is as sure as usual, but the real significance resides in her appearance and manner. This is the first hint of the part she will eventually play in real life—the seen-it-all, no-flies-on-me, sassified sophisticate. This is the prototype of the Judy Garland that the cult would crystallize around. It's Judy Garland à la Kay Thompson, but still vulnerable as only Judy could be vulnerable. From this point on, the two of them would be great friends and Kay Thompson would take her place alongside Roger Edens as Judy's musical and stylistic mentor. As Freed's right-hand man, Edens now had many other responsibilities and his name was beginning to show up on film credits as associate producer.

Ziegfeld Follies.
*The Great Lady
Gives an Interview.*

141

Chapter 2
Coming Apart

For some time Judy had been pressing Arthur Freed and the front office for an opportunity to do a nonsinging role and finally they agreed to give her one. Probably everyone was curious about what future she might have as a straight actress, and since Judy had been difficult of late, someone might have suggested it would be a good idea to humor her. There was no great risk involved. A nonmusical would be relatively inexpensive to produce and Judy was by now a big enough star to survive even a total disaster.

The story they found for her was *The Clock,* by Paul and Pauline Gallico, which was adapted for the screen by Robert Nathan and Joseph Schrank. It was a simple enough tale. Set and shot in 1944, the picture tells how a young soldier (Robert Walker) meets a girl (Judy) while on a forty-eight-hour furlough in New York City. He woos her and, after a number of everyday Manhattan mishaps, they marry before he ships out to the front.

To direct the film, Freed picked Fred Zin-

nemann, a young Austrian who had recently graduated from the shorts to features. On August 24, 1944, after a little over three weeks' work, the picture was closed down. It seems Judy and Zinnemann had not gotten along well and the footage up to that point was very unsatisfactory. Despite the problems she was having with the director, Judy was still desperate to make the picture, but Mayer and his production committee saw no point in continuing with it under existing circumstances. In a last effort to keep the project alive, Judy called Vincente Minnelli and asked him to have lunch with her (Minnelli thinks Arthur Freed may well have suggested the meeting). They ate at the Players' Club and Judy asked Minnelli to try and salvage the movie. He agreed to at least look into the possibility and ran the existing footage. Every scene seemed to belong to a different picture. Pressing further, he decided that much of the problem sprang from the screenplay, which looked fine on paper but which played badly for some reason or other.

M-G-M glamour pose.

He felt he could rectify this and told Judy he would try to revive the project only if Zinnemann did not object to his taking over, and on the condition that he be given a completely free hand. Zinnemann admitted he was very irritated by Judy's lack of confidence in him but said he would not stand in Minnelli's way. Meanwhile, Mayer, Freed and the production committee were delighted to let Minnelli take the project over and allowed him to make whatever changes he thought were necessary. Almost $200,000 had been put into the picture already. One set that had been built was a full-scale replica of the interior of Pennsylvania Station.

Minnelli scrapped everything that had been shot up to that point and started anew. His idea was to make Manhattan a third character in the story—a difficult enough notion since the entire film would have to be made in Culver City. Careful planning was necessary. Backgrounds shot by a location crew would have to be combined with studio footage to create the required atmosphere. (This was done so successfully that no one viewing the completed film would suspect that the scenes set in Central Park, or on a Fifth Avenue bus, were in fact shot thousands of miles away. Watching *The Clock,* one is always aware of the city as a modifying influence on the relationship of the young couple.)

There were numerous conventional and sentimental incidents in the existing script that needed attention. Early in the story there is a scene set by the model boat pond in Central Park. As written, this had the hero befriending a small boy and helping him rig the sails of his boat. The boy is convinced that his boat will be of little service in the war effort and Walker persuades him he is mistaken. When the boy falls into the pond and a policeman tries to arrest him for swimming, Walker and Judy pretend to be his parents, thus extricating him from his problem. Finding this trite, Minnelli changed things around so that when Walker attempts to befriend the boy he gets a kick in the shins for his trouble. His difficulties with children continue through the film as a leit-

The Clock. *With Keenan Wynn and Robert Walker.*

145

motif. Small but considered changes of this sort were made all the way through the movie, and the love affair is believable because the characters and situations that surround it are believable.

The film's aims were modest but, within its self-imposed limitations, it was almost perfect. Minnelli, working with George Folsey again, adapted his predilection for boom shots to the demands of this film, without becoming too mannered or intrusive. There are some fine secondary performances by Keenan Wynn, James Gleason and others, and the whole thing is underpinned by a strong George Bassman score.

Judy was well behaved throughout the shooting of *The Clock*. The only problem Minnelli had with her was that she was taking her acting a little too seriously and he had to convince her that her natural talent was all that was called for. Seeing her performance today, we can judge how well he succeeded; she seems devoid of affectation.

While Judy was in relatively good shape, Robert Walker was a mess. His marriage to Jennifer Jones had fallen apart and he was drinking heavily. Aware of his problems, Judy did everything she could to nurse him through the picture. Knowing he was on a bender one evening, Judy and Dottie Ponedel went from bar to bar until they found him, then took him home and managed to get him into shape for the next day's shooting. Despite his problem with the bottle, Walker turned in one of the best performances of his career, low-keyed and touching.

Judy's domestic arrangements had been rather loose for some time. After breaking up with David Rose, she rented a house in Beverly Hills, but sometimes she returned to her mother's home. Judy was not the kind of person who could stay on one tack for any length of time. She became bored easily and was no sooner into a situation than she wanted to be out of it. She bounced from crisis to crisis. A depression might send her home to Mother and then, a few days later, a manic rage would send her storming out of the house, denounc-

ing Ethel as a witch. In her mother's home there was always an identity problem—should she expect to be treated as Judy Garland or as Frances Gumm? Yet often this was the only continuing relationship she could fall back on.

During the filming of *The Clock* her romance with Minnelli warmed up again, and he treated her as Judy Garland. She moved in with him once more, this time giving up her rented house. Ethel disapproved very strongly, and said so in no uncertain terms. By now there were many things she was prepared to close her eyes to, but living together without a marriage certificate was not one of them. Minnelli assured Ethel that his intentions were honorable, pointing out that he could not marry Judy until her divorce from David Rose was final, but she refused to be placated.

Up to this point the affair had been conducted on Judy's home turf. Now the studio organized a promotional junket to New York which would give Minnelli the chance to play the seigneur for a while. As well as introducing Judy to his New York friends, Minnelli enjoyed taking her to the spots he had re-created for *The Clock*—they ate in an Italian restaurant in the theater district that had been reconstructed in Culver City for the film. They were reliving the screen romance at one remove and fact spilling into fiction made it just the kind of trip that Judy most enjoyed.

Minnelli was aware of Judy's dependence on pills—she had told him about it early in their relationship—and obviously was concerned, but felt he could not simply order her to stop taking the drugs. Instead, he recalls, he appealed to her to give them up and she agreed to try. Minnelli understood only too well the pressures that had driven Judy to this dependence. He was a sensitive, creative person, capable of imagining himself in her predicament, and because of this empathy he acted less decisively than he might have.

Back in California there were new assignments waiting. While Minnelli was scheduled to direct Fred Astaire in *Yolanda and the Thief,* Judy was set to star in *The Harvey Girls* —a musical that would feature her as a wait-

Playing softball while on location for The Harvey Girls. *With Judy is George Folsey, director of photography on several of her pictures.*

ress in one of the Harvey House restaurants in the period when the railroads had opened up the West but before the frontier was completely tamed. The film was to be directed by George Sidney, who had also directed Judy's first screen test.

The good will Judy had displayed during the making of *The Clock* did not continue into this new project. The picture was hardly into rehearsal when the trouble began, and the following memos—sent by various people to Arthur Freed's office—give some idea of how frustrating her behavior was becoming:

1/10/45

Judy Garland had an 11:00 ready call this A.M. to make wardrobe tests; she arrived in studio at 10:45. At 12 noon she called Griffin, assistant on the picture, to say she couldn't be ready till after lunch. We went to lunch at 12:30 and on return she still was not ready; she arrived on the stage at 3:07 P.M. all made up but not in wardrobe; she came on set dressed at 3:25. At 4:00 she left the stage without making a test, for a conference with LB and did not return to the stage again.

1/11/45

Judy Garland had a 10 A.M. makeup call to be ready on the set at 1 P.M. She arrived at the studio at 12:12 and came on the set at 1:48.

1/12/45

Last night Judy Garland was given a call for this morning, by the assistant, 8:00 in makeup, 10:00 ready on set. She told him she wouldn't be in until 8:30 as she didn't need more than an hour and a half for makeup. This morning she arrived at the studio at 9:25, onstage at 10:50, went into her dressing room and didn't come on the set until 11:25.

1/26/45

Miss Garland called at 3:20 this morning to say that she was not feeling well and could not come to work today. We will try to shoot whatever we can without her. . . .

It was not uncommon for Judy to call in sick at 3:20 in the morning, but it was not always possible to shoot around her. Often calls would go out to the entire company at four and five in the morning, telling them not to report for work. Her pattern of lateness became so taken for granted that when she did turn up on time, surprised memos would be sent out noting the fact. At the beginning of March the situation became ridiculous and the following exasperated memo was sent to Freed by an assistant named Dave Friedman:

3/2/45

The company was informed by Evelyn Powers, Judy Garland's secretary, that as of this date use of her Webster phone number was to be discontinued and that a new address but no phone number would be supplied to us March 3rd. Our contact with Judy Garland from now on is to be through Evelyn Powers and a call bureau. This, of course, will be of inconvenience to the company and of greater inconvenience to Judy Garland should we ever wish to change a call to a later hour. She is aware of the latter possibilities.

This last move led to a confrontation between Judy and the front office and her attendance became a little more regular.

Being a movie star was no way to start the day. You got up at dawn and headed for the lot, down Doheny or Robertson, often beneath the drab overcast that comes in from the Pacific at night. If your name was Judy Garland, you were a nervous driver and preferred to be chauffeured to the studio; you might swallow a couple of wake-up pills in the back of the limousine, or you might have taken them before you left the house. An anxious assistant director would be waiting for you at the East Gate, noting your exact time of arrival, and before you were fully awake you would find yourself seated under a bright light in front of a makeup mirror, your ears assaulted by unwanted greetings, your nostrils challenged by a pungent blend of cosmetics, coffee and perspiration. Someone would be dragging a comb laden with setting lotion through your hair, or sponging something icy cold onto your face. While your mind was trying to piece together

Relaxing on the set.

the events of the previous evening, these busy beauty technicians would be painting your skin and teasing your hair and trying to make you look like a Harvey Girl. All the while the assistant director hovered nearby, ready to rush you down to the set. It was not a dignified way to begin the day. Judy Garland hated it more than most but, for a while at least, she forced herself back into the routine and kept her displays of temperament to a minimum.

Even without Judy Garland as its star, a film was subject to thousands of minor irritations. To start with, the producers had to concern themselves with the stringencies of the Breen Office, the means by which the American film industry censored itself. (It was named for Joseph Breen, who administered the Production Code.) Close attention had to be paid to a constant stream of notes, such as the following apropos of *The Harvey Girls,* dated January 16, 1945, and addressed to L. B. Mayer:

With L. B. Mayer and Vincente Minnelli on the occasion of her marriage to Minnelli.

Regarding the can-can number . . . please note that it will not be acceptable to show the "can-can" dancers with garters above their stockings. To be acceptable, the stockings should be full length, with no flesh showing between the top of the stocking and the crotch.

In addition to the Breen Office, the producers of *The Harvey Girls* had to contend with the Harvey organization, which was very much a going concern (the founder was still alive). A representative of the company was assigned to the film to keep an eye on historical accuracy; had he confined himself to this, no one would have found his presence abrasive. Unfortunately, he insisted on suggesting little bits of comedy business and even submitted some ideas to improve the lyrics that Johnny Mercer had written for "On the Atchison, Topeka and the Santa Fe," feeling that the line "And they'll all want meals Fred Harvey style" could be interpolated at some point.

Then there were the nagging accidents common to all movie sets. Two of Judy's co-stars received minor injuries during the making of *The Harvey Girls*: Ray Bolger was scalded by steam from a locomotive, and John Hodiak was hurt during a fight scene when a blazing beam fell on him. Several stunt men were also hurt, and one extra dropped his lighted pipe onto the voluminous Victorian skirt of another, causing it to catch fire.

On top of all of these problems, Judy's behavior must have seemed intolerable at times. The moment she stepped on set, however, and began working, she became the old adorable, quick, funny Judy everyone remembered, and suddenly all the anger was forgotten. She could turn these situations around in a flash. She might be mooning around in her trailer, keeping everyone waiting, then out of the blue something would strike her as amusing and all at once she was out on the set, joking with the grips, demanding action. The whole company would come to life, the sound stage would be full of activity, all of it seeming to revolve around her. She was the sun, and when she came out from behind the clouds, everyone was happy. One moment, people were furious at her; the next, fawning over her. And she seemed to be able to produce this transformation by sheer willpower.

Her periods of misbehavior were usually precipitated by fatigue. This is not to say that no psychic wounds were involved, but only

that her adrenalin level was usually high enough to keep them under control. Judy's energy was her great defense against all her demons, but it was bound to give out from time to time—despite, or because of, the supercharge of Benzedrine, and when that happened, she was a mess, unable to handle even the simplest everyday problems. In this condition she would become bitchy and malicious, but the moment the energy returned (and she had a remarkable ability to mine fresh resources), she was once again witty, bright, charming, almost overpowering in her sheer vitality. Being such a remarkable performer, she was able to communicate almost anything effectively—and that included her pleas for forgiveness: "I'm sorry, I didn't mean it, I love you, please love me." She could convey this without saying a word, and when she was sure it had struck home, she would change the tone a little, beginning to banter and tease, so that whoever had been angry at her would begin to think it was his fault for being so foolish as to have taken the whole thing seriously in the first place. And anyway, she had had that terrible childhood and that monster of a mother—as she had told everyone a hundred times!

Judy Garland would be playing this scene for the rest of her life—with husbands, lovers, friends, producers, directors, with fans and with hangers-on, with anyone who would fall for the bait.

The Harvey Girls is by no means a landmark musical, nor one of the highpoints of Judy Garland's career, but it's an entertaining movie and her performance gives no hint of the troubles behind the scenes. Along with "On the Atchison, Topeka and the Santa Fe," the Johnny Mercer-Harry Warren songs included one other fine number, "It's a Great Big World." The film, as usual, belongs to Judy, but Angela Lansbury has some good scenes in the role of Em, a dance hall queen with a pragmatic disposition.

Just before Judy finished work on *The Harvey Girls,* her divorce from David Rose became final. On June 15, 1945—five days after her twenty-third birthday—she married Vin-

cente Minnelli in a quiet ceremony at her mother's house. Betty Asher was maid of honor and Minnelli's good friend Ira Gershwin was best man. Minnelli confesses that his memories of the occasion are vague but, in his book, he reports Gershwin's recollections:

Ira swears that at the end of the ceremony, the minister brought out a symbolic wooden staff. He asked Betty to grasp it first, then Ira, followed by Judy and me. Then, out of nowhere came an alien hand and grasped the staff by the knob on the top. It was Louis B. establishing his territorial imperative.

The Minnellis honeymooned in New York, renting an apartment on Sutton Place, but even here they were not completely free of the studio's demands and Judy found herself making broadcasts to promote the upcoming release of *The Harvey Girls.* Minnelli recalls their honeymoon as the occasion of a significant gesture. Walking by the river one night, Judy produced a bottle of pills and threw them into the water. Minnelli was certainly too knowledgeable about these things to imagine that this was the end of the problem, but he did see it as a welcome sign of Judy's good intentions.

The honeymooners were scheduled to re-

On the set of Till the Clouds Roll By, *with Minnelli and Jerome Kern. Kern died a few days after this picture was taken.*

151

turn to Hollywood early in the fall so that Judy could begin rehearsals for her next film, *Till the Clouds Roll By*. They arrived back with a piece of information that demanded an immediate change of plans. Judy was pregnant.

They half-expected the studio to take this news badly, but nothing of the sort happened. Plans for *Till the Clouds Roll By* were modified so that Judy's scenes could be shot immediately, before her pregnancy became too obvious. The picture had been planned as a full film biography of the composer Jerome Kern, but Kern died just as the movie went into production and the script had to be modified, for legal reasons, into a rather unsatisfactory blend of fact and fantasy. Judy was cast as Broadway star Marilyn Miller and her part in the film was to consist of a few dramatic scenes and three musical numbers.

Richard Whorf was set to direct the movie but it was decided that Minnelli should handle all Judy's scenes. He managed to wrap them

up in a little over two weeks. Her numbers were "Sunny," "Look for the Silver Lining" and "Who?" "Look for the Silver Lining" was staged with Judy half-hidden by a pile of dirty dishes and it's been commonly assumed that this was a device to conceal her swelling stomach. It may have served that purpose, but in fact this was exactly how Marilyn Miller had introduced the number on stage. According to Minnelli, Judy was very amused at the notion of performing "Who?" in her condition. This number had her running up to one male dancer after another, singing "Who stole my heart away? Who?"

It would be more than a year before Judy worked again.

The marriage surprised many people in Hollywood. We've already noted that Judy and Minnelli seemed an unlikely match, though in fact they probably had a good deal in common, both hailing from the Midwest and both having become familiar with the backwaters of show business before graduating to the big time. Having touched base on Broadway, however, Minnelli was assumed by many to be too polished for a movie brat like Judy. Physically they were like a pair of matching bookends—both small, nervous, frail, breathless, birdlike, with large, brown, permanently surprised eyes. Looking at photos of this couple, one detects something close to a family resemblance and it's impossible to resist the thought that Minnelli may have reminded Judy of her father.

Throughout her pregnancy Judy stayed off drugs except for those prescribed for her. Her mental condition was good and she showed no unusual fears of childbirth, even when she was told that a caesarean section would be necessary because of her narrow pelvis. Minnelli remembers this as a happy time, with Judy amusing herself around the newly decorated house on Evansview Drive, high in the hills above Sunset. She played the newlywed to the hilt, trying her hand at cooking and housework, then leaving the mess for the help to clean up while she retired to her mirror-lined dressing room to curl up with some light reading on a fur-covered chaise.

On the set of Till the Clouds Roll By, *Judy—in the part of Marilyn Miller—is watched by Vincente Minnelli, on the camera boom, and Roger Edens, on the stairs nearest the camera.*

The caesarean was scheduled for March 12, 1946. There were no complications in the delivery, but a postoperative condition demanded additional surgery, which was performed on Judy by her father's old friend, Dr. Marcus Rabwin.

Names had been settled well before the child was born. If it had been a boy, he would have been christened Vincente. Since it was a girl, they called her Liza May—Liza for the Gershwin song and May for Minnelli's mother, who had died just a short while before her son's wedding. Kay Thompson and her husband Bill Spear were asked to serve as the child's godparents.

Everything seemed fine, but during the next few months Judy's mental state began to deteriorate again. Perhaps this can be attributed to postpartum depression, or perhaps it had something to do with her fear of resuming the crippling work schedule she had managed to escape for a while. Whatever the explanation, she became neurasthenic and jittery. For the first time in her life, Judy Garland—the girl who thrived on candy and potatoes—was unable to eat. She became physically weak and painfully thin.

Gradually, however, she began to pull out of this downswing and to show some enthusiasm for the project that was to be her first vehicle on returning to the studio. This was *The Pirate,* and it would be directed by her husband.

*T**he Pirate* does not belong to the mainstream of Judy Garland musicals. Almost all her films have artificial plots, but usually they are built on rather commonplace fantasies, and in most cases it's from precisely this that they derive their charm. We see the everyday become magical, the daydream

brought to life. *The Pirate,* on the other hand, is artificial in quite another way—as different from, say, *Babes in Arms* as a Dresden doll is from a Raggedy Ann.

Minnelli remembers that he first discussed the idea of making this picture with Judy when they were honeymooning in New York. *The Pirate* had begun life as an S. N. Behrman play, written for Alfred Lunt and Lynn Fontanne. It was, as it happened, the only Broadway show the Lunts ever did that was not a success, but most people in the business had liked it a great deal. The setting was a Caribbean island in the 1830s—a period when the West Indies were dotted with lively cosmopolitan outposts —and the story concerned a young woman, Manuela, in love with the stories she had heard

153

about a notorious pirate, Macoco, known as Mack the Black.

Since *For Me and My Gal,* the Freed unit had been looking for an opportunity to pair Judy with Gene Kelly once again, and Kelly's athletic style made him the obvious choice for this project. He had liked the show onstage and since, with Robert Alton, he would do most of the choreography, he began to work with Minnelli right away. Albert Hackett and Frances Goodrich adapted the story and dialogue to accommodate the special talents of Garland and Kelly, and Cole Porter was commissioned to write songs for the film. (It was Porter who renamed the pirate Mack the Black, in honor of a friend.)

Minnelli started out with the premise that the film would have to be totally artificial. It told a story that could never have happened, but it would have to be presented as though it had. To transform the M-G-M sound· stages into a fanciful tropical island, he drew on all his early experiences as an art director, working closely with his designers, Cedric Gibbons and Jack Martin Smith, and with Irene Sharaff, who was to be responsible for the costumes. Over the years Minnelli had built up an extensive library of books and clippings to provide himself with visual inspiration, and *The Pirate*

Preceding pages: With Vincente Minnelli on the set of The Pirate *and (below) with Minnelli and Liza.*

allowed him to give free rein to his natural eclecticism. He montaged an exotic environment that was wholly a product of the imagination. By the time it reached the screen, even the color (photographed by Harry Stradling) would seem faintly unreal.

Unfortunately, with the exception of "Be a Clown," the songs were not among Cole Porter's best but, given that limitation, the musical numbers were inventively staged and Kelly in particular has some splendid moments. Judy's Manuela is a strange little neurotic. Her touch with comedy was as sure as ever, but throughout the film she seems nervous and aflutter, her eyes darting everywhere and her hands never still for a moment (her lifelong mannerism of playing with the rings on her fingers is nowhere else so much in evidence on film as here). Kelly attributes some of her nervousness to her fear the picture would not appeal to her grass-roots public, and, despite some good reviews, it was a relative failure (though, like all her M-G-M movies, it did show a profit). Most critics praised Kelly's performance, deservedly, since it was the energy of his Fairbanks-Barrymore parody that held the story together.

The Pirate is another Garland film that has developed a cult following and, in all fairness, it does have many merits. But its particular brand of artifice lacks roots in the Hollywood tradition without managing to establish any other. The staging of the movie has all the fey eccentricity of a novel by Ronald Firbank, but the story does not advance with the lightness of a Firbank plot nor does the dialogue have a brittle enough edge to it.

One by-product of *The Pirate* was that it established a close working relationship between Kelly and Minnelli which would come to fruition later. Some hint of Judy's mental state at the time can be found in the fact that she became irrationally jealous of their professional intimacy, going so far as to interrupt one work session with a violent scene, accusing them of using the picture to advance themselves at her expense.

This display of paranoia was by no means

an isolated incident. When Hedda Hopper visited the set, she found Judy in her trailer, shaking like a leaf and on the verge of hysteria. She told Hopper that everyone had turned against her, that she had no friends, and accused her mother of having tapped her phone. Judy became so agitated that she was eventually carried from the trailer—still in costume and makeup—and driven from the studio in a limousine.

Minnelli was in a difficult position, split between responsibility to the studio and responsibility to his family. At home, he was again divided, between responsibility to his wife and responsibility to his daughter. When she was well, Judy was a very giving mother. During the bad periods, however, Liza needed extra attention from her father.

It was obvious that Judy was taking pills again, but there was very little her husband could do about it. Like most addicts, she was sneaky about her habit and there were plenty of places about the house where she could conceal emergency supplies. Inevitably, there were squabbles over this and over Judy's general behavior. Minnelli had only to make some slight criticism to send Judy into a towering rage. She would accuse him of not loving her and walk out of the house, sometimes staying away for days at a time.

Minnelli did his best to protect Liza from the emotional crises, and he also tried to defend their privacy in the hope that something could be worked out. Meanwhile, at the studio, Judy was into her pattern of absenteeism again —in one spell she stayed away from the lot for three consecutive days—and the picture ran behind schedule and over budget.

After a period of time, during which Judy had not been seeing a psychiatrist, she returned to Dr. Simmel—this time at Mayer's suggestion and the studio's expense. During the filming of *The Pirate,* Simmel died, which only added to Judy's emotional problems. Another psychiatrist was called in and he suggested that Judy should spend some time in a private sanitarium.

The place chosen was in Compton, between

On the set of The Pirate, *Dottie Ponedel repairs Judy's makeup.*

Long Beach and downtown Los Angeles. Later Judy liked to tell the story of her arrival there. Heavily sedated, and in the middle of the night, she was driven to the sanitarium where two hefty attendants helped her out and supported her, one on either side, as she crossed the grass to her accommodations. It was a terrifying experience because she found herself tripping and falling every few paces. Something seemed to be grabbing at her feet and the thought that crossed her dazed mind was that it was all over, that she had finally gone over the edge into total insanity. Under the influence of the sedative, she fell asleep. When she awoke the next morning, she looked out of her window and saw what had been grabbing at her feet. It was the croquet wickets dotted about the lawn.

The grounds and accommodations at Compton were pleasant, but Judy soon discovered that this was not the Beverly Hills Hotel: "It didn't take me long to realize that my bungalow was next to Ward Ten, the 'violent' ward. The sounds they made were strange and scary." In her *McCall's* memoirs she talked about her encounters with some of the other inmates:

157

I met some of the most charming people there, sensitive, intelligent, humorous people. As far as I could gather, not one of them was demented in the common sense. Most of them were just too highly strung and too sensitive for reality. . . .

Judy recognized that these people were, psychologically speaking, mirror images of herself. They had not, of course, gone through the alienating experience of force fed Hollywood celebrity, but they did share many of her problems. This stay in the sanitarium did, then, give her an opportunity to discover that she was not unique in her inability to deal with everyday reality. This knowledge seems temporarily to have neutralized her sense of isolation.

The inmates were not the only people Judy came into contact with. She was fascinated and disturbed by a nurse who crept into her bungalow every morning at about five o'clock. Due to her insomnia, Judy would be dropping off to sleep about then. She would open her eyes and watch in amazement as this woman made a systematic search, going through every drawer, every closet, every stitch of clothing. After this had been repeated several times, Judy finally challenged her:

"Look," I said, "I don't know what you're looking for, but it isn't here. I haven't got any pills, dope, money or whisky. I don't mind you looking for them, because that's your job, but does it have to be at five o'clock in the morning? At these rates!"

The woman paid no attention and refused to answer. The next day she was back as usual.

After this stay in the sanitarium, Judy spent some time at the Riggs Foundation in Stockbridge, Mass., but within a few weeks Judy was back at the studio. Retakes for *The Pirate* were the first order of business, then she went into rehearsal for *Easter Parade,* which was planned as a follow-up vehicle for Judy and Gene Kelly, this time with music by Irving Berlin. Minnelli was scheduled to direct, but just as he was ready to begin casting the supporting roles, he was taken off the picture and replaced by Chuck Walters.

This happened without warning. Minnelli was called into Arthur Freed's office and found Freed in an uncharacteristically somber mood. He told Minnelli that Judy's psychiatrist had suggested that it would be a mistake for them to do another picture together.

Minnelli was understandably stunned. He could follow the doctor's reasoning, but he found it difficult to accept the fact that Judy had not told him herself. When he got home that evening she behaved as if nothing had happened. Although angry, Minnelli respected her silence and she never made any attempt to explain her feelings. Probably she was genuinely relieved at not having to work with her husband. Their problems would only be magnified if they continued to spend twenty-four hours a day together—if they had to work them out in front of a crew on a busy sound stage. She may also have suspected that their artistic relationship was becoming unhealthy. As her director, Minnelli could remake her image to suit his fantasies—and, given the pliability of her tremendous gifts, it would be hard to resist the temptation. *The Pirate* certainly represented his taste rather than hers. Despite all her insecurities, she did have a clear idea of what a Judy Garland movie should be, and she may have felt that Minnelli was pushing her in the wrong direction.

Curiously enough, the new director—Chuck Walters—had once come close to marrying Judy himself. They had been friends since working together on *Presenting Lily Mars,* but *Easter Parade* was only Walters' second picture as a director and Judy did not mean to let him forget it. Walters described her attitude in an interview he gave the magazine *Films and Filming*:

Judy loved to growl, loved to *pretend,* and when she heard I was assigned to *Easter Parade* she said, "Look sweetie, I'm no June Allyson, you know. Don't get cute with me. None of that batting-the-eyelids bit, or the fluffing the hair routine for me, buddy! I'm Judy Garland and just you watch it!"

Rehearsals were under way and the film was

158

almost ready to go into production when another change had to be made. Gene Kelly broke an ankle playing touch football in his backyard. There was only one possible replacement—Fred Astaire—and he was nominally in retirement. Without work to occupy him, however, Astaire was getting restless and, as he recalls it today, did not have to think for long about taking the part. He had known Judy for years and says that they had often talked, half seriously, about doing a picture together someday:

I loved to work with a talent like Judy, of course. She was a super talent—great sense of humor.... She wasn't basically a dancer, but she could dance.... If she felt like it, she could do it ... and learn it just like that— very fast.

His decision to take the part may have been influenced by the word that Judy was in one of her upswings. She was jittery at times but, for the most part, the atmosphere on the set was good and things went rather smoothly.

Irving Berlin came out to California to visit the company and spent much of his time at Judy's voice rehearsals and recording sessions. He adored her and was openly in awe of her talent, but he could not resist suggesting, once in a while, how one of his songs should be phrased. Judy poked a finger into his stomach, one day, and pushed her face a few inches from his.

"Listen, buster," she hissed. "You write 'em. I sing 'em."

Berlin was delighted.

For the last time on the M-G-M lot Judy got through an entire movie without provoking coronaries, and the result was one of the most delightful pictures she ever made. Garland and Astaire made a charming, if unlikely, duo and Walters handled them with a light touch that was just right for the material. The plot is basically a Pygmalion variant, with Astaire picking Judy out of a seedy chorus line as a prospective dancing partner. The movie is peppered with Berlin songs, including "A Fella

with an Umbrella," which Judy sings with Peter Lawford, and "A Couple of Swells," with Astaire and Garland as bums. The latter is one of the four or five best things Judy ever did on screen and later it became a high spot of her stage act.

Preparing for "A Couple of Swells," Astaire —compulsively neat—had difficulty in deciding on his tramp's costume. Each day he came to Judy with something a little different, but he never looked worse than a particularly well-groomed Fuller Brush man at the end of a hard day. Every time he would ask her the same question: "Is this too much?" Judy, amused, made polite comments until she had perfected her own ensemble for the number. Then she got into full costume and makeup—the clown's shoes, the baggy pants, the monstrous coat, the burnt cork and the blacked-out tooth—and knocked on the door of Astaire's trailer. He opened the door and looked out in disbelief. "Is this too much?" she asked.

It was apparent to everyone that *Easter Parade* was going to be a winner. They had rediscovered the "real" Judy and began to plan for her future. She had been promised an extended vacation when the film was over, but already everyone was thinking about a follow-

With Fred Astaire in a scene from Easter Parade.

159

up to *Easter Parade*—another vehicle for Garland and Astaire. The property they decided on was *The Barkleys of Broadway,* and since Judy had worked so well with Chuck Walters, he would be in charge again. The vacation plans were curtailed and the picture went into rehearsal.

This time, things did not go as well. Rehearsals began June 14, 1948, and for two weeks Judy's behavior was exemplary. She missed a single day through illness, otherwise she was on time or just marginally late, and she was working without signs of temperament. On June 30, however, she did not show up at the studio. This caused a little nervousness, but there was a general sense of relief the next day when she was on time for wardrobe fittings. Then, as the fourth week began, she failed to show up once more. From July 7 to July 12 they waited for her; finally the production was closed down until a replacement could be found.

Judy was at home and miserable. The good spirits of the previous several months had dissolved and she was a mental and physical wreck again. She was in one of those phases when she could hardly make the decision to move from one room to another without bursting into tears or throwing a tantrum. She was back on a steady diet of amphetamines, which killed her appetite for food and brought her weight down to close to ninety pounds once more. She refused to have anything to do with anyone from the studio, seeing them all as part of some Kafkaesque conspiracy against her.

A call went out to Ginger Rogers, then semi-retired on her ranch in Oregon, who agreed to replace Judy and renew her partnership with Astaire for a salary of $12,500 a week—more than twice what Garland had been getting.

With Mickey Rooney, recording "I Wish I Were in Love Again" for Words and Music.

Soon after shooting began, the company received an unexpected visit. Just as Miss Rogers was about to go before the cameras one morning, Judy showed up on set in full costume and makeup. She acted as if this was in no way odd and began joking with the crew and cast (except for Miss Rogers, whom she chose to ignore). Nobody knew quite what to do about this—after all, Judy Garland was still a star—and Ginger Rogers withdrew to her trailer in considerable distress. Chuck Walters finally managed to persuade Judy to leave.

Later, in *McCall's,* Judy would recall this as a period in which she felt abandoned: "Hollywood is a strange place when you're in trouble. Everyone is afraid it's contagious." This comment was not quite accurate since, with all the pain she seemed to attract to herself and those around her, Judy was adored and there were dozens—probably hundreds—of people in Hollywood who wanted desperately to help her. She had close and supportive friends such as Humphrey Bogart and Lauren Bacall, and Kay Thompson and Bill Spear. She had old studio allies like Roger Edens to turn to, and old family friends like Marcus Rabwin.

Among those closest to her were Sylvia Sidney and her husband Carleton Alsop. Alsop was able to manage Judy's moods better than most people and she, in response, placed a good deal of trust in him, so that he became a go-between in the increasingly frequent disputes between Judy and her husband. The Alsops made their home available to her during her separations from Minnelli (later she rented a second home, at 10,000 Sunset Boulevard, so this kindness was no longer necessary). Alsop, more or less by default, became Judy's de facto business manager and began to act as her liaison with the studio. Mayer was anxious to see Judy return to work and was looking for a way to ease her back into the studio routine. The Freed unit was developing a film biography of Richard Rodgers and Lorenz Hart, starring Tom Drake and Mickey Rooney, and Mayer hit on the idea of having Judy do a guest spot in the picture. Alsop at this point was prepared to take M-G-M to

160

Words and Music.
Judy's guest spot with Rooney was the last time they worked together at M-G-M.

court since the studio had withheld $100,000 of Judy's salary on the grounds that she was not living up to her side of her contract. Mayer told Alsop that he would pay Judy $50,000 to make an appearance in *Words and Music,* the Rodgers and Hart movie—an appearance which would consist of one number and a few lines of dialogue.

She came through so well on the first number, "Johnny One Note" that she was asked to come back for a second outing, this time to sing a duet with Rooney. The price tag was another $50,000—the remainder of the withheld salary.

Judy and Rooney prerecorded the song, "I Wish I Were in Love Again," without mishap, then Judy had a sudden relapse. Twice she came to the set in costume, and twice she was unable to go out in front of the cameras and perform. The entire company was concerned, except for Rooney who assured everyone that Judy would come through and that she would be as good as ever. For a while it seemed he would have to swallow his words but, at the third attempt, Judy got through the number without difficulty—appearing, in fact, relaxed and healthy.

In the three weeks between the two numbers Judy had been on an eating binge and had

gained almost thirty pounds. Both songs were supposedly performed at the same party, but nobody seemed to mind about the weight discrepancy. Everyone was happy to have Judy back. Her extreme weight fluctuations over short periods of time, however, would become a serious problem in future Garland movies. Dottie Ponedel was adept at adjusting Judy's makeup to keep her facial structure stable in closeups, but the wardrobe department was sometimes reduced to despair.

Judy soon began rehearsing a new movie, *In the Good Old Summertime*—to be made by the Pasternak unit—but she was not entirely happy with her role. It was a period piece, a remake of Lubitsch's *The Shop Around the Corner,* set in Chicago at the turn of the century. Judy played a shopgirl conducting a romance by mail with an unknown young man who turns out to be her despised co-worker, played by Van Johnson. Pasternak had chosen the subject largely because it offered a good role for his friend S. Z. "Cuddles" Sakall, who was cast as the owner of the store. The romance between Sakall and Spring Byington is actually more engaging than the Garland-Johnson dalliance. Worse still, from Judy's point of view, the songs she was asked to sing offered relatively little. The whole production was something of a comedown after what she had been used to.

To complicate matters, Minnelli—who had been inactive since being taken off *Easter Parade*—had been approached by Pandro Berman with the idea of making a screen version of Flaubert's *Madame Bovary*. This soon developed into an exciting project with a cast that included Jennifer Jones, Louis Jourdan and James Mason. Minnelli, quite reasonably, hoped that Judy would share his excitement about this project since she knew how difficult his period of forced inactivity had been for him. Instead, she was dejected—complaining that she was stuck playing a dull little shopgirl while he could lose himself in a challenging project like *Madame Bovary*. Minnelli tried to rationalize this in terms of her mental fatigue and the toll the pills had taken, but he could not disguise the fact that he was badly hurt once again.

The small child seen in the closing seconds of *In the Good Old Summertime* is the young Liza Minnelli. At two and a half, she could still be insulated to some extent from her parents' problems—professional help and an adoring grandmother helped cushion her from the depressions and rages. Although Judy was now on very cool terms with Ethel, she made no attempt to keep her away from Liza at this time. It was Ethel who sent Liza to her first dance class.

Because of her periods of sickness, Judy's own relationship with Liza was somewhat intermittent, but there were enough good times to permit a strong bond to form between them. It's been said of Judy that she was capable of loving more intensely than anyone else could imagine, and that much of her unhappiness sprang from her expectation that the object of her affections would match this intensity, so that constant disappointment was inevitable. This may be an adequate description of her relationships with adults, but nothing is stronger than a child's love for its mother, and in Liza, she at last found the ideal partner, someone who could balance the equation.

In the Good Old Summertime was completed without too much disruption and, once more ignoring its promises of an extended vacation for Judy, the studio decided to rush her into a new picture. In contrast to the last movie, this one was being planned as a blockbuster. She would be back with the Freed unit and they would be developing a story that had been bought especially for her at enormous expense—the highest price ever paid for a movie property of any kind up to that time. This was to be a picture on a par with *The Wizard of Oz* and *Meet Me in St. Louis*. The property they had acquired was the Irving Berlin musical *Annie Get Your Gun*.

Judy was enthusiastic—at least she felt she was getting her due for once—but she was more in need of that much postponed vacation than of this role. Everything was conspiring to make the project a disaster for her. Before *Annie* even went into rehearsals, she lost her director. Chuck Walters had been assigned to the picture because, besides being a first-rate director of musicals, he had shown himself capable of handling Judy. Unfortunately, Walters became involved in a contract dispute with the studio and the front office decided to remove him from the project. The choice of a replacement could hardly have been less fortunate. The man picked was Busby Berkeley —a genius, perhaps, but someone Judy held a grudge against.

Despite rumors to the contrary, Judy and Berkeley seem to have gotten along reasonably well while making several films in the late thirties and early forties. He may have driven her too hard at times and there may have been some friction at the beginning of *Girl Crazy,* but even that is far from certain. The most probable explanation of the grudge is that, during the intervening period, Judy's galloping paranoia had magnified some small incident into a full-blown feud. Presumably she had not informed the front office of her hostility toward Berkeley, but it was certainly common knowledge around the lot and it's difficult to understand why the assignment was made since it was bound to lead to trouble. Judy was capable of extreme malevolence toward people she felt had slighted her.

Aside from that, her physical condition was deteriorating again. The insomnia had returned, she was putting on weight once more

In the Good Old Summertime. *A Bob Moore caricature.*

At Romanoff's with Minnelli and Joan Blondell.

and her hair had begun to fall out. All of this was, presumably, a reflection of her mental and emotional states, and it's a measure of her inner turmoil that for the first time in her life she had difficulty in learning lines.

She still had incredible reserves of energy and some days she seemed almost her old self. Certainly, she went into the project with all possible goodwill. She had loved the show when she had seen it on Broadway, and she knew that the movie was potentially as important to her as *The Wizard of Oz* or *Meet Me in St. Louis*. But this time she was unable to rise to the occasion and she must have realized that it was only a matter of time before she foundered.

Things started out quietly enough. The first call was for March 8, 1949. Judy was on time; she reported to the wardrobe department at 10 A.M., then went on to a rehearsal. The following day she was thirty-five minutes late, and on the 10th she was called for 11 A.M. but phoned in to say she would be late and did not appear till 2 P.M. Her punctuality then improved, until the 17th, when she called in sick. This did not cause any great inconvenience since her co-stars, Howard Keel and Frank Morgan, were also ill that week. On March 25 the first two songs for the movie—"Doin' What Comes Naturally" and "You Can't Get a Man with a Gun"—were prerecorded. Judy was on time for this session and her punctuality continued to be exemplary through April 1, when the recording sessions were concluded without serious problems.

Listening to these recordings today, they sound below Judy's usual standard. Only one track—"I'm an Indian Too"—is downright bad, but none is quite up to her general level of excellence. You can sense the weariness behind the voice. *Annie* contains some of Irving Berlin's wittiest songs and, at her best, Judy could have worked miracles with something like "Doin' What Comes Naturally." Instead, she turned in an adequate but relatively mediocre performance.

Filming began on schedule, April 4, without Judy, who was not needed that day. She began work on April 6, reporting fifty-five minutes late. With or without Judy, shooting plans had to be modified because Howard Keel had broken a leg and would not be available for several weeks. Everything was rescheduled so that the company could shoot around him, which would put more weight on Judy's shoulders. For a while, at least, things went reasonably well, and surviving footage shows her in good form, laughing and joking when she blew her lines. At this point she was working mostly with the second unit under the direction of Robert Alton, so there was no friction with Berkeley. For almost a month she was reasonably punctual and did not cause any major delays. When possible, she was given a late call.

Things began to deteriorate again, however, and on May 3 there was a serious blowup. Judy was back on pills and in no condition to give any kind of performance. She could not think straight and had become pathetically thin. Minnelli recalls trying to take a bottle of pills away from her and precipitating a violent rage. On the set her anger was directed at Berkeley. On May 4 the director did not put in an appearance and Judy went home before noon, claiming to be ill. On May 5 Berkeley was taken off the picture and replaced by Chuck Walters, who had settled his contract dispute. Judy spent three hours in his office, nominally discussing story problems.

In his *Films and Filming* interview, Walters recalled that meeting and the events that led up to it:

Well, I got an urgent call from Arthur [Freed] to come in and look at the *Annie* footage . . . and it wasn't going well . . . it was horrible! Judy had never been worse. She couldn't decide whether she was Mary Martin, Ethel Merman, Martha Raye or herself. . . . "She's a mess," I said. Arthur nodded sadly. "I want you to take over the picture," he said. "O.K., but the first thing to do is have a long talk with Judy," I replied. So lunch was set up for Judy in my office. And we talked and talked. "It's too late, Chuck," she cried. "I haven't got the energy or the *nerve* any more."

Judy and Liza pose at the door of Judy's trailer. Liza is in costume for her appearance in the final scene of In the Good Old Summertime.

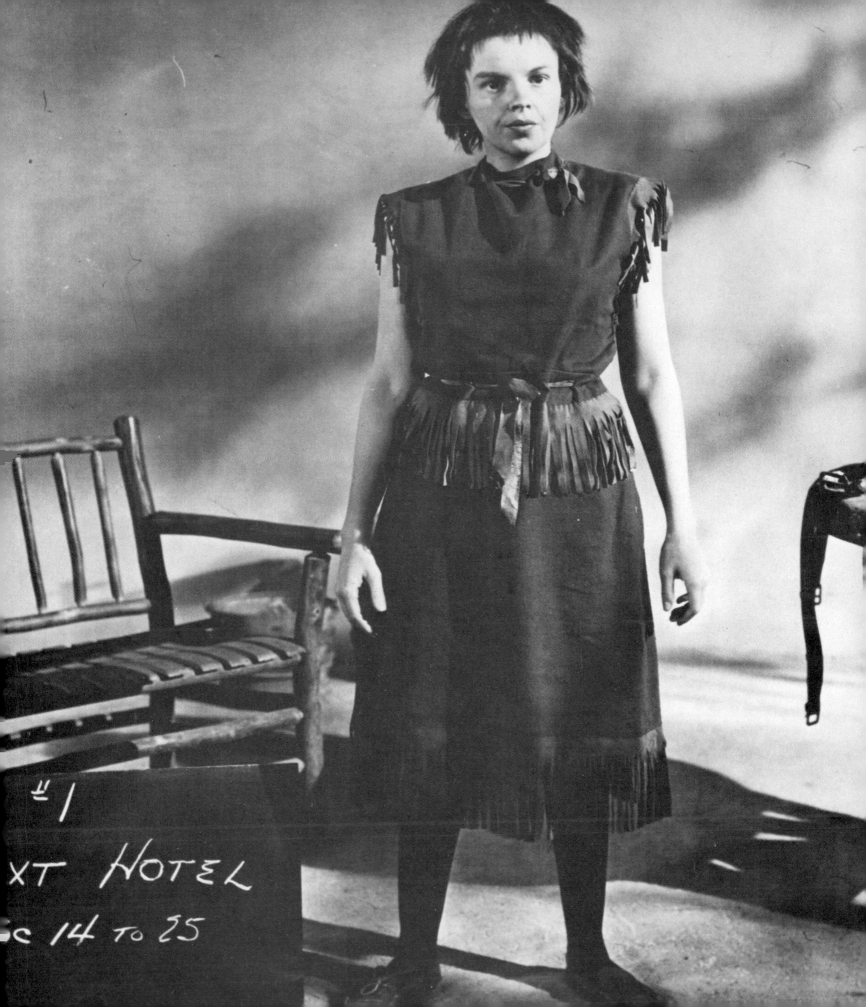

"/1

XT HOTEL

c 14 TO 25

The footage he is referring to here is apparently not the relatively happy material shot under Alton's direction, but rather the later scenes directed by Berkeley: "...nothing Buzz shot was usable. He had been very theatrical in shooting the whole thing like a stage play. Everyone would come out of the wings, then they'd say their lines, then they backed away up stage for their exits." After the meeting between Judy and her new director, it was decided to abandon shooting till the next week. Things had gone too far, however. Judy was coming apart at the seams. On May 10, 1949, she had a 9 A.M. call. She arrived on set at 11:18. It was obvious she could not continue. Later that day the studio suspended her.

Annie was eventually begun again with Betty Hutton in the title role and George Sidney directing. Meanwhile, the studio did not abandon Judy completely. Mayer met with Carleton Alsop, and it was decided that Judy should receive medical attention, with Metro footing the bill. Accompanied by Alsop, she took a train east and checked into Peter Bent Brigham Hospital in Boston.

Amphetamine and barbiturate withdrawal can be more painful than withdrawal from heroin. Unless it is undertaken under medical supervision, amphetamine withdrawal sometimes leads to seizures and brain damage. Barbiturate withdrawal can cause death. At Peter Bent Brigham, Judy was not in danger of dying, but the hospital had no way of sparing her the miseries of withdrawal. Subjected to a sudden barrage of pain and indignity, she pleaded to be released. Alsop refused to listen to her and gradually her condition began to improve. While taking a series of tests at nearby Children's Hospital, Judy began to take an interest in the youngsters in one of the wards. She asked for permission to make further visits and the time she spent with the unfortunate children there proved to be beneficial both for them and for her. It was exactly the therapy she needed.

As her health improved, she was allowed visits from her husband and daughter. Away from the pressures of Hollywood, she was able to enjoy simple pastimes—liking nothing better than to sit in the stands at Fenway Park and watch Ted Williams hit another one over the right field wall. At the end of three months Judy was feeling fitter than she had in years. Arthur Freed came out to visit and told her the studio wanted her back, and that a property had been lined up for her. A few days later she was discharged—posing cheerfully with her nurses and telling the press she was anxious to return to work.

The script that was waiting for her was *Summer Stock*, to be produced by Joe Pasternak. It was far from an innovative vehicle; in fact, it harked back to the "let's put on a show" musicals she'd made with Mickey Rooney ten years earlier. In this variation on the theme, show business comes to a near-bankrupt farm operated by Judy and Marjorie Main, and the screenplay provides Judy with an opportunity to get worked up over the purchase of a new tractor. This time it was Gene Kelly who brought the Great White Way into the barnyard. Under ordinary circumstances this script would have found its way into Kelly's wastebasket. He agreed to do the film only because

A wardrobe test picture for Annie Get Your Gun. *This costume was made for "Doin' What Comes Naturally," one of the two numbers shot before Judy left the movie.*

(Below) On location for Annie Get Your Gun, *with Frank Morgan (as Buffalo Bill) and J. Carroll Naish.*

of his friendship for Judy and to pay back the kindness she had shown him when he arrived in Hollywood. Chuck Walters accepted the chore of directing the film for similar reasons. Another good friend, Phil Silvers, would be in the cast, and two more, John Green and Saul Chaplin, would be in charge of the music.

Everyone was anxious to see Judy back on her feet, and for a while things looked promising. She was glad to be home. Her marriage was going through a relatively peaceful stage and she and Minnelli were seen out together more often than before—frequently dining at the La Rue Café. It was only a matter of time, though, before the seesaw began to tip back the other way.

To begin with, she reported for work fifteen pounds overweight and immediately began to diet, which, as usual, proved to be a prelude to disaster. Working conditions were far from ideal. Her every move was watched by a psychiatrist that the studio had flown out from Boston to keep an eye on her. Supposedly he was there to help her, but she resented his presence on the set, and often refused to have anything to do with him. There were frequent calls on Minnelli's time when he was the only person Judy would deal with. She also felt the picture was beneath her talents and that depressed her. Shooting dragged on interminably. Some days Judy called in sick or arrived late; on others she showed up on time but then locked herself in her dressing room and refused to step in front of the cameras. It was a struggle to get her to do anything, as Chuck Walters recalled in *Films and Filming*:

God, she was a problem on that picture— her nerves were shot, there was the weight thing, everything. We never knew what time she'd come in—or whether she was prepared for anything when she did. She'd come storming in and say "Look, buddy. If you expect any acting out of me today, forget it!" And I had to sort of josh her out of it, had to pretend that I didn't care if she worked or not. "Let's just have a cup of coffee and talk a bit," I'd say. There's a number in that picture, "Friendly Star," which I think is one of the best

things she ever did. . . . We were moving in for a giant close-up. Judy looked up with those great liquid eyes of hers and it was the most fantastic shot in the world. "Cut," I yelled. "Will someone please hand me a towel. I've just come!" Now that might be thought indelicate, but Judy loved that kind of foolishness. . . . You always had to keep her spirits high. Once you had her in the mood for work, you had to keep her there. Not that it was always easy. What was that number on the tractor? Oh, "Howdy Neighbor!" The days we spent on that. I can see her sitting on that damn thing mumbling, "What am I doing here? Please send for Vincente to take me home."

Things were going so badly at one point that Joe Pasternak, who is on record as believing Judy to be the greatest musical talent of her generation, went to Mayer and asked him to close the picture down, saying that Judy had become impossible to work with. Now, Mayer's own power was beginning to wane—Nicholas Schenck had already brought in Dore Schary as head of production—but for a little while longer he would still have the final word at M-G-M and Judy's fate was in his hands. He told Pasternak to be patient with her. He talked about her in fatherly terms, not forgetting to add that this "little girl" had earned millions of dollars for the studio. He made it quite plain that, as long as he was in charge, the picture would continue.

It continued. The production went on for so long that a distinctive subculture began to develop on and around the set. According to Saul Chaplin, "All those dancing kids had such a long job, because of the delays, it was almost like belonging to a college class. They were constantly having parties for people leaving for other jobs."

The finale of the film includes one of Judy's most famous numbers—"Get Happy"—in which she looks so trim and energetic that people have sometimes assumed it was shot earlier, for a different picture, and then tacked on to the *Summer Stock* footage in order to liven it up. "Get Happy" was, in fact, filmed for *Sum-*

mer Stock—but under slightly unusual circumstances, as is explained by Saul Chaplin:

It's customary to save the soloists' numbers until the end of the shooting schedule, because then you can get rid of the chorus girls and take them off salary. It was always planned that there should be a solo spot for Judy, in the finale, but the song hadn't been written, because nobody could decide what it should be. It would be the last thing to be shot—but Judy got sick and disappeared. She had gone up to Santa Barbara with a hypnotist, hoping that he could help her relax and lose weight. She did not return for several weeks. By the time she came back, the songwriters were off someplace else, but we all thought we needed a number from Judy. I went to her home and she said she'd always wanted to do "Get Happy." We talked about it, and I said, "Okay, I'll make an arrangement." Which I did. After I finished it, I played it for Chuck Walters and then I took it to Judy's house and played it for her. She was lying on the sofa—she still wasn't well—and she loved it. It was a Friday and we were going to prerecord the number the following Tuesday or Wednesday—less than a week later. And she did the song in three takes. You could play anything to her and she'd sing it right back at you. She had a memory like a vacuum cleaner.

The reason "Get Happy" looks as if it was shot for a different picture is that it shows a much thinner Judy Garland than in any other part of *Summer Stock*. During her stay in Santa Barbara she had lost fifteen pounds.

The film's original choreographer, Nick Castle, had long since departed for another project so Chuck Walters devised the "Get Happy" number himself, evolving a routine that would team Judy with a group of boy dancers against a simple background of painted clouds. The costume she wore for the number —consisting of leotards, a man's tuxedo jacket and a black fedora tilted over one eye—had first been worn for a number that was cut from *Easter Parade*. It was apparently based on an outfit Tamara Geva had worn on stage. It became one of the standard ensembles that Judy would wear over and over again.

When she came on the set for the shooting of "Get Happy" she was in a somewhat manic state and her breath reeked of paraldehyde —a chemical that is sometimes used as a sedative and also as a hypnotic. Paraldehyde gives off a strong, sweet odor which some people find pleasant but which can become quite overpowering. The dancers had good reason to notice this since Judy was in a mood to convey to them certain notions she felt could only be spoken in a whisper. She pointed out a member of the crew—a small, inoffensive man who had been at the studio for years—and began to recite accusations against him under her breath. "He's been after my body since I was thirteen years old" was the general drift of her monologue. Eventually, she called the man over and, as soon as he was within range, high-kicked him in the teeth. Then she went about her business, more brilliant than ever, committing the difficult routine to film in a couple of takes.

Judy had promised to return to Boston for further treatment when filming was completed. Now she backed out of this agreement and instead rented a house at Carmel where she hoped to find the peace and quiet she needed to rebuild her strength. She was planning to spend at least six months there, but she had

A Summer Stock *script conference. Gene Kelly in the light jacket, and Chuck Walters, with the cigarette.*

been in residence for less than three weeks when a call came from the studio. June Allyson, scheduled to make *Royal Wedding* with Fred Astaire, was pregnant and Judy was asked to replace her. After the fiasco of *Annie Get Your Gun* and the agonies of *Summer Stock,* it's difficult to understand how the studio could expect to get a decent performance out of Judy. The decision to put her into *Royal Wedding* is inexplicable.

June Allyson had reported her pregnancy on May 19, 1950. Judy came in for her first rehearsal on May 23, arriving on time. She was happy to be working with Astaire again and things went smoothly for a few days. Then, at the beginning of June, her usual pattern reasserted itself. June 1: Miss Garland half an hour late. June 2: three and a half hours late. June 5: fifteen minutes late. June 6: forty-five minutes late. June 7: half an hour late. June 8: forty-five minutes late. June 9: two and three-quarter hours late. June 12: three and a half hours late. June 15: fifty minutes late. June 16: fifteen minutes late. Even when she was on the set, there was no guarantee she would perform. Warnings and thinly veiled threats were issued: If Judy did not shape up, she would be suspended again.

At first the hints were verbal, but then a written warning was delivered to Carleton Alsop by messenger. When Alsop tried to see Mayer, he was sent downstairs to the office of M-G-M's corporate attorney, who handed Alsop Judy's suspension. To add ingenuousness to insult, the lawyer made a pompous speech designed to demonstrate that Judy had cost the studio a 20 percent premium on each of her recent films. Alsop countered that Judy had earned the studio $36,000,000, and pointed out that M-G-M's regard for her health and well-being compared unfavorably with the attention lavished on Mayer's racehorses.

Amid mutual recriminations, Judy Garland was severed from the M-G-M payroll on June 17, 1950, just a week after her twenty-eighth birthday and a little short of fifteen years after the day her father had brought her to Culver City to audition.

Summer Stock. *Performing "Get Happy."*

171

Chapter 3
Picking Up
the Pieces

Three days later, on June 20, Judy was at 8850 Evansview Drive, discussing her future with her husband and with Myrtle Tully, her personal secretary. Minnelli recalls that Judy seemed rather subdued and resigned. Without any display of emotion, she left the discussion and went to a bathroom. Suddenly there was a sound of breaking glass and a scream. Minnelli rushed to the bathroom door and found it locked from the inside. Judy yelled at him, "Let me alone! I want to die!" Finally Minnelli managed to break the door down with a chair, smashing a mirror on the inside in the process. He found Judy standing with a broken glass in one hand. There was blood on her neck. Myrtle Tully tried to comfort her while one of the staff called a doctor and Carleton Alsop, who lived nearby. It was 6:30 in the evening. By the time Alsop arrived, minutes later, Minnelli was hysterical and Alsop had to slap him to get him under control.

In the panic of the moment it was somehow decided that Judy should not be found at Evansview Drive so they decided to move her to 10,000 Sunset. (Even before the doctor arrived, it was evident that she wasn't seriously hurt.) Not wanting to tie up the house phones,

Alsop ran down the hill to the Mocambo to call an ambulance. On the way into the club he was buttonholed by a gossip columnist who asked if it was true that Judy had tried to kill herself. Alsop was shocked and amazed. The whole incident had happened only half an hour earlier. He told the columnist that as far as he knew, there was no truth to the story. By the time he got back to the house, it was already surrounded by newsmen.

With the press in attendance, an ambulance was out of the question, so Judy was smuggled away by car. In no time at all the reporters and photographers found their way to 10,000 Sunset and resumed their vigil there. Alsop continued to deny all rumors but a man sent over by the M-G-M publicity office, wanting to score points with the press, gave the story away. The doctor who had been called had placed Judy under sedation, confirming that the wound was superficial. Perhaps because of this, he did not report the injury as a suicide attempt for more than fifteen hours. Meanwhile, the story had been broken by Florabel Muir in the Los Angeles *Mirror* and the New York *Daily News*.

Finding itself accused in some quarters of

Judy's first trout, Sun Valley, Idaho, August, 1950.

having precipitated Judy's desperate gesture, M-G-M released a defensive statement to the press:

Following completion of *Summer Stock*, and after consultation with the doctors in Boston, the studio placed [Miss Garland] on vacation status. After a rest . . . Miss Garland reported that she was feeling fine, and physicians of her own choosing considered her all over her difficulties.

Some time thereafter, we learned that June Allyson, who was to appear in *Royal Wedding,* was to have a baby. With assurances from Miss Garland that she was in top physical condition, we submitted the script to her and she appeared most eager in accepting the role, promising there would be no difficulties.

Within a matter of a few days, delays already had begun, and these delays increased as time went on during rehearsals. She was then told by the producer that a warning letter was to be sent to her, but that he would ask to have it stopped if she would promise to cooperate. But the delays continued.

With the responsibility and in justice to other artists, the studio had only one recourse, which was to take Miss Garland out of the picture, assuming whatever losses were involved, recast it and go ahead.

The substitution of an artist in any picture is never made on an arbitrary basis, and certainly a person of Miss Garland's talent is not easily replaced.

The replacement is not a hasty move, prompted by pique or irritation. It is the last resort, arrived at with great regret after all other means have failed.

The statement contained no expression of corporate sympathy for the unfortunate young woman who had tried to take her own life.

The story remained on the front pages for days. Some of the tabloids hyped Judy's desperate gesture as an event on a par with the bombing of Pearl Harbor. Meanwhile, Judy rested in the besieged house, receiving very few visitors. A relatively new friend—and one she was in awe of—Katharine Hepburn, was one caller who was welcomed. She berated the newsmen, informing them they had no right to be there and defying them to take just one picture of her: "Do anything like that and I'll kill you." Inside the house she gave Judy a little pep talk, telling her she was one of the world's greatest talents and that now that she'd hit bottom, there was no place to go but up. When Miss Hepburn left, the newsmen followed her and she evaded them by vaulting over a wall into the grounds of Greta Garbo's home.

Another visitor was Ida Koverman. Some years earlier she and Judy had had a bitter disagreement over some romantic attachment that Koverman disapproved of, and their relationship had been strained ever since—especially since Koverman had tended to support Ethel in her differences with Judy. All this was forgotten now and Ida Koverman stayed for an hour. Like Miss Hepburn, she refused to talk to the press.

Ethel herself got to Judy's side as soon as she could. Up until the time of Judy's first suspension, a little more than twelve months previously, Ethel had received a regular allowance that came out of Judy's salary. When this ended, Ethel had moved to Dallas, where Virginia was now living with her second husband, John Thompson, and found a comfortable niche for herself managing the Coronet Theater. Now she flew to California to be with her daughter. The press was told she would stay until Judy had recovered, but her visit did not lead to any reconciliation.

The papers also discovered that, after a dozen years of stardom, Judy Garland was virtually broke. Contrary to some reports, Ethel was not the person responsible for this state of affairs. The available evidence indicates that she managed Judy's money quite sensibly—rather conservatively, even—as long as she was legally responsible for Judy's welfare. Once on her own, Judy was careless and did not always take good advice. On top of this, taxes and medical expenses had taken huge bites out of her capital.

One person who certainly knew all about her financial embarrassment was Louis B. Mayer. He came to the house and spent more

174

than an hour alone with his former *wunderkind,* in what we can assume was a tearful meeting on both sides. A few days later he met with Judy's attorney, Lloyd Wright, and proposed a plan that would allow Judy to receive money from the studio until she was well again. This plan had to be approved by Nicholas Schenck, however. Schenck was completely unsympathetic to Mayer's idea and vetoed it. For a while Mayer paid Judy out of his own pocket—a gesture that was not as uncharacteristic as it may seem at first glance. He had proved himself capable of treating her as a piece of merchandise, but he was also genuinely fond of her. Judy's suicide attempt had torn her free from his orbit, and now that he could no longer use her in his Monopoly game, he began to relate to her as a human being for perhaps the first time.

Mayer was one of the few people who knew that this was not Judy's first attempt on her own life. There had been another similar episode three years earlier. This time he took her desperate gesture more seriously.

In August Judy took a trip to Lake Tahoe—staying at the Cal-Neva Lodge, which was now part-owned by her friend Frank Sinatra—and to Sun Valley, Idaho. She was photographed landing her first trout. Toward the end of the month she traveled to New York with Dottie Ponedel, announcing that she wanted to attend the World Series.

On September 5, 1950, Judy was spotted in the Capitol Theater on Broadway during a screening of *Summer Stock,* which had opened to good business a few days earlier. People near her began to call out, "We're with you Judy." Hearing these shouts, other members of the audience tried to get closer for a glimpse of her and, in the enclosed space, it became a little scary. When Judy's party left the theater, she found herself at the center of a Times Square mob that gave her an impromptu ovation. She had been in crowds of well-wishers before, but this time it was different, the level of excitement was higher. People were screaming, "We're all for you, Judy" and "We're with you, honey." The crowd would

hardly let her move. It was exciting and frightening at the same time. There was no longer an aesthetic distance between these people and Judy Garland. She had not been stripped of her deity, but suddenly everyone felt closer to her. When she finally reached her car and was driven off (slowly because of the crush), the mob followed her to her hotel, screaming the words she would hear echoed for the rest of her life: "Judy! We love you Judy!"

Nothing would be the same again between Judy and her public. That little scratch on her throat was as important as "Over the Rainbow." The fans still saw Dorothy, but a changed Dorothy who had been pushed to the point of attempting suicide. By walking to the very edge of the cliff and surviving, Judy had been miraculously transformed, the fans sensed, and they wanted her to know that they understood what she had been through. They wanted her to believe that they would always be there from now on—whatever happened. It was in the wake of this 1950 suicide attempt that the Garland cult came into being. It was almost as if she had actually come back from the dead.

She didn't know it at the time, but this was another albatross for her considerable collection. For the rest of her life, she would have to bear the weight of being a living legend.

On her return from New York, in September, 1950, Judy is greeted by Liza and a Minnelli dog.

Chapter 1
Phoenix

The great popular entertainers are alchemists. They take base materials—a flimsy joke, a banal story, a trivial lyric—and transmute them into gold. Their imitators—the ones who fall below greatness—are conjurers: their gifts are put to the service of illusion. By sleight of hand they succeed, occasionally, in persuading us that they have mastered the trick; but it remains just that—a trick—and the gold they produce turns out to be pinchbeck.

Judy Garland's fans wove a mystique around her, but she had no use for mystery because real stars do not traffic in cheap illusion. Like any performer of consequence, she developed a technique, and like any original personality, she had mannerisms that could be isolated and mimicked—but there was never any trick involved. Whether playing a simple comedy scene, reaching for an emotional climax or soaring on a Harold Arlen melody, everything was out front. At her best, she had that ultimate directness that jolts the brain like a massive dose of caffeine.

When Judy made concert appearances men and women crowded around the stage, reaching out to touch her. She would respond by reaching back across the footlights, grasping hands, completing the energy cycle generated by her performance and by the accumulated memories of her earlier performances.

This lust for physical contact was not, of course, unique to the Garland cult. All celebrities, whether athletes, politicians or entertainers, are subject to it and many of them exploit it with enormous skill. Garland, however, neither exploited it nor shrank from it. She gratefully accepted it. There was a curious understanding between Judy and her admirers. They were in awe of her talent, but they were not in awe of Judy Garland as a person. It was precisely this that made her—after the 1950 suicide attempt—*more* than a star. As she sometimes remarked, sympathy was what she inspired in her audiences. Her fans understood very well that despite her extraordinary gifts as an entertainer, she was subject to pain just as much as they were; and this bond was

At the Los Angeles Philharmonic, April, 1952.

177

strengthened when they realized that the pleasure they received from her was somehow linked to her suffering. They knew that she could be wounded—she had the scars to prove it. They wanted to return some of the positive energy that, in all innocence, they had taken away from her, and they reached out to her physically and emotionally in an attempt to bridge the gap created by her brilliance as a performer.

When she performed, her whole being was involved in the act of communication. There was no Cartesian advisor reminding her body what was expected of it. (Everything was planned, but when a plan is executed perfectly, the planning is forgotten.) Each nerve ending knew exactly how to respond. Since she could not rely on physical beauty, she learned how to use every other weapon in the entertainer's armory. Above all, she relied on the devastating effectiveness of her voice.

An interesting analysis of Judy's voice is to be found in Henry Pleasants' book *The Great American Popular Singers*:

She had the most utterly *natural* vocal production of any singer I had ever heard. Probably because she sang so much as a child, and learned to appreciate the appeal of her child's voice, she made no effort as she grew older to produce her voice in any other way. It was an open-throated, almost birdlike vocal production, clear, pure, resonant, innocent. One keeps coming back to that word *innocent,* again and again. It was not just an innocent sound, it was a sound innocent of anything that smacked of artful management.

This almost certainly explains a conspicuously limited vocal range. . . . I can think of no other singer whose top was so low. One reads of Judy's occasional troubles in reaching for high notes. Those notes were not so very high, no more than Cs and Ds, and not a soprano's high Cs and Ds, but the Cs and Ds an octave lower. She never extended that range by recourse to head voice or falsetto as other popular singers have done. She just sang naturally and purely as far as she could go without vocal expertise, and that was that.

She hadn't much at the lower end of the range, either.

Mr. Pleasants' analysis continues by touching on the well-known analogy between singing and playing the violin:

In this analogy, the passage of breath over the vocal cords is equated with the drawing of a bow across the strings of a violin—or any other instrument of the viol family. All schooled singers are aware of it, and all schooled fiddle players, too. But I can think of few other singers in whose work I have been so continuously aware of the singer's breath being used as a bow.

The quality, or character, of the voice itself had something, possibly everything, to do with this. It was a viola-like voice that responded almost electrically to every variation in the weight of breath imposed upon it. This may have been due as much to the absence of any muscular restriction or pressure as to the intrinsic timbre of the voice, fine as that timbre was. Judy sang freely, which is why she could sing as many as twenty-five songs a night without developing any symptoms of vocal fatigue.

The voice responded more amiably to light than to heavy bowing, and most amiably to the lightest.

This detailed discussion of Judy Garland's voice and vocal style also includes the following comments:

Another natural phenomenon that she exploited skillfully was vibrato. It could become intrusive when she was not in good shape. In the precarious circumstances of her last public appearances it was more tremulous than vibrant. When she was at her best, however, it contributed importantly to the heart-throb quality of her singing. It was, if I hear it correctly, a controlled vibrato, the control possibly intuitive rather than witting. . . .

Judy's enunciation was exemplary. She knew it and cultivated it, which may be why in ballads she tended to favor very slow tempi, giving herself and her listeners time to savor not only the words but also the delicate shading she could achieve with the bow of her breath. . . . Like Sinatra, she was a master—or mistress—of *rubato*. She relished and managed well the light blues-derived trail-offs to unidentifiable pitches at phrase endings, where the singing voice merges with the speaking voice to sustain the narrative character of the song.

This business of the singing voice merging with the speaking voice is perhaps the key to Judy's power. She could slip from an aside to a song without any apparent change in tone. From speaking to singing, there was a continuity of personality that is rare in any kind of performance. Belting out a climax, or just breathing a casual remark, she was always Judy Garland.

In the months following her suicide attempt the question was who was going to give her a chance to be Judy Garland? M-G-M could have prevented her from working—her contract had two years to run—but Mayer released her from this obligation, so she was a free agent. There were many rumors, but the only work that materialized was on Bing Crosby's Chesterfield-sponsored CBS radio show, and Crosby's kindness to her at this period should be mentioned. On September 20, 1950, she was in the Hollywood studios of KNX radio, recording the first Chesterfield show of the season with Crosby, Bob Hope, Ken Carpenter, John Scott Trotter's orchestra and the Rhythmaires. Plugging *Summer Stock,* she sang "Get Happy," did a couple of numbers with Crosby and Hope and participated in the comedy sketches. When the show was aired on October 11 the reactions were good. Judy sounded fine and for the rest of the season she was a semiregular on Crosby's programs. Later, when Crosby's first wife, Dixie, became fatally ill, Judy took over as guest hostess.

There was talk in the trades of her making a picture at Paramount with Crosby and Hope. It was also rumored that Richard Rodgers and Oscar Hammerstein wanted her to take over from Mary Martin in the Broadway production of *South Pacific,* but that the backers thought Judy would be too unreliable. Other studios and shows were mentioned, but none of these possibilities came to anything.

As for Judy's marriage to Minnelli, it was finished. Having developed a hatred of 10,000 Sunset, she moved back into the Evansview Drive house for a few weeks, but by Christmas the Minnellis had definitely separated. Later that winter there were rumors of a reconciliation and hints that they had taken an apartment in the Sunset Towers building, but the gossip proved to be groundless. Late in 1950, on a trip to New York, Judy had met Michael Sidney Luft.

Sid Luft had the build and looks of a Warner Brothers heavy—perfect down to the scar on his face—and the reputation of being the kind of man who took life by the throat, as a coyote takes a jackrabbit. Before the war he had been Eleanor Powell's personal secretary and business manager, and he had gone into the custom car business with Jackie Coogan. Later he flew for the Royal Canadian Air Force, which led to a brief career as a test pilot for Douglas Aircraft. Then, in the late forties, when married to actress Lynn Bari, he became a producer of B movies. These were mostly standard action programmers that failed to win him much of a reputation, but they were successful enough commercially to allow him to indulge his passion for racehorses. Normally a somewhat plainspoken man, he became a poet when he discoursed on the subject of thoroughbreds.

By the time he met Judy, Luft and Lynn Bari were already headed for divorce. To Judy, used to the company of rather gentle men, Luft must have seemed like a creature from Mars—but she was intrigued. He was the kind of man Ethel and the studio had tried to protect her from and she found his uncomplicated manner and frank masculinity distinctly refreshing. His extrovert energy somehow meshed with her own nervous vitality, which at this point had an edge of desperation to it. For his own part, Luft seems to have had an immediate intuition that his destiny was tied to Judy's.

Her divorce suit against Minnelli came before Superior Judge William R. McKay in March of 1951. Dressed in black and white, Judy gave her testimony with the air of someone who was accustomed to delivering lines in a professional manner:

When we were first married, we were very happy. We had many interests in common, and many mutual friends. But sometime later, without any explanation, my husband withdrew himself and shut himself out of my life.

I had to appear in public without him. It was very embarrassing. Finally I didn't go anywhere myself because it was too difficult to explain his absence.

I was terribly lonely, I frequently became hysterical. I had to go under a doctor's care. I just couldn't understand [my husband's] attitude. He lacked interest in me, my career, my friends, everything.

Judy was granted custody of her daughter on the understanding that Liza would spend half the year with her father, and that this would be managed in such a way as to avoid undue regimentation in her life. Division of the estate was relatively uncomplicated since they were virtually broke. In return for a consideration of $25,000, Minnelli gave up all claims on the Evansview Drive house and on a beach house at Malibu. He agreed to pay $500 a week child support while Liza was with Judy, and to be responsible for his daughter's medical bills. Judy and her ex-husband remained friends.

Luft's divorce from Lynn Bari the following year was anything but friendly. Miss Bari, accustomed to playing "the other woman" on the screen, found herself cast in real life as the woman who has been wronged. Through her attorney, she told the court that Luft had a standard routine: "I'd ask him where he was going and he'd say, 'Just out to get the papers.' And then he wouldn't come back till next morning."

By this time Luft was serving as Judy's manager and she was called as a witness to testify on his financial affairs apropos of child support for Luft's son John. The first time Judy was subpoenaed, she failed to appear in court. The second time, she was several hours late and a warrant for her arrest had been issued by the time she put in an appearance, armed with the argument that court appearances caused her "psychic trauma."

This brush with the law followed closely on another. A little after 2 A.M. on September 30, 1951—a rainy night—Sid Luft was involved in an automobile accident at the intersection of La Cienega and Beverly Boulevard. According to newspaper reports published at the time, when the police arrived on the scene, they found Judy in the vicinity—disgruntled and apparently drunk—but Luft insisted she had not been in the car at the time of the accident, explaining that she had been waiting for him in a nearby bar. A student who had been in the car Luft collided with insisted that Judy *had* been in Luft's vehicle but that she had wandered off after the crash, returning a little while later. This same witness claimed Judy had taken a swing at him, knocking off his glasses and breaking them. Another witness, a tuxedo-clad dentist, accused Luft of punching him on the nose when he offered his assistance. Luft, it should be noted, had a reputation for getting into fights which dated back to 1945, when he had been involved in a well-publicized brawl with Dead End Kid Bobby Jordan.

Luft was charged with drunken driving and became very agitated because he could not find his gun. The weapon, a .38 revolver, was later recovered from his car and its serial number traced to the director of security at the Douglas Aircraft plant in Santa Monica, who had reported the gun missing. In addition to the original charge, Luft was also booked for driving without an operator's license and carrying a concealed weapon.

One occupant of the other car demanded $10,000 for injuries he claimed had been sustained in the accident. The dentist asked $15,000 damages for the beating he accused Luft of administering, charging that his nose had been broken and his face cut. When the case

180

came to trial, Luft pleaded guilty to drunk driving and paid a $150 fine in lieu of spending thirty days in jail. The other charges were dismissed.

Sid Luft's social demeanor did nothing to endear him to some of Judy's old friends, but her own image of Luft was influenced by the fact that he seemed to have the ability to make things happen in her life. He seems to have sensed that the only way to restore Judy to health—or at least to get her fit enough for work—was to let her indulge herself for a while. Further dieting and repression would only lead to renewed crises. He encouraged her to relax—to stop punishing herself—and she began to put on weight and feel better.

What Judy needed more than anything else was to get back to work. Sensibly she realized that it would probably be a mistake to plunge back into the killing grind of movie making. It was time for her to set off in a radically new direction. She had an established image and a repertoire of songs that were closely associated with her, the ideal raw materials for a personal-appearance career. She was still very much a star (*Summer Stock* was playing to enthusiastic audiences), so the momentum was there. All she had to contend with were her shattered nerves and any prejudice that might have carried over from the publicity surrounding her suicide attempt. Not that this publicity had engendered hostility, but it had caused her to seem pathetic and made it likely that any live appearances she made would be treated as a comeback—a comeback from her confrontation with oblivion. Everything would have to be planned very carefully. This "comeback" would have to begin in just the right place. Judy decided to present her first stage show at the London Palladium.

She could not have made a better choice. The British had been relatively isolated from Judy's recent troubles, and they adored her. *The Wizard of Oz*—and especially "Over the Rainbow"—had a special significance in Britain. The movie had been released there just as the British Isles became cut off from the rest of Europe by the Nazi advances of 1940. "Over

the Rainbow" was accorded the reverence that is normally reserved for such establishment ditties as "Rule Britannia" and "Land of Hope and Glory." The song was heard everywhere—in pubs, in theaters and in air raid shelters. Because of it Judy Garland had always been more, far more, than just another Hollywood star to the British.

In the summer of 1950 the Hollywood trade papers reported that the Palladium had offered Judy $15,000 a week to appear in London, and it seems the offer had first been made as much as two years earlier. Now it was raised to $20,000 a week and Judy agreed to a four week engagement. Over the years she had made occasional live appearances, mainly promoting her films, and during the war she had

Judy at the London Palladium.

gone on several USO tours. In 1943 she had been the star of a huge open-air concert at Robin Hood Dell in Philadelphia. Lately, however, she had seldom played to anything larger than a radio studio audience, and the thought of working the Palladium brought on a terrific attack of nerves and she almost backed out at the last moment. Legend has it that Fanny Brice heard of this funk and marched into Judy's home to give her a tremendous tongue lashing. Still anxious, Judy slipped and fell on opening night—but she turned it into a joke and the audience was enchanted. The show was an enormous success.

She played to full houses for the entire run, then toured other British cities and gave a single concert in Monaco. She was enthusiastically received everywhere. Luft joined Judy in London and helped organize the British tour, becoming her de facto manager. Buoyed by the responses of European audiences, he set about continuing the plan on the other side of the Atlantic. His target was the Palace Theater in New York—the same Palace Theater Judy had aspired to reach on screen in films like *For Me and My Gal*. Since the thirties the Palace had been exclusively a movie theater and there were many people who doubted that anyone could successfully revive vaudeville on Broadway in 1951. The idea seemed so anachronistic that when Judy Garland opened at the Palace on October 16, the Time-Life organization did not even bother to assign a photographer.

This proved to be a miscalulation. Before the show Times Square was jammed like New Year's Eve, and inside the theater the packed crowd—studded with celebrities—waited patiently through a mixed bag of opening acts till the band of dancers billed as "Judy's Boyfriends" appeared to introduce her. Then the cheering began, and when Judy stepped into the footlights the crowd stood and gave her an eight-minute ovation. The performance she gave justified the reception. Her opening night at the Palace was one of the most smashing successes Broadway had seen in years. Critics stretched back into vaudeville history to find something it could be compared to. The only name they came up with was Jolson.

At the Palladium Judy had presented a fairly straightforward program of songs from her movies, closing with "Over the Rainbow." She would conclude with the same song at the Palace, but this time the program was more carefully planned, with special material written by Roger Edens, and the whole show was staged by another old friend, Chuck Walters. Hugh Martin, who had written some of Judy's biggest hits, was at the piano and her wardrobe was designed by Irene Sharaff and Pierre Balmain.

Edens had the idea of having Judy sing "Over the Rainbow" in her tramp costume and makeup and, to allow for the necessary transition, "A Couple of Swells"—which Judy loved to do—was slotted into the program immediately before it, setting up the ritual climax that worked again and again for thousands upon thousands of people. On opening night Judy performed "A Couple of Swells" with Chuck Walters.

Judy was held over for nineteen weeks, during which time $750,000 was grossed. Tickets advertised at a top of $4.80 were sold out weeks in advance and were being offered by scalpers for $30.00 a pair.

Not that the Palace run was without its mishaps. During the fourth week, an hour or so before the Saturday matinee, Judy complained of feeling unwell. The house doctor could not be contacted, so an outside physician was called in. He saw that Judy was running a temperature, ordered her not to perform and shot her full of sedatives. She went to sleep in her dressing room.

The audience was already seated. Luft apparently was not at the theater and, in his absence, someone—it's not clear who—woke Judy and sent her out onstage—presumably expecting her to pull herself together when confronted with an audience—but the sedative had made her too groggy to handle the challenge. She was unsteady on her feet and slurring her words. From the orchestra seats, she appeared to be drunk. She kept forgetting

After her fall on opening night at the Palladium, Judy is helped to her feet by her accompanist, Buddy Pepper.

182

lyrics and, completely losing track during the course of "Rock-a-Bye Your Baby with a Dixie Melody," began mumbling something about "that stupid man Al Jolson." People started to boo. Judy left the stage and Vivian Blaine— then Miss Adelaide in *Guys and Dolls*—came out of the audience to take over. She performed for twenty minutes and comedian Jan Murray finished the show.

Preceding pages: Taking bows at the Palladium.

(Right) At the Palace, 1951. A break during rehearsals.

This episode precipitated several canceled performances—attributed to influenza—but Judy settled down again and completed the run without further problems, though it became common for the show to begin forty or fifty minutes late.

Closing night, February 24, was almost as spectacular as the opening. Since it was a Sunday, the audience was full of Broadway personalities taking advantage of their night off. Many people there had seen the show two and three times before. After "Over the Rainbow" they wouldn't let Judy go. She made speeches. She performed three encores. Finally, prompted by Sid Luft, the audience began to sing "Auld Lang Syne." Halfway through this bit of communal schmaltz, Metropolitan Opera tenor Lauritz Melchior stood up to lead the singing. The entire house rose for the final bars.

In a popular entertainment context a performer may work with banal material as long as the experience of the performance is not banal. Judy's secret was that she gave her fans something to hold onto, something they could take with them when they left the theater. She made herself the content of the show, and if some of the numbers she performed were in themselves negligible, she gave them meaning by making them metaphors for episodes in her life—which had been public enough for people to recognize the allusions.

The critics persisted in talking about a revival of vaudeville, but audiences were in fact experiencing something else—a novel kind of Broadway musical, the words and music by various writers and composers, the book by Judy Garland, with the formidable assistance of the entire Hollywood press corps. To the audience, the book was Judy Garland's life story.

Later in her career Judy would be extremely nervous before stepping on a stage, but she was relatively relaxed during this engagement at the Palace, seeming eager to work. Between shows, she liked to take it easy with the gypsies —her male dancers—gossiping and playing card games or memory games, which she particularly enjoyed because of her unusually retentive memory. One game she liked to play involved passing around a sheet of paper bearing numerals from 1 to 100, on which everyone was invited to write common nouns alongside the numbers. When the sheet was filled, it was handed back to her and she would study it for a few seconds, then hand it to someone and ask how they would like to test her. Should she recite the words from 1 to 100? Or would they prefer to hear the list backwards? Or would it be amusing to take odd numbers only? Or would someone like to pick a number at random, and have her give the word that goes with it? She took her ability to do things like this very lightly.

At Halloween she insisted that the gypsies accompany her on a trick-or-treat expedition. Dressed in her tramp costume, she led them through Park Avenue apartment buildings, ringing doorbells and delighting in the shock of recognition she provoked.

By the way of serious relaxation, she took to heavy housework and it was not uncommon to walk into her apartment on East Seventy-fourth Street and discover her scrubbing the kitchen floor. Missing Liza, who was in California with her father, she loved to baby-sit. Jack Regas, one of her dancers, had a two-year-old and Judy would beg his wife to allow her to sit for them.

In some ways, then, this was a good period for Judy, but it did correspond with the esca-

lation of some of her problems. By now, for example, she was supplementing her intake of pills with morphine. The morphine habit may, in fact, have begun before she left M-G-M. Years later, Harry J. Anslinger, former U.S. Commissioner of Narcotics, told a reporter on the Chicago *Sun-Times* how a Los Angeles police officer who knew of Judy's drug problems had come to him and asked for his help. Anslinger discovered that Judy was getting the drug from a doctor who was himself an addict. When Judy refused, or was unable to, break her dependence on this doctor, Anslinger put pressure on the man to leave her alone. Evidently she found other sources of supply.

Anslinger also reported that he had once approached a top M-G-M executive (apparently L. B. Mayer himself) with the suggestion that Judy be given a year's vacation to allow her to overcome her drug problem. This idea was rejected on the grounds that the studio had $14,000,000 tied up in Judy and that she was the studio's biggest asset.

Later Judy told Anslinger that she took amphetamines when she got up in the morning, minor stimulants during the day, a shot of morphine before night time engagements and a sleeping pill before going to bed.

In April of 1952, after a vacation in Palm Beach, Judy brought her show to the Philharmonic in Los Angeles—this time opening to an audience of her Hollywood peers. It was another triumph, though one reviewer found the California audience less warm than the crowd that had cheered her at the Palace, suggesting that movie dignitaries turned their applause on and off like a faucet. After the concert she entered Romanoff's on Luft's arm and was given a standing ovation by a crowd that included Bogart and Bacall, Burns and Allen, Claire Trevor, the William Goetzs, Eleanor Parker, Jean Simmons, and Joan and Harry Cohn. Wearing an ermine coat over red velvet, Judy swept across the floor to Louis B. Mayer, planted a huge kiss on his forehead, then hugged three other M-G-M alumnae—Joan Crawford, Esther Williams and June Allyson

—who were seated nearby.

The general mood of gaiety and good will might have been muted a little if any of these celebrities had been present earlier in the evening when Judy's mother had attempted to visit her. Virginia, who was not present either, received a report on the incident from Ethel:

Mama's allowance was cut off when Judy was first suspended by M-G-M. She had saved enough to get along okay, for a while, but then she needed a job. She was real good friends with Ida Koverman and Ida found her a job at the Douglas Aircraft factory. I think she made $90 a week. We didn't have much, but we sent what we could and—with what she made—she could manage. But she was going to lose her life insurance because she couldn't keep up the payments. And that was all she had.

So she got in touch with Sid and told him she wanted to talk to Judy, and Sid said, "Come on down to the Philharmonic." She did, and she went backstage, but Judy wouldn't see her. Sid asked Mother what the problem was and she told him about the life insurance. He said, "We'll take care of that. Just sign it over to Judy." She said, "I am not going to sign it over to Judy! It's in the names of all three girls." Sid said, "Okay, leave it that way and we'll take care of the payments."

There was something else Mama had to pay for—her car, I think—and she said, "I hate to

With Chuck Walters, walking through "A Couple of Swells" on the Palace stage.

189

ask this, but do you think Judy could let me have a couple of hundred dollars, as a loan?" Sid said, "I'll tell you what—we'll send you $25 a week to help you out." My mother got very insulted—after all the years she'd worked with Judy—and she left in a huff.

The mitigating factor here is that if Luft believed half the stories Judy had told him about her mother, he probably thought that $25 a week was a generous offer.

After the Philharmonic appearance Judy took her show to San Francisco. During her run there, two days before her thirtieth birthday, she and Luft slipped off to the ranch of his friend—oil millionaire Robert Law—inland from Salinas, where they were married in an informal ceremony.

In July, 1952, Judy Garland was the second woman ever to be roasted by the Friars Club. (Sophie Tucker preceded her.) In November Judy gave birth to a second daughter, Lorna, delivered, like Liza, by caesarean section.

This time, no psychological problems followed the birth and Judy was soon ready for work again. The question was, what next? The time seemed ripe for her return to the picture business—it was more than two years since she had last worked on a sound stage—and Luft began to explore the available opportunities. There were producers around who owned properties they thought might gain luster from Judy's participation, but these producers wanted her on their terms, whereas Luft had in mind an arrangement that would give him and his wife a large measure of control over the product, and give Judy a degree of latitude as far as schedule and punctuality were concerned. The live performances had confirmed Judy's undiminished box-office appeal, but every studio executive in Hollywood was acutely aware of her reputation for demolishing budgets and shooting schedules.

According to Hollywood legend, the stone wall was cracked because of a debutante party. Jack Warner's daughter Barbara was to come out in January of 1953, and reputedly told her

father that she desperately wanted Judy Garland to sing at her party. Her father warned her he thought it would be impossible to arrange, but promised to try. When he contacted Sid Luft, Luft suggested terms that included a movie deal. Eventually an agreement was hammered out and a title was selected. The property they decided on was a remake of the 1937 Janet Gaynor-Fredric March classic, *A Star Is Born*. It was not a casually made choice. The role of Esther Blodgett–Vicki Lester might well have been created with Judy in mind, and she had fallen in love with the part more than ten years earlier when she played it, alongside Walter Pidgeon and Adolphe Menjou, on CBS's *Lux Radio Theatre*.

Judy's mother was still working at Douglas Aircraft in Santa Monica. The job Ida Koverman had found for her in the personnel department there paid even less than Virginia remembers—exactly $61 a week. According to some sources, Judy did attempt to pay Ethel an allowance following the incident at the Philharmonic, but Ethel was too proud to accept it. She did, however, own a comfortable house on Darlington Avenue, near the Brentwood Country Club, said to have been worth about $40,000 at the time.

When Ethel's circumstances came to the attention of the press, considerable interest was aroused and the hostility between mother and daughter came out into the open. In June of 1952, for example, Ethel was quoted by Sheilah Graham in her *Daily Variety* column: "Judy Garland's mother tells me she feels like a cross between Marjorie Main and Stella Dallas. And added—'Judy and I never had a quarrel, she just brushed me off.' " Elsewhere, Ethel complained, "I always seem to be in the way." Judy frequently threatened to tell her side of the story, but didn't till some years later—by which time she was more concerned with mythologizing her career than with the truth.

Ethel spent Christmas of 1952 in Texas with Virginia and her husband, then returned to Los Angeles. On January 4, 1953—an over-

cast, drizzly day—she was found dead in the Douglas parking lot at Twenty-seventh Street and Ocean Park Boulevard. She had fallen between two cars, slumped in a half-kneeling position. Her face and mouth were bruised and her dentures had fallen out. The cause of death was a heart attack. Judy was in New York to sing at Barbara Warner's party.

Ethel's death was treated as a major news story and there was plenty of comment from the columnists. Some attacked Judy for neglecting her mother, but others defended her on the grounds that Ethel had tried to run her life—suggesting that it was Ethel who had ruined Judy's finances. Within a year or two of Ethel's death—and despite the mass of evidence to the contrary—the latter viewpoint had won out entirely.

Though Judy never expressed any sense of guilt regarding her mother's death, it must have stayed with her, like a dripping faucet sent to tease her insomnia.

Meanwhile, *A Star Is Born* was taking shape amid a cloudburst of rumors, keeping Louella Parsons and her competitors gainfully employed:

Henry Fonda will return to the screen in *A Star Is Born*, opposite Judy Garland, if deal now well along in negotiations is finalized.

Marlon Brando will be Judy's husband in the picture. . . .

Yesterday I told you that Cary Grant was being sought for both *Sabrina Fair* and Judy Garland's pic—*A Star Is Born*. Now I can tell you that Judy gets Cary.

One of these rumors was not without foundation. Grant came very close to playing Norman Maine—he actually began rehearsals for the movie before backing off.

There was also considerable doubt for a while as to who would direct the film. At first, it was stated that Charles Vidor (related by marriage to the Warners) would be at the helm, but eventually a more considerable artist—George Cukor—was given the assignment.

At an early rehearsal for A Star Is Born, *1953.*

Aside from these preproduction personnel changes (and others of secondary importance), there was at least one major technical change after shooting had begun. Following rumors that the picture would be shot in 3D, it was started in standard aspect ratio three-strip Technicolor, but almost immediately the decision was made to switch to CinemaScope, making *A Star Is Born* one of the first feature films in the new format. Commercially, this may have been a sound decision, but Cukor and most of the people working with him regarded the change as a pain in the neck. It entailed adapting to an unfamiliar aspect ratio—one that made all the old ideas about composition outmoded—and it also meant that they would have to deal with a new and relatively untried color system. Working closely with his art director, Gene Allen, and his color consultant, George Hoyningen-Huene, Cukor was obliged to rethink his entire approach. (Much of the energy of these three men was spent circumventing the cautious advice of the people who had been assigned to the project as CinemaScope experts.)

When shooting got underway in earnest, Judy was nervous. Despite the success of her concert appearances, she evidently thought of this as the real test, the real comeback, and she was feeling the pressure, but—for a while at least—she managed to keep her self-doubt under wraps. The only outward sign of anxiety during those first weeks was her tendency to gain or lose weight almost from day to day (these fluctuations are quite evident in the finished product).

It had been estimated that *A Star Is Born* would cost about $3,000,000, and the agreement between Transcona—the Lufts' production company—and Warner Brothers apparently called for a straight fifty-fifty split in financing. Warner Brothers does not seem to have placed any ceiling on the arrangement, merely agreeing to match whatever Luft raised —assuming, it can reasonably be guessed, that this matching requirement would keep spending within limits. But Transcona had the backing of a wealthy Garland aficionado who was

prepared to bankroll the project to an extent no one at Warners had bargained for. As the weeks went by, the cost began to soar. Vincente Minnelli had just completed *The Band Wagon* back in Culver City, and it was reputed to have cost M-G-M $6,000,000. Judy seemed anxious to make sure that *A Star Is Born* would top that record. She and Luft were spending money as if that in itself would ensure the quality of the film. Inevitably they came into serious conflict with the Warners. Harry Warner was disparaging about Luft's absence from the set, remarking, "He's the only producer I know of who has his office at Santa Anita." This reference to the racetrack seems to have been misplaced. What should have worried Warner was the fact that Luft spent so much of his time away from the lot raising money. No final accounting was ever made public, but it was generally admitted that the eventual cost of the film was over $10,000,000 and there are those who think a true figure would be closer to $20,000,000.

Judy's disinclination to abide by a regular work schedule contributed to the extravagant cost, but this had been anticipated to some extent and written into the budget. Some of her other habits were less predictable and chillingly irrational. Sometimes they seemed to verge on madness.

Judy's wardrobe (most of it designed by Mary Ann Nyberg, the balance being by Jean Louis and Irene Sharaff) cost a small fortune. Some costumes consumed thousands of dollars in fabrics and labor. Judy knew when each one was finished because she would be photographed in it as a wardrobe record. If she liked the dress, she would go to Jack Warner and tell him that she simply had to borrow it for such-and-such a party or premiere, arguing that it would be valuable promotion for the picture if she was seen wearing these things. One dress had been made from dozens of yards of rare French lace, specially dyed by an old—and highly dangerous—technique that uses heated gasoline as its base. It required several hours of work in a room filled with potentially explosive fumes, but everyone

194

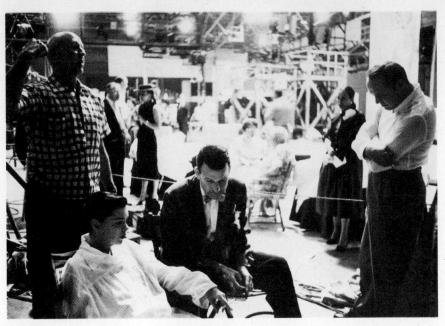

Preparing for the "Born in a Trunk" sequence, with George Hoyningen-Huene, in checkered shirt, Roger Edens, seated, and Sid Luft.

agreed the results were worth it. Judy borrowed the dress before it had been used in the film, and returned it in shreds and matted with a variety of foreign substances, the origins of which could only be guessed at. The condition of the dress was such that no one in the wardrobe department would touch it and it was destroyed immediately. It had to be replaced at the same expense and the same risk. And this was not an isolated incident.

For the Academy Awards sequence, which is one of the high points of the movie, Judy was originally supposed to wear a predominantly white dress—intended to emphasize the innocence of her character. When this garment was completed, she loved it so much that she decided she must keep it for her personal use. Warning Mary Ann Nyberg that she would hate her for what she was about to do, Judy proceeded to throw a tantrum for the benefit of Jack Warner and others: "Look at this thing! How can you expect me to wear this! It makes me look like the great white whale!" So the white dress was put away for Judy's future pleasure, and a new one—black with purple overlay—was made to replace it.

Mary Ann Nyberg's experience of this film seems typical enough. Never having worked with Judy before, she went into the project with some trepidation and a good deal of excitement. At first she thought Judy one of

the most delightful and charming people she had ever met. The star put their relationship on a chummy girl-to-girl basis, and this happy state of affairs continued for several months. As Judy became exhausted, however—and she drove herself mercilessly—her mood shifted and the tantrums and bitchiness began. At first there were occasional outbursts, then they became regular occurrences. The atmosphere changed.

Miss Nyberg managed to stay on reasonable terms with Judy till Easter. For some time everyone had been working seven days a week. Easter was the first break they had taken in months. That morning, however, Judy called Mary Ann Nyberg to ask her to fetch some fabrics from the studio so that Judy could give them to her own dressmaker. Not prepared to be treated as a servant, Miss Nyberg stormed out in a rage—which led to her being dropped from the picture.

As the tension grew, Judy added a voracious sexual appetite to her usual array of hungers for food and drugs and reassurance. A steady stream of men found their way into her dressing room. Nothing could provide her with relief, however. Under pressure her needs became inhuman.

Everything was redeemed by her performance, though. George Cukor, interviewed by Gavin Lambert for his book *On Cukor,* commented on her abilities as a dramatic actress:

Until *A Star Is Born,* Judy Garland had only played musical comedy. A lot of people in musical comedy are like mimics or impersonators, which is not real acting. They promise more than they deliver. You think, "If only they could play out a scene, how good they'd be," and very often you're wrong. But Judy Garland was a very original and resourceful actress.

Cukor goes on to describe her ability to deliver under pressure:

Towards the end of shooting, we had to do a scene when she's in a state of total depression after her husband's suicide. While we lined it up, she just sat there, very preoccupied. We'd talked about the scene only a little, but we both had a general idea what it should be. The basic note was her melancholia, her state of total depression. Just before the take, I said to her very quietly, "You know what this is about. You really know about this." She gave me a look, and I knew she was thinking, "He wants me to dig into myself because I know all about this in my own life." That was all. We did a take. If you remember the scene, she has trouble articulating anything, she seems exhausted and dead. A friend . . . comes to see her to try and persuade her to go to a benefit performance that night . . . gets deliberately rough with her—and she loses her head. She gets up and screams like somebody out of control, maniacal and terrifying! She had no concern with what she looked like, she went much further than I expected, and I thought it was great.

Cukor continues by saying how he was afraid the actor, Tommy Noonan, might be thrown by this display, but that Noonan hung in and spat back his lines with the necessary force:

The lines were meant to shame her—and her reaction was unforgettable. She turned around and you saw that all anger and madness and fear had disappeared. Her face looked very vulnerable and tender, there were tears in her eyes. So I said, "Cut!" and then "Quick, let's do it once more!" . . . So Judy did it again—differently but just as stunningly. . . . Anyway, when it was over, I said to Judy, "You really scared the hell out of me." She was very pleased, she didn't realize what an effect she'd made. And then—she was always funny, she had this great humor—she said, "Oh, that's nothing. Come over to my house any afternoon. I do it every afternoon." Then she gave me a look and added, "But I only do it once at home."

Despite the brilliance of Judy's performance, James Mason's equally remarkable effort and the excellent work of the supporting cast—and notwithstanding Cukor's distinguished direction—*A Star Is Born* is a disappointing movie, full of marvelous things but fatally flawed. The plot is familiar enough. An alcoholic movie star, Norman Maine (James Mason) meets a band singer, Esther Blodgett

(Judy Garland), when she saves him from making a complete fool of himself at a charity performance. Recognizing Esther's great talent, Maine gets her a movie contract at the movie studio owned and operated by Oliver Niles (Charles Bickford), where she soon becomes a star herself, and marries Maine just as his career is going into a rapid decline. Although still deeply in love with Esther, Maine cannot handle this reversal of fortune and, after slipping deeper into alcoholism, commits suicide to save his wife's career. Gloating over all this is Libby (Jack Carson), head of publicity at Niles' studio, a man who has despised Maine for years.

The screenplay, by Moss Hart, was based on the scenario for the 1937 version, which had been written by Dorothy Parker, Alan Campbell and Robert Carson. The Esther Blodgett character was changed to the extent of making her a singer, to take advantage of the star's obvious talents, and special musical material —including "The Man That Got Away" and "It's a New World"—was written for her by Harold Arlen and Ira Gershwin.

All the ingredients were there, but unfor-

Hoyningen-Huene, Gene Allen and Irene Sharaff.

197

tunately the film was cut to ribbons by the studio before it was released. In *On Cukor* the director gave some indication of what is missing from the version we see today:

They cut so many important scenes. The romance between Judy Garland and James Mason was much more clearly developed. There was an excellent scene when they quarrel and she runs away, and he tries to find her. He finally tracks her down to one of those terrible Los Angeles apartment buildings— she's on the roof, drying her hair, very embarrassed at being found there, and there's a rather spectacular vista of the whole city from this ugly, dreary roof. Then they go to a preview together, a charming scene when she's so nervous that she runs out, says, "Pardon me," and throws up near one of the big downtown oil pumps. And when he proposes to her, there's a wonderful number with both of them on a sound stage, she's recording a song, and there's an open microphone and everyone around can hear him proposing.

On the set of A Star Is Born, *Del Armstrong assists Judy with her makeup while Liza clowns for her nanny.*

Asked whether the cuts were made because "they" considered the picture was too long, Cukor replied:

Yes, but it was ridiculous because they put more numbers in. When they added "Born in a Trunk" they made the picture twenty minutes longer. I knew it was too long but I told them that Moss Hart and I . . . could sweat out the twenty minutes and they'd never miss them. They refused, just went ahead with these lethal cuts and threw all the material away.

Asked who, in this case, "they" were, Cukor had the following observation to make: "I made the picture for Warner Brothers. But in the end *they* are always the same people. . . ." Judy described the whole mess more succinctly when she told Vincent Canby, "They didn't cut the picture. Harry [Warner] gummed it to pieces."

The "Born in a Trunk" sequence, staged by Richard Barstow after Cukor had left the picture, is one of the most extended and unsatisfactory numbers in any Judy Garland movie. A stylized recapitulation of the singer's rise to

198

fame, it is trite and garish and serves only to interrupt the real action of the movie. Cukor's account of the missing scenes is a partial one. The lost sections have been published in script form by Los Angeles County Museum, allowing us to see exactly what has been cut and to make some kind of guess at just how fine this picture could have been. It's sufficient to say here that vital continuity links are missing and that what we see in theaters today, or on television, might best be described as a vandalized masterpiece.

When *A Star Is Born* was previewed, uncut, at Huntington Beach, word leaked out and hundreds of fans lined up outside the theater for hours before the screening began. Hedda Hopper was observed munching fried chicken in the back row, and when the picture finally started, the dialogue was drowned out by applause for a full fifteen minutes. It was an event.

At the end of the preview, Judy—who had been seated in the balcony—walked down the aisle to a standing ovation. Looking nervously at her delirious fans, she was heard to ask, "Do you think they *really* liked it?"

Similar scenes greeted a second preview and the official premieres in Hollywood and New York. Despite the flaws that now seem so obvious, the movie received ecstatic reviews and both Judy and James Mason were nominated for Academy Awards. Judy was heavily favored to win, and on Awards night was in the hospital, having given birth to her third child, Joseph, just twenty-four hours earlier. Anxious to capture the great moment for the doting masses, however, the network carrying the Awards broadcast had television cameras installed at the hospital—one at Judy's bedside and another mounted on a special platform that had been built outside the window of her room. If and when her name was pulled from the envelope, Judy would talk to Bob Hope from her bed. When at last the envelope was unsealed, though, the name that emerged from it was not Judy Garland but Grace Kelly. Judy

and her husband watched disconsolately as the cameras were removed, the cables rolled up, the lights taken down, unused. To make the scene still more pathetic, she had been told that her son was very frail—one lung had failed to open—and had only a moderate chance of survival. He did survive, however, prompting Judy to refer to him as her Academy Award.

Most observers found it incredible that Miss Kelly's performance in *The Country Girl* should have been chosen over Judy's Esther Blodgett. The explanation seems to be that many voting members of the Academy tended to consider box-office success—and hence the fiscal health of the industry—a prerequisite for this ultimate accolade, and the rumor making the rounds was that *A Star Is Born* would lose money. By normal standards, it was doing very good business, but the picture had cost several times as much as most feature films. Moreover, many people in Hollywood had heard the stories that had originated on the set and they blamed Judy for the excessive cost of the movie. By 1955 Hollywood was becoming conservative and it's probably fair to say that there were people who voted against Judy as a form of reprimand.

Warner Brothers managed to extricate itself from the multipicture deal they had originally agreed to with the Lufts, and the period that followed the release of *A Star Is Born* proved to be one of relative stagnation for Judy. The momentum of the picture's publicity carried her to a successful television special—*The Ford Star Jubilee*—in 1955, a program that borrowed its format from the Palace show. The following year she was back at the Palace, where she drew full houses and received good reviews but did not generate quite the same level of enthusiasm as she had in 1951. Also in 1956 she made her cabaret debut at the Frontier in Las Vegas—an engagement that brought fresh plaudits—but there was a definite loss of energy, a gradual running down over a two- or three-year period, a phenomenon that was reflected in her weight, which began to balloon toward 150 pounds.

A Star is Born. *On the set with James Mason.*

201

Chapter 2
Flying High
and
Lying Low

When *A Star Is Born* was released, Judy was thirty-two years old. Some days she looked fifteen years older than that, and behaved fifteen years younger.

The passage to adulthood is difficult under the best of circumstances. For someone who has grown up as a movie celebrity, it can be a dozen times worse, especially when—as in Judy's case—adolescence had been artificially prolonged by her studio, both on screen and off. Judy discovered that her only effective weapons were those of a teenager. She learned to rely on tantrums and irrational outbursts, and she developed an emphatic certainty in the rightness of her own convictions even when all the evidence contradicted her. Since she never fully grew up, she had the rest of her life to hone these weapons, and to use them against her oppressors—both real and imagined. For support and approval, she looked to her peer group—other performers living their own sustained adolescences, immature adults from other backgrounds and actual teenagers. The

breach with M-G-M had been equivalent to leaving home. Judy had found herself, for the first time in her life, free of external discipline, but she was ill equipped to replace it with any kind of self-discipline. It seems likely that without Sid Luft she would have fallen apart.

Judy Garland had the body of a woman and had seen just about everything there was to be seen. Emotionally, though, she was a child bride. Thus it's hardly surprising that her marriage to Luft was a stormy one. Once it was over, Judy delighted in telling reporters that the union had been an unhappy one from the very beginning. This was hardly fair of her. Certainly the relationship was tumultuous but it seems to have been exhilarating too—in the early years, at least—to both parties. In Judy's defense, she generally took her share of the blame, explaining that she seemed incapable of learning the lessons of marriage, saying that she knew how to hold an audience but not a husband. The dynamics of the relationship was made up of alternating cycles of strong mutual attraction and violent disputation. More than

In the driveway of their Holmby Hills house, the Lufts receive a visit from their neighbor Lauren Bacall.

one divorce suit was first brought and then subsequently dropped.

The Lufts had bought a large house in Holmby Hills, south of Bel Air, a neighborhood of quiet, meandering streets where massive and mostly rather ugly villas hide from the world behind high walls and hedges. At that time it was the home of the Rat Pack, and those were the people—the Bogarts, Sinatra, Peter Lawford and the rest—with whom the Lufts spent a great deal of their leisure time.

The Rat Pack came into being as the result of a chance remark made by Lauren Bacall. Entering Romanoff's restaurant one evening, she looked around and said, "I see the rat pack is all here." Later that night, after a good deal of drinking, the Rat Pack was inaugurated with mock solemnity. Doubtless it would have been forgotten about immediately, except that Joe Hyams wrote the whole thing up in his column for the *New York Herald-Tribune:*

The Holmby Hills Rat Pack held its first annual meeting last night at Romanoff's restaurant in Beverly Hills and elected officers for the coming year. Named to executive positions were: Frank Sinatra, pack master; Judy Garland, first vice president; Lauren Bacall, den mother; Sid Luft, cage master; Humphrey Bogart, rat in charge of public relations; Irving Lazar, recording secretary and treasurer; Nathaniel Benchley, historian.

The only members of the organization not voted into office are David Niven, Michael Romanoff and James Van Heusen. Mr. Niven, an Englishman, Mr. Romanoff, a Russian, and Mr. Van Heusen, an American, protested that they were discriminated against because of their national origins. Mr. Sinatra, who was acting as chairman of the meeting, refused to enter their protests on the minutes.

The Rat Pack described itself as being against everything and everyone, including themselves, and the Lufts certainly found this to be the case—as indicated by a couple of anecdotes recounted in *Bogie,* Joe Hyams' biography of Bogart:

In front of the Holmby Hills house. Left to right: Lorna Luft, Judy, Liza Minnelli, Joey Luft, Sid Luft and John Luft— Sid's son from his previous marriage to Lynn Bari.

One night . . . Humphrey Bogart expounded on the subject of "class" before a gathering of the Hollywood elite. Sid Luft . . . had just purchased a Rolls Royce. That item of conspicuous consumption, along with the bench-made English shoes and a butler who doubled as chauffeur, spelled class to Luft. Then Bogart took the floor. In a voice honed with sarcasm he announced, "You can't buy it and you can't acquire it like a suntan. And I can tell you you don't have it, my friend, and you never will. I know what I'm talking about because I was born with it. I've had it all my life—and I can also do without it."

The Lufts were apt to turn up on a friend's doorstep with a recital of their family troubles, a habit that apparently got on Bogart's nerves at times. Hyams quotes Richard Burton's account of one of these occasions:

Bogie told Sid and Judy to get out, stay out, and never come back, that he was fed up with their problems. He added a few choice epithets and ended by admonishing Sid to "take that dull wife of yours with you."

At this juncture, according to Burton's story, Luft threatened to bust Bogart's face in.

Bogart backed off a few steps, grinned, and said, "Sid, you won't lay a hand on me."
Nonplussed, Luft stopped a haymaker in midair to ask, "why not?"
"Because, Sid, you're my friend," Bogart said gently. . . .
Arms around each other, Bogart and Luft strolled over to his bar, raised glasses, and the incident was closed.

The Lufts' new home was huge, but not huge enough to insulate their frequent fights from the world at large, and these battles were usually loud and inventive. Having been blessed with a voice that carried, Judy could sometimes be heard throughout the neighborhood. The gentlemen of the press dutifully reported the more spectacular outbursts for the benefit of those readers who were not fortunate enough to live in Holmby Hills. Everyone seemed to agree that Judy and Luft were well matched in these contests; neither could be accused of tyrannizing the other. Inevitably, however, these fights must have had a lasting effect on their relationship.

When the other children said unkind things to Lorna, Judy would give her lines to deliver to the culprits the following day. "Where were you born?" she'd have Lorna ask. "Under a rock?"

There were other problems in the Luft household. The family's finances were so erratic that—despite the house and the servants and the publicity—the cupboards and refrigerators were sometimes virtually bare. Then Judy would have to go back to work, no matter what state she was in at the time.

On New Year's Eve, 1958, Judy opened at the Flamingo in Las Vegas and encountered open hostility from the audience. She was grossly overweight and some of the people out front, well oiled by the time she appeared, let her know how they felt about this. Judy got through the opening numbers without any serious interruptions, but she hadn't been onstage for more than ten or fifteen minutes when the catcalls began. As the performance continued, the barrage of jeers and insults grew steadily worse. Quite a few of the comments took note of Judy's obesity.

Some members of the audience tried to quiet things down, but the rowdy element easily drowned them out. Judy persevered until two women climbed onto the stage and performed a drunken hula dance. Judy stormed off and refused to fulfil the rest of her engagement. The management sued her, but judgment was made in her favor.

It is not too difficult to imagine the sheer terror she must have felt. She was used to crises in her private life, and to violent squabbles with her peers—but this was revolution, this was the storming of the Bastille. Was the mob finally ready to sacrifice her? To obliterate Dorothy? This was not the kind of thing that was supposed to happen to Judy Garland. It was as if a salesclerk had asked her for proof of identity.

But to see her at this time was, in fact, to question her identity, because she was swollen to twice her normal size. She was a million miles from the spunky kid who had made her way to the Emerald City. She looked like a peasant who had suddenly come into a fortune and gorged herself on starchy foods, trying to hide the damage under expensive, voluminous clothes. She continued to perform, even playing the Metropolitan Opera House in New York—where she was sadly below her best—but this was not the real Judy Garland. She had become a grotesque, a fact that she tried to joke about but which nonetheless caused her considerable anguish. The incident at the Flamingo was followed by others less well publicized but no less painful. She began to overhear unflattering remarks about her weight wherever she went, and she did not always find it easy to laugh them off.

In an effort to get herself back into shape, Judy spent several weeks at a health ranch situated to the northeast of Los Angeles, in the mountains near Thousand Oaks. This establishment was run by Kay Mulvey—who, as has been mentioned, knew Judy at M-G-M in the thirties—and by her husband. It was an exclusive place, patronized by movie celebrities and West Coast socialites, and the Lufts managed to blend in with the general ambience of calm and tranquillity. There were no fights. Judy played tennis every day and stayed on a strict diet. When presented with a bill she told the proprietors that she would have to defer payment.

Her physical condition appeared to have improved as a consequence of this interlude, but the improvement was short-lived. In the fall of 1959 she collapsed, in New York City, and was rushed to Doctors Hospital. The public was told that she was suffering from an acute form of hepatitis. Cynics, believing that Judy had been drinking heavily, concluded that hepatitis was a euphemism for cirrhosis of the liver. Judy announced that the specialists had told her that she would be a semi-invalid and that she would never work again. For the time being, she seemed to accept this as final.

Not made public at the time was the fact that the doctors had told her that she probably had only five years to live. Released from the hospital, looking much slimmer, she spent some weeks in California then took a plane to London, flying by herself—"to prove to myself that I could function as a halfway intelligent woman"—despite her fear of planes and her usual habit of traveling with as large an entourage as possible. Later Luft joined her, bringing Liza, Lorna and Joey. For a few months they led a relatively idyllic life, living in a comfortable rented house and even enrolling the children in English schools. During this period, Judy visited a number of U.S. service bases in Europe to campaign for the election of John F. Kennedy.

According to Judy—and this may be part of the self-generated legend—she could not sleep one night and locked herself, as usual, in the bathroom. She began to sing and realized that she had to return to the stage. A few weeks later she was back at the London Palladium. She remained a little heavy, but no longer obese, and the British audiences still loved her. Her confidence began to return. She toured the British Isles and played several dates on the continent.

It's significant that performers often select their metaphors from the language of assassination: "I killed them tonight..." "I wiped them out . . ." "I destroyed them . . ." "I murdered them. . . ." Performers are successful to the extent that they are able to manipulate an audience, and murder is the ultimate form of manipulation. But this is a two-way street: the performer is always laying himself open to manipulation by the audience. When things go wrong, the metaphor is reversed: "I died out there tonight. . . ."

For anyone working at Judy Garland's level, each performance is an act of courage. As for the phenomenon of the comeback, though its annals are strewn with clichés, there can be no denying that any comeback demands enormous quantities of nerve, tenacity and effort. The risk involved is always great, and for Judy it was doubly risky because this was her second comeback.

Despite favorable reports of her European dates, Judy's return to the United States was not greeted with a flood of offers—in fact, it stirred very little interest in professional circles. The only serious approach she had was from Freddie Fields and David Begelman, who were just setting up in the management business. Remembering Judy's smashing success at the Palace in 1951, they realized that while the risk of employing her was considerable, the potential payoff was enormous. They decided to take the gamble, picking up the reins dropped by Sid Luft, who was beginning to ease out of the picture (though he would never vanish entirely).

For years Judy and her husband had sustained their relationship on a steady diet of domestic warfare—each of them dishing out verbal violence with equal gusto—which was nonetheless based on mutual respect and need. Now they had exhausted one another, and soon after their return to America on New Year's Eve, 1960, they separated. Probably this rift was inevitable—the pressures had been building up for a long time—but it was unfortunate. Whatever his faults, Sid Luft was the one man in Judy Garland's life who both loved her and had the strength to stand up to her. Without him she was more vulnerable.

Judy's first engagement under her new managers was, of all places, at the Concord Hotel—a resort in the Catskills. She was rather shaky, but thanks to the skill of Mort Lindsey, who had agreed to lead the band just this once, the date was not a total disaster. By the time she played Washington, D.C., a few weeks later, she had regained most of her confidence and gave one of the strongest concerts of her career. Mort Lindsey was now permanently installed as her musical director and momentum began to build toward the climax of this second comeback.

The concert Judy gave at Carnegie Hall in New York, on April 23, 1961, ranks with her opening night at the Palace, ten years earlier, as one of the great triumphs of her personal appearance career. The word was out that although her weight problems and emotional difficulties had not vanished, she was in complete control of her talents again. Tickets to the concert were sold out almost immediately, and on the night of the concert there was a mob scene on Fifty-seventh Street, aggravated by the fact that somebody (no one seems quite sure who) ordered that the doors remain closed until the very last minute so that everybody—men in tuxedos and women with fur wraps over evening gowns—was kept waiting on the sidewalk. While the scalpers' prices crept higher and higher, so did the pitch of anticipation. Then, when the doors were finally opened, people barely had time to find their seats before the buzz of conversation was stilled by the dousing of the house lights. Suddenly Mort Lindsey was taking the orchestra into the overture, drawing the evening's first burst of applause.

It all happened so quickly that the crowd had no chance to lose itself in self-contemplation, hardly had time to take note of the celebrities in the stalls—Henry Fonda, Myrna Loy, Richard Burton, Julie Andrews, Rock Hudson, Carol Channing, Spencer Tracy, Maurice Chevalier and dozens more—before they were sucked into the breathless moments that preceded the star's entrance.

The story that circulated the next day was that Judy had been so nervous that she had frightened herself into a state of near catatonia and had had herself placed in an iron lung, protesting that she was unable to breathe. This, it was said, was why the doors had not been opened until the last minute. Until Judy left the iron lung, nobody could be sure that the concert would start at all, and naturally the idea of risking a riot inside Carnegie Hall was unthinkable. According to this same story,

208

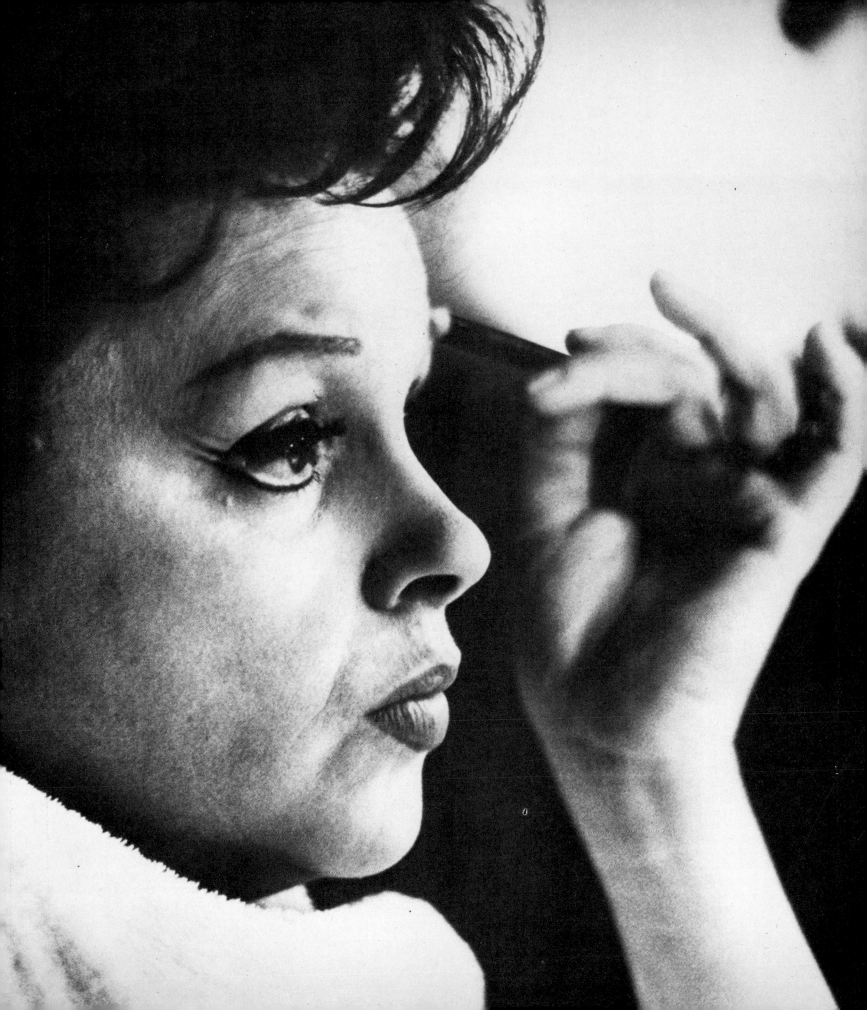

Judy was finally teased out of the iron lung by a dwarf. Dwarfs, the perpetrators of this yarn explained, always cracked Judy up.

Most people preferred to believe that the reason for keeping the doors closed so long was sheer showmanship—a deliberate effort to eliminate the period of transition between street and concert—and this is a more likely explanation. The iron lung story does have a certain symbolic validity, though, since Judy was chronically nervous before going onstage. Like many performers, she was terrified that her voice would desert her, or that her fans would turn on her—as they had done in Vegas—and she could not overcome these fears until she was standing in the wings listening to the overture. Then she would begin to stamp her feet—arms folded, chin tucked into her neck—and she would yell to her musical director, "Hit it, Mort!"

Meanwhile, out in the darkened auditorium, the audience was waiting. At Carnegie Hall they could tell—from the first bars of the overture—that tonight at least she would not have to fight the orchestra, as sometimes happened. Lindsey had put together a group of top New York session men. From "The Trolley Song" they slipped into "Over the Rainbow," and followed this with "The Man That Got Away." Then there was a brief recapitulation of "Over the Rainbow" and Judy was there, skipping out into the footlights.

She was heavy still, but it was unmistakably the old Judy. She was wearing a black sheath and a blue satin jacket top by Norman Norell—her hair short, looking a little mannish. She grinned and bobbed and waved while the audience went wild, and finally the cheering died down as the orchestra went into the introduction of "When You're Smiling." By the time the song was over, there was no doubt that she was as good or better than ever.

It was all there—the ad-libbed (or apparently ad-libbed) humor, the whole unmistakable repertoire of mannerisms. She played with the hand mike and yanked the cord draped over her shoulder. She hugged herself and tugged at her own sleeves. She played with her

ring finger and dabbed at her eyes with her free hand (left-handed, she usually held the mike in her right hand so that the left was free for gestures). She stabbed at the air to accentuate phrases. She planted her feet wide apart and rocked from side to side—shifting weight from one foot to another like an overgrown child. She would glance at the floor—as though gathering strength from some hidden source—then stare intently out into the auditorium as she launched into a new chorus.

Best of all, the voice was flawless. It had never sounded better. It had all the liveliness of the young Judy Garland's voice and a new dimension of maturity. Experience may not have benefited her in her everyday life, but it had had a profound effect on her art. Now the voice had everything. Technically, it was marvelous, with a rich, controlled vibrato; emotionally, it was devastating.

"When You're Smiling" built to a climax that would have been strong enough to close the show for most singers. The applause was an expression of sheer delight. Judy swung into "Almost Like Being in Love," handling it lightly against a background of jabbing brass, then she modulated down to "This Can't Be Love," bouncing along on the drummer's rim shots and the four-to-the-bar guitar chords. More applause, then she began a very slow, very silky version of "Do It Again"—her voice approximating the timbre it had had in the early forties, Judy at her most stylish working against a delicate choir of strings and woodwinds. Toward the end of the song her voice opened up again—became the voice of a thirty-eight-year-old woman—and at the finish she reached for a high note, but fell away from it poignantly—a brilliant little gloss, whether deliberate or otherwise. The crowd was yelling titles by now, but this was a carefully planned performance with a definite shape. "You Go to My Head" was the next number, opening with a Latin beat, Judy sounding rather like Sarah Vaughan at her sassiest. About halfway through, she stumbled over the lyric for a moment—one of her very few slips through the entire evening—but she picked it up again

immediately. She was flying now and nothing was going to stop her.

The concert spanned two and a half hours and twenty-eight songs, building steadily as it went along. It showed Judy in all her moods —from clown to mistress of melodrama— drawing on a wide and varied repertoire to do so. There were songs she had first performed as a member of the Gumm Sisters. She had sung "Puttin' on the Ritz" at Maurice Kusell's *Stars of Tomorrow* back in 1931. Thirty years later she handled it as a brisk throwaway routine with flashes of dixieland from the pit. Then there was "Stormy Weather"—one of Judy's staples in 1933 and 1934, at which time she had deliberately imitated Helen Morgan's delivery. Now she held back for the first chorus and then built to a tremendous climax, moving up through several keys as she did so. (During her early days at M-G-M Roger Edens had had difficulty persuading Judy she was too young for this kind of material. Now she was proving she had earned the right to it.) She also performed a very straightforward, free-swinging version of "Zing Went the Strings of My Heart," her audition song and the song she had sung as her father lay dying.

There were the dependable show-stoppers like "San Francisco" (with her jocular recitative verse: "I never will forget Jeanette MacDonald . . .") and a lot of reliable standards. She turned "How Long Has This Been Going On?" into a spine-chiller, leaning on jazz phrasing of the Lester Young school, allowing little heart-stopping breaks to creep into her voice. In "I Can't Give You Anything but Love" she hung back against the beat, very controlled, producing a dead hush in the auditorium, wringing every last nuance from the lyric (helped by some delicate scoring and a strong Ben Websterish tenor solo) and ending to wild applause. There were others: "Just You, Just Me," "Come Rain or Come Shine," "A Foggy Day," "That's Entertainment." Then there were Judy's songs, the numbers from her movies, the ones that were always her own.

One of the biggest cheers of the evening came not quite halfway through the concert when the audience recognized the familiar introduction to "The Man That Got Away"— trombone and muted trumpets—and the climax of the show was reached by way of a medley of some of her biggest hits: "You Made Me Love You," "For Me and My Gal" ("Sing it with me, please . . .") and "The Trolley Song." This led to another show-stopper, "Rock-a-Bye Your Baby with a Dixie Melody." Judy is perhaps the only performer who has ever gotten away with singing Al Jolson's songs, and she did so because she avoided the Jolson mannerisms—so tempting to the lesser performers—and just sang the numbers straight and unadorned. Later she would borrow another song from Jolson, but first she launched into "Over the Rainbow"—the planned conclusion of the show—and the crowd went beserk (people were scrambling down the aisles now, crowding around the stage, yelling and screaming). Her voice broke on the first phrase—the hint of a sob—then she was the brave little girl facing the troubles of the world, but still pleading: "Why, then, oh why can't I?" And as she finished, the roar was deafening.

The orchestra began to recapitulate the melody, this time as her signature tune, but no one imagined for a moment this could be the end of the performance. The audience was on its feet and more people were pushing down the aisles as she sailed into "Swanee" (another roar), at the end of which the band began "Over the Rainbow" again, and Judy headed for the wings, but turned before she reached them and, back at center stage, sang "After You've Gone." She was show-boating now— serving a side of corn with the meat and potatoes, the greatest short-order singer in the world—and everybody loved it. Sober men in tuxedos stood on their seats and yelled "Bravo!" Again the orchestra played "Over the Rainbow" and again the crowd yelled for an encore.

"Do you really want more?" she asked. "Aren't you tired?"

Warning the crowd that this was her last song, she sang "Chicago." She sounded just as fresh as she had at the beginning of the evening.

Judy with her fans, Carnegie Hall.

And then it was really over.

"Good night! I love you very much! Good night! God bless!"

The cheering still came in waves, but finally —after innumerable bows—she was gone and the stage was empty.

Not every performance was as happy as the Carnegie Hall concert. Throughout the sixteen-city tour she undertook, Judy was in reasonably good shape, but conditions were not always ideal. Aside from Mort Lindsey, she traveled with just three regular musicians—a pianist, a drummer and a lead trumpet (the last never called her anything but "man")— and the rest of the orchestra had to be recruited from local musicians. In some smaller cities this method was disastrous and Judy found herself fighting the band. Lindsey recalls that he generally had only a few hours to rehearse this pick-up unit, and that in a few instances he dared not even rehearse them because the musicians were so obviously subprofessional that he knew if he did he would end up with an epidemic of split lips among the brass players before the concert began.

With Spencer Tracy on the set of Judgment at Nuremberg.

The nomadic life dictated by her concert schedule—overnight trips from hotel to hotel —was not always to Judy's liking. She did not mind dealing with strangers, so long as they were polite, but she loathed the types she met all too frequently who treated her as if she were a public property, and she did not hesitate to turn the cutting edge of her wit on them ("I've got rainbows up my ass, honey!").

Carnegie Hall was far from her only triumph that year, though. There was a magnificently bizarre concert at the Hollywood Bowl— 30,000 people listening in a steady downpour, not one of them leaving till the last encore was over. And this same year Judy made her return to film, taking the small but important part of Irene Hoffman in Stanley Kramer's *Judgment at Nuremberg*.

Kramer had wanted to make this picture with unknowns, but United Artists refused to agree to this so he ended up with an all-star cast that included Spencer Tracy, Burt Lan-

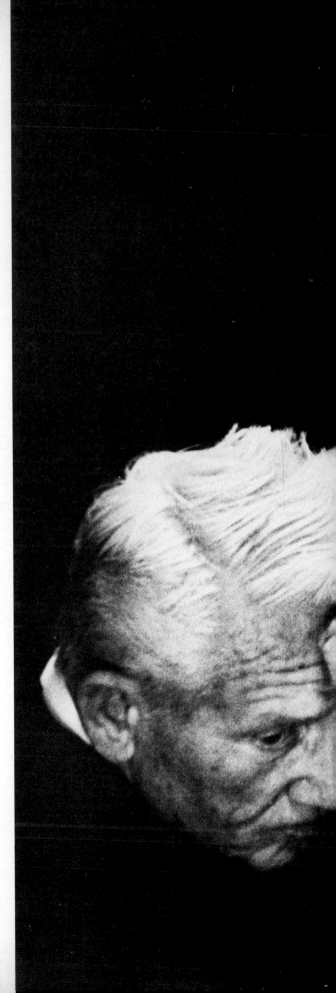

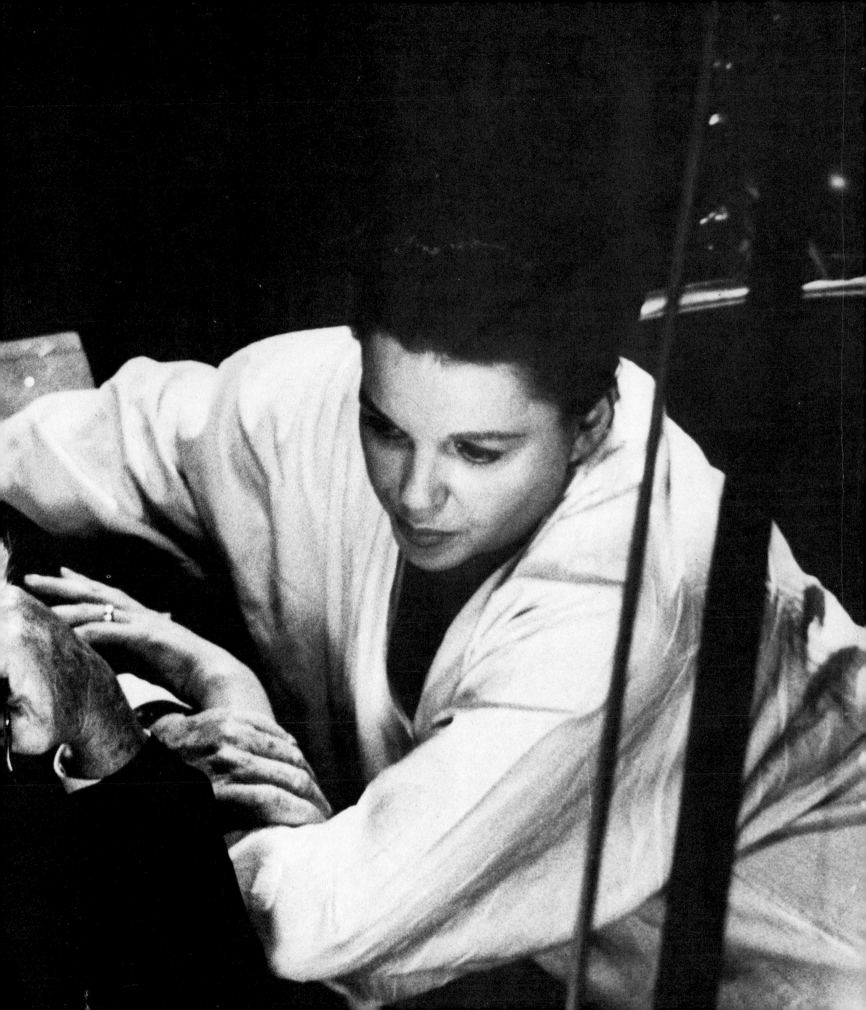

caster, Richard Widmark, Marlene Dietrich and Maximilian Schell. One part that had been difficult to cast was that of Rudolph Peterson, a witness at the Nuremberg War Tribunals who had been sterilized by the Nazis and is on the verge of insanity. Kramer hit upon the idea of using Montgomery Clift—who was, by then, severely disturbed—for the role and this, as Kramer remembers it, triggered the notion of asking Judy to take the role of Irene Hoffman, a woman whose existence had also been laid waste by trauma.

Kramer figured that he would be able to get four weeks of good work out of Judy, whatever her problems. As it turned out, he had no major difficulty with her; she was a model of cooperation and punctuality. Judy was, in fact, enormously grateful for being given this chance, and Kramer attributes the easy time he had with her in part to the fact that she was not required to look even approximately slim or glamourous (though she did give the make-up department a few bad moments). She was playing a German hausfrau called upon to bear witness to a Nazi atrocity, and it was appropriate that her face looked puffy and her eyes welled with exhaustion. The only problem Kramer had was that her interpretation of the role tended to be influenced by the last person she had spoken to. Because she had understood his viewpoint perfectly on Monday evening did not necessarily mean he could count on her agreement on Tuesday morning. He often had to convince her all over again.

Monty Clift's segment was finished by the time Judy's began, but he hung around the set, watching everything that was going on. When Judy did her big scene, breaking down under Richard Widmark's probing, Clift sat watching her in a corner—"like a little animal" Kramer describes him—with tears pouring down his cheeks, his shirt and jacket drenched. At the end of the scene he made his way to where Kramer stood and, still sobbing, mumbled his opinion: "She played that all wrong."

Judy received another Academy Award nomination for her role in *Judgment at Nu-*remberg—this time as best supporting actress—and the next several months saw her involved in a flurry of film activity. She was the voice of Mewsette, an animated cat in a UPA feature-length cartoon titled *Gay Purr-ee*. Despite songs by Arlen and Harburg, the film can best be described as an exercise in archness. *Newsweek*'s reviewer detected an effort to reach "a hitherto undiscovered audience—the fey four-year-old of recherché taste."

A Child Is Waiting was another Stanley Kramer production, starring Burt Lancaster as the superintendent of an institution for mentally retarded children, and Judy as a music teacher, new to the staff, who becomes emotionally involved with one of the youngsters.

Kramer had hoped to direct this picture himself but, when this proved impossible, John Cassavetes was called in to take over. The screenplay had been tailored to suit Kramer's talents and Cassavetes seems to have had difficulties coming to terms with it.

The film is a failure, but it has a number of touching scenes and Judy has some fine moments with the children, most of whom were patients of the Pacific State Hospital in Pomona. Had the production worked, this might have been one of Judy's most interesting —if least typical—roles. There are enough good scenes to demonstrate that it presented her with a challenge she was quite capable of meeting.

Before *A Child Is Waiting* was released, Judy went to England to make another movie —*I Could Go on Singing*. Directed by Ronald Neame, the picture featured Judy as Jenny Bowman—a singer-celebrity à la Judy Garland—who seeks out her former lover, now a successful London physician (Dirk Bogarde), hoping to see their son, whom she gave up to him as a baby. The film does not pretend to be anything but a tearjerker, with a few songs thrown in for good measure, but even at this level it does not work. Jenny Bowman is too close to the real Judy Garland to make this soap-opera treatment palatable. Given the limitations of the script, Bogarde is fine, as is Gregory Phillips, who plays the disputed son;

I Could Go on Singing.

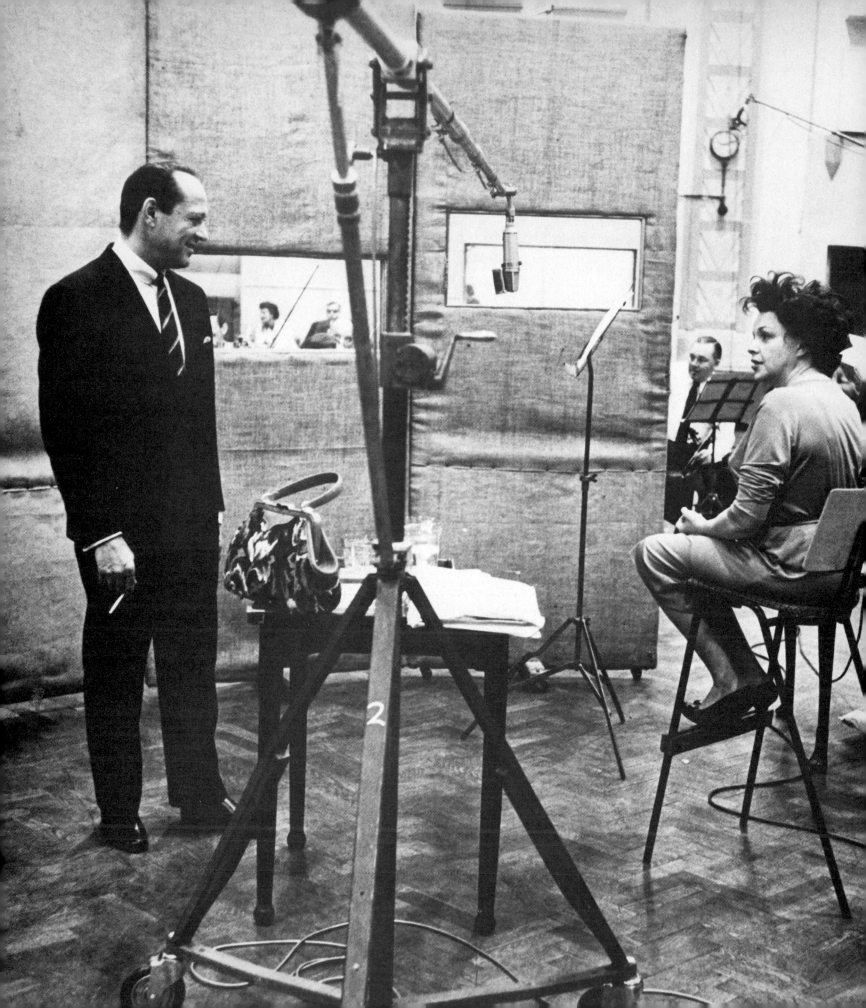

and there are some fascinating quasi-documentary glimpses of Judy backstage at the London Palladium, but the whole picture is pervaded by an atmosphere of compromise. Had it attempted to portray more of Judy's real-life problems, it might have been much better. Instead it tried to capitalize on the public's awareness of these problems without confronting them, and this left the film with a soft center.

During production Judy was her usual unpredictable self. Saul Chaplin was musical supervisor on the film and recalls that her punctuality was as erratic as ever:

I had a rehearsal set up with her for eleven-thirty in the morning, and she arrived at seven o'clock at night—and didn't think anything was wrong. Now, you'd expect some kind of apology—but no. Nothing. Her attitude was, "What's wrong with that?" She wasn't being temperamental or playing the star. It was just that she seemed to have no sense of time. When she got there, she'd be fine. She'd work till seven the next morning, if you asked her to—so you couldn't get mad at her.

Before shooting began, Dirk Bogarde—a long time friend—had told Judy how much he had looked forward to working with her. She told him to try it for a couple of weeks before he made up his mind. Feeling very insecure, once again, Judy made huge demands on Bogarde's patience, which eventually led to friction between them. By the end of the picture they were good friends once more, but the quarrel was bitter while it lasted and for a while Judy was taking it out on everyone, as Chaplin remembers:

There was one scene in which she had a lot of props to carry, and she was complaining to Ronald Neame. He said, "Let's do it once more." Ordinarily that wouldn't have bothered her at all, but this day she flew into a rage. Really she was mad at Dirk, but she was taking it out on Neame.
Neame said, "Judy, you're marvelous. But, as a director, every once in a while you get the feeling that someone you're working with could do it better—it's not something you can

At a London recording session for I Could Go on Singing, *Judy talks with her estranged husband, Sid Luft, while Saul Chaplin, back to the camera, and Mort Lindsey stand by.*

219

put your finger on. That's the only reason I'm asking you to do it again."

She calmed down immediately.

Despite Neame's charm and diplomacy, the work schedule was disrupted sufficiently to necessitate David Begelman's flying out from New York to smooth things over. At one point Judy threatened to take the next plane back to America, and the only thing that prevented her from doing so was that she had given her passport to the British authorities so she could be issued a work permit. To add to all this, there was another apparent suicide attempt—this time an overdose of pills—while she was in London.

The film was released in London to moderately favorable reviews, but nobody except the most fanatical of Judy's followers went to see it. In the United States the story was much the same. As a movie star, Judy was finished. *I Could Go on Singing* was her thirty-second feature film. It was also her last. At this stage in her career she needed the unpredictability of her live performances to pull in the crowds.

On either side of this fiasco, Judy did two television specials for CBS—the first with Frank Sinatra and Dean Martin, the other with Phil Silvers and Robert Goulet.

She was losing weight again. In 1962, while in Tahoe to establish residency qualifications for a Nevada divorce from Sid Luft, she went on a crash diet and touched nothing but two cups of unsweetened tea a day. This led to an attack of acute pyelonephritis of the right kidney, an extremely painful condition that put her in the hospital once again. She recovered in time for a six-week season in Las Vegas, at the Sahara this time, then stayed on in Nevada with her children, waiting for her divorce. Luft, however, was countersuing in California and that effectively neutralized her efforts.

Both parents wanted custody of the children, which led to an ugly situation. Luft argued that Judy was unfit to have custody, and Judy became obsessed with the idea that he was going to kidnap the children; she began to take all kinds of precautions. Having been befriended by John F. Kennedy—whom she met through Peter Lawford, then the President's brother-in-law—she took advantage of an opportunity to spend some time in a guest house adjacent to the Kennedy compound at Hyannisport, apparently figuring that her husband would hardly be able to penetrate the security provided by the President's Secret Service men. In 1962, immediately before *I Could Go on Singing,* Luft shut himself in a room at the Stanhope Hotel in New York with Lorna and Joey. Assisted by friends and three private detectives, Judy snatched the children back and—stopping to pick up Liza on the way —rushed by limousine to Idlewild Airport where she and the children boarded a London-bound plane. Within a few days, however, Luft followed them to England and he and Judy were soon back on amicable terms.

Judy's children grew up quickly. Liza, at the age of fifteen, made her professional debut with a small part in *Take Me Along* at the Hyannisport Summer Playhouse. Not asking for help from either of her parents, she made her own way and, in 1963, landed the third lead in an off-Broadway revival of *Best Foot Forward*. Judy, pretending she had been given the wrong date, did not make an appearance on Liza's first night. Liza was hurt until she realized that her mother had stayed away deliberately, knowing that if she was there she would have drawn attention from Liza. (Needless to say, Judy was there the next evening.)

In 1963 Judy herself began a new career. She and the Columbia Broadcasting System had had their differences in the past, but CBS executives were desperate to break *Bonanza*'s stranglehold on Sunday evening television and decided Judy might be just the person to do it. Terms were agreed to and Judy

220

was signed to a full season of hour-long weekly shows.

The men who made this decision—William Paley, Dr. Frank Stanton, James Aubrey and Hunt Stromberg, Jr.—must have realized the risk involved. Making a movie, Judy's erratic work habits could be absorbed to some extent —the picture might run over schedule and budget, but it would still end up as a Judy Garland movie and stand a good chance of making a profit. Television was an entirely different situation. A weekly show has to stay within a strict budget and production delays can be disastrous. Given Judy's history, it should have seemed inevitable that difficulties would arise sooner or later.

For some reason, more words have been expended on this television series than on any of Judy's greatest movie successes—and most of these words have tended to paint a negative picture of the entire enterprise. Let's begin then, by saying that, at its best, *The Judy Garland Show* was remarkably good and provides us with the most comprehensive record we have of Garland the entertainer as opposed to Garland the movie star. There were some weak programs, but the series afforded many glimpses of Judy near her peak, and included four or five shows as good as anything that has been done within the television variety format.

The Judy Garland Show was taped at CBS Television City in Los Angeles—a huge modern complex built on the former site of the New Gilmore Stadium, the scene of one of the Gumm Sisters' early triumphs, the *Movie Star Frolic* of 1934. Studio 43, one of the largest in the complex, was completely redesigned for the show, with a large turntable stage area and a projecting apron runway to bring Judy close to the audience. Seating was provided for about 300 people.

George Schlatter was engaged to produce the show and a team of seasoned talents was assembled around him, including Johnny Bradford as head writer and Bill Hobin as director. Mort Lindsey was the natural choice for musical director and he was given the assistance of Mel Tormé, who was hired to write special

Reunited with Mickey Rooney at CBS Television City, June, 1963.

vocal arrangements for Judy, and Jack Elliott, who would act as musical coordinator. Nick Castle was the choreographer and Gary Smith the scenic designer and associate producer. Judy's wardrobe was in the hands of Ray Aghayan (who may have done more for her than any other designer), and the unit manager was George Sunga.

Everyone made a tremendous effort to create an atmosphere Judy would find agreeable. Her portable dressing room was decorated in the same style as her new home (on Rockingham Drive in Brentwood), and a yellow brick road was painted on the floor outside. People told raunchy jokes and dressed up in costumes to keep her amused. They stood on their heads to make Judy happy.

A couple of days before the first taping Freddie Fields called a staff meeting. It was held behind closed doors in Schlatter's office. Everyone but Judy was present.

Fields was straight-faced and solemn. He told them he was grateful for the way they had catered to Judy. She had needed all the support she could get and they had been right to concentrate on developing a relaxed atmosphere at the studio. Now, however, a change in attitude was called for. This series meant life or death for Judy. If it failed, she was finished. This was her last chance—it was as simple as that. The time had come to quit clowning and get down to the serious business of making this show work. It was up to everyone in the room to stand behind Judy and give her strength. "We have to be as strong," Fields proclaimed, "as U.S. Steel." The speech lasted close to twenty minutes, all of it in this vein.

As Fields concluded, there was total silence. People glanced at one another nervously. Then there was a knock on the office door. Fields opened it to reveal Judy, standing there in a preposterous costume—half-bum, half-lunatic—one tooth blacked out and a grin a yard wide on her face.

"Can anyone spare a dime for a girl who's down on her luck?"

Everyone cracked up.

Fields' speech had been set up and everyone

222

loved the fact that the professional jokers had been beaten at their own game. Yet there was something horribly appropriate about this gag because in a very real sense this series *was* life or death for Judy. The successful continuation of her career hung on it.

Judy had slimmed down to close to one hundred pounds and looked better than she had in years. More important, her voice was sound. She was too notoriously unpredictable to allow for a sense of security, but there were grounds for optimism around Studio 43.

On Friday, June 24, 1963, the first *Judy Garland Show* was taped. Along with the star and her regular second banana, Jerry Van Dyke, there would be at least one guest on most shows and, logically enough, the first one selected was Judy's old buddy Mickey Rooney. The show went well and Judy and her production staff were happy with the results. On Monday morning the network offered its own opinion, and it was not flattering. The men in the front office felt Judy had been presented as "a little old lady"—a serious mistake—and they were very disturbed because she seemed unable to talk to anyone without touching them. (She did have a need for physical contact with people and was always grabbing them, nudging them, tugging at their clothing.)

The second show, taped a week later, had

Rehearsing with Liza.

Count Basie and Mel Tormé as guests. The emphasis was on music, which should have been to Judy's advantage, but the material was not right for her. The show was run of the mill, and the network brass pointed this out in no uncertain terms.

The third show was much better. Judy's guest was Liza and there was a real chemistry between them which was quite evident in the studio and which came across well on screen.

The fourth show taped was a nightmare. Lena Horne and Terry-Thomas were the scheduled guests, but Judy was conspicuously absent from rehearsals and on tape day she fluffed lines, scraping home on a wing and a prayer.

The next show featured Tony Bennett and Dick Shawn and, apart from Judy's closing "Born in a Trunk" segment (a regular feature which was designed to spotlight songs associated with her past career), the whole thing was rather mediocre.

The following Monday, the axe fell, Schlatter was fired. The writers were fired. Wholesale changes were announced. The music department—Lindsey, Tormé and Elliott—remained intact, and Hobin, Sunga and Aghayan were still there; but all the people responsible for the format of the show were replaced. The network took responsibility for these changes—Judy had seemed happy with Schlatter's team—but it was later rumored that Kingsrow Productions, Judy's company, was in complete sympathy with this move, feeling the time had come for radical surgery. All this happened before a single segment of *The Judy Garland Show* had been aired.

Norman Jewison, who had produced a successful special for Judy, was called in as executive producer and Gary Smith was promoted to producer.

These changes happened to coincide with a disruption in Judy's private life. She had been seeing a singer called André Phillipe, but that relationship was suddenly over. Taking everything into account, it was decided there should be a production break and Judy flew to New York for a short vacation. When she returned, she had a new beau—Glenn Ford.

224

The first show under the Jewison regime featured June Allyson and Steve Lawrence. The atmosphere on tape day was very relaxed. Judy usually had a glass of chilled Liebfraumilch within reach, and this particular Friday she began drinking early in the day. Miss Allyson seems to have kept pace with her and the taping was very loose—perhaps too loose to make for a really good show. Afterwards there was a Laurel and Hardy fight with a large, frosted cake that had been brought to the studio for Mel Tormé's birthday.

The next show featured another old friend, Donald O'Connor, and this was the first to be aired—on September 29. The reviews were generally good and Judy was thrilled to get a telegram of congratulations from President Kennedy; but the figures showed they had not made much of a dent in *Bonanza*'s rating. (Coincidentally, Judy's first husband, David Rose, was musical director of *Bonanza*.) Almost before the general public was aware of its existence, *The Judy Garland Show* was well on its way to being tagged a failure.

There were some fine individual shows ahead—a marvelous head-to-head encounter with the young Barbra Streisand, two solo concert performances, a Christmas show with her three children—but somehow everyone knew the series was doomed. Further staff changes did little to alleviate the feeling.

Judy began to hold rehearsals at home and there were more and more phone calls summoning staffers to Rockingham Drive in the small hours of the morning. There were tantrums and panics and lost days; on the whole, though, Judy stuck to her chores as well as could be expected. There were no complete disasters and she continued to try to make something of the show long after she might have been expected to give up all hope.

Immediately before Christmas she broke up with Glenn Ford, ending a relationship that had briefly promised something approaching stability. That split, however, was eclipsed by an event that had happened less than a month earlier—the assassination of John F. Kennedy. Predictably, Judy was shattered by the news.

She had identified with the President. He represented politics at a level that she could understand—the President as star. His career had followed a scenario the M-G-M publicity department could not have improved on.

When she pulled herself together, she announced that she wanted her next broadcast to be based on a medley of American patriotic songs. The idea struck everyone on the production staff as very fitting, but the network vetoed it, arguing that the public had had enough of the assassination without being reminded of it in music. They were counting on Judy to provide a show that would signify the return to business as usual. She was hurt and angry and found it impossible to forgive CBS for this decision.

Later, when the assassination was safely behind everyone, the network did allow her to put on a show similar in concept to her earlier idea. Meanwhile, less than a month after the President's death, she secretly slipped in a blood-curdling rendition of "The Battle Hymn of the Republic"—an effective tribute to the man she considered a friend.

Some of Judy's best performances were toward the end of the series, but by then everything was coming apart. When she brought pianist-arranger Bobby Cole in from New York, it led to friction with Mel Tormé, who eventually left the show feeling slighted. The circumstances led to a court case. There were other legal proceedings and the good will that had existed at one time was gradually eroded. In the end the Judy Garland television series just petered out. The final taping, on March 13, 1964, was truncated by the star's inability to face the studio audience for the last time. A segment from an earlier show had to be spliced into the air tape to complete the hour.

Commercially, the show had not been a success, and emotionally it had put a tremendous strain on Judy. Yet we have reason to be thankful she had this opportunity to work on television since it left us a remarkable record of the way she worked when she was unencumbered by the paraphernalia of movie plot and situation.

Chapter 3
Swan Songs

Judy had a little more than five years to live, and the television series was the last sustained effort of her career—the last project that commanded her interest, even spasmodically, for any length of time. Until now, she had always had enough vitality to give her career a definite momentum, a semblance of direction, however erratic. Now what energy she had left was absorbed in neutralizing her day-to-day problems and she began to drift. Her life became increasingly confused and chaotic.

Much of her confusion derived from her chronic and crippling shortage of money. Over the years she had made millions, but somehow she had managed to stay broke almost the whole time. The enormous sums of cash that had flowed, however erratically, through her bank accounts had destroyed her sense of reality concerning her purchasing power. During Judy's prime, her talent had been so lavishly rewarded that she came to think of it as being readily convertible into material

goods. Even when she was heavily in debt and being hounded by the tax authorities, she could not conceive of denying herself the comforts to which she was accustomed, and this created some very serious problems.

At times not a supermarket within a couple of miles of Rockingham Drive would extend credit to Judy Garland, and local pharmacies refused to make up her prescriptions because her bills had not been paid for over a year. So she would hoard the prescriptions, and she would try to get by without the pills for a few days; then she would panic at four in the morning and some unfortunate friend would be sent to scour the city for an all-night drugstore.

She always managed to hang on to a staff at the house, but often these people were living off their savings—bound to Judy by her extraordinary personal magnetism. She still went on occasional eating jags. Loving potatoes, she would order a large bowl of potato salad to be waiting for her when she returned late. In the crunch, however, pills usually won out over

At the Palace, 1967.

food. Having developed an amazing level of tolerance, she would gobble down handfuls of pills, terrifying witnesses not familiar with the extent of her habit. Sometimes there were phony suicide attempts, calculated to keep people on their toes. Liza Minnelli, quoted by Tom Burke in *Rolling Stone,* recalled these episodes with something that resembles affection since, given the passage of time, they came to seem like moments in some bizarre comedy she had once been privileged to play in:

Life with her was theater of the absurd. When I was a little kid, she started locking herself in the bathroom, announcing that she was going to OD, and I soon discovered that what she'd done was empty half an aspirin bottle into the john. I once took some big shears and cut through the screen and climbed in, and that's what she'd done. All she wanted was attention.

But the problem was that her appetite for attention varied in its intensity. Sometimes Judy would be satisfied with opera buffa, but there was no telling when she would try to pull the real thing and her actual suicide attempts lent a good deal of dramatic suspense to the playacting. It also led to extreme caution among members of her household. They would secretly empty Nembutal capsules and replace the contents with glucose or some other nontoxic substance. The stomach pump was a familiar instrument to people close to Judy Garland.

Yet through all these crises she managed to generate the same high intensity of love and affection as always, and it was this which saved her, since her friends and family returned it in kind. There were any number of blowups when Judy became intolerably demanding, but they would evaporate as suddenly as they materialized. At times Liza must have felt that she was Judy's mother. A catalogue of Judy's fits and breakdowns would demand a volume to itself.

Judy's first major endeavor after the termination of her television series was a tour of Australia and the Far East, which turned out to be an exercise in futility, near-catastrophe and rampant misunderstanding.

Although the tour was arranged by Fields and Begelman, neither of them accompanied her. Instead her intimate in the traveling entourage—the man who would bear the brunt of keeping Judy amused and on the rails—was Mark Herron, a young actor who had become one of the courtiers (halfway between friends and fans) who were in regular attendance at the house on Rockingham Drive. The tone of social gatherings at Judy's Petit Trianon was sometimes rather shrill and Herron seems to have distinguished himself by striking a comparatively gentle note. He was amusing, but he did not grate. Judy became attached to him during the final weeks of the CBS series and he seemed a natural choice for her companion on this tour. He could hardly have bargained for the consequences.

Like the British, the Australians were longtime Garland fans, but they did expect value for money and Judy was not in good shape. In Melbourne her concert was a disaster. Though her voice gave out, she stood there for forty-five minutes trying to salvage a performance from the wreckage. The fans felt they had been cheated and booed her. She stormed off the stage in a fury.

The following day Mark Herron's picture was seen in newspapers around the world. Looking somewhat haggard, he was shown escorting Judy—herself on the point of hysteria—to an airplane to fly out of Melbourne. Overnight he became a name for the columnists to toy with.

Shortly after this incident, Judy and Herron arrived in Hong Kong. Almost at once she was in the hospital again. This time the ailment was reported as a heart attack, but some people thought it was a breakdown. Others said it was an overdose, and there were those who insisted she had tried to slash her throat again. It seems, in fact, that her throat was injured when her stomach was pumped after an overdose.

By this time, though, there had been so many flirtations with death—deliberate and accidental, real and imaginary—that it hardly

With Mark Herron at the London airport.

mattered which, if any, of these explanations was the true one.

While Judy was in the hospital Mark Herron was hounded by photographers and reporters. At the Hilton one evening he found the press waiting for him in the lobby and, before they spotted him, dodged into a dining room where two young Australians—known professionally as the Allen Brothers—were entertaining. Herron stayed through their performance and told them afterward he was sure Judy would love their act and promised to bring her over as soon as she was released from the hospital. The young Australians were perhaps less impressed than they might have been, knowing nothing about Judy beyond what they had read in the papers.

The following day Herron told Judy about the Allen Brothers, and she—annoyed that Herron had been out on the town while she was stuck in a hospital bed—tried to have herself discharged immediately. A few days later, she accompanied Herron to the Hilton (causing something of a stir since rumors had it she was at death's door). As Herron had guessed, Judy was indeed very taken with the Allen Brothers, especially with Peter Allen, who recalls that she made it clear she had no intention of ending the evening when their scheduled performance was over:

When she'd heard the act, she said, "You're the greatest thing since Fred Astaire. . . . Where can we go?" I said, "There are after-hour places [in Kowloon] where you can get a beer, play pool. . . ." So we went over on a ferry, and we went to this place and had some drinks, and Judy was playing pool and a man insulted her—accused her of cheating or something—so she hid behind some curtains and threw a pool ball at him and hit him on the head. . . . The man thought Mark Herron had thrown it, because she blamed it immediately on him, so she and Mark had a really big argument. . . . They were almost the first Americans I'd ever met. I thought, "Bizarre people, these Americans. . . ." So, now they weren't speaking, and the only way back to Hong Kong—because all the ferries had

stopped—was to hire a little man to row us back. Judy sat at one end of the boat and Mark sat at the other and I sat in between and the little man rowed, and Judy said to me, "You're a singer—sing." I said, "I can't, I have to have my brother here, I only know harmonies." She said, "No. You must sing." So I sang. She said, "You're a wonderful singer." I thought she was quite crazy, but she made the man row round and round in the harbor while I sang to them till she and Mark finally made up.

This was the first of a number of battles in which Peter Allen found himself acting as go-between, and the first of a number of low-life expeditions. Another incident he recalls occurred when they were driving back from Victoria Peak one day:

She and Mark had a fight. . . . He was talking about acting [saying that he wouldn't take such and such a part, suggesting it was beneath him], and she said, "You don't know anything about acting . . . [what counts is] a part that entertains people." She stopped the car and rolled down the windows, and people started crowding round—none of them spoke English—and she said, "That's when you know. . . . That's it. . . . When people in Hong Kong recognize you. . . . That's acting. . . . This is my audience. . . ."

When she had completely recuperated, Judy and Mark Herron, along with Peter Allen and his stage brother, took a President Lines boat to Japan, where the Allen Brothers had a booking at the Tokyo Hilton. Somewhere along the way Judy jokingly signed an autograph, "Judy Garland: Mrs. Mark Herron," and by the time they boarded the boat for Japan the rumors this provoked had swelled to banners saying "Welcome Mr. and Mrs. Herron." When members of the press asked about this, Judy told them they had been married by the captain of a German freighter. Herron, in the meantime, insisted they had been joined in a Buddhist ceremony.

Back in the United States, Judy's representatives and friends did their best to pour cold water on this story, pointing out that she was not yet divorced from Sid Luft. This did nothing to discourage newsmen, who simply invented a Mexican divorce to overcome these objections.

In the midst of Judy's Far East tour her sister Suzanne took her own life in Las Vegas. After her marriage to Lee Cahn broke up, she had married another musician, Jack Cathcart—the same Jack Cathcart who had given the Gumm Sisters the call that brought them their break at the Oriental Theater in Chicago. Cathcart had become musical director at the Riviera in Vegas, but his marriage to Sue had ended in divorce and he married a younger woman. Sue had taken overdoses of Nembutal on several occasions and finally succeeded in killing herself. Shortly after this happened, Virginia spoke to Lloyd Shearer about it:

It was a sordid domestic mess. Living in Las Vegas, that's not a particularly tranquil atmosphere—the gambling, the girls, the temptations. When Jack and Sue obtained a divorce—that was the end for her. She went the sleeping pill routine. Somehow the Garland females can't stand loss of love.

Judy did not make any great public display of emotion over this loss, but there is reason to think she took it badly. It seems that Sue had called Judy several times at the time of the divorce, looking for help, but Judy—in far from great shape herself—had not always been able to offer much in the way of practical support, though she had rushed to Sue's side at the time of an earlier suicide attempt. Her relationship with Sue had had its ups and downs, but Sue had always managed to keep it alive. Virginia, by this time, had broken with Judy because of Judy's treatment of their mother, but she remembers that Sue struggled to get along with their sister:

I couldn't be around Judy any more . . . because she'd destroy your life if you let her.
I always felt sorry for Susie, because Susie was so vulnerable to Judy. She treated her like she was her child—and in later years Judy did awful things to Susie. She'd have her phone

number changed and not tell Susie. Judy would do really devastating things, things there's no explanation for.

Sue had always tried to stay close to Judy's children and this, Virginia recalls, led to some bizarre situations:

Judy flipped, one time—she was mad at Sid —and had her will rewritten and left the children to Susie. Susie was panicked. She called me and asked, "What am I going to do?" It was the craziest thing.

November of that same year found Judy in London again, performing at the Palladium—this time with Liza. Judy was not in the best of voice, but her concerts were a box-office success. Then, during the next several months,

With Mark Herron.

231

she played a number of engagements in the United States, sometimes concerts and sometimes cabaret dates.

The Allen Brothers were now opening the show for her. Judy had been very anxious for Liza to meet Peter Allen, and practically pushed them together when they arrived simultaneously in London. Initially they recoiled from the prompting, but later struck up a relationship on their own, and eventually, in March of 1967, they were married. Meanwhile, in November, 1965, Judy's divorce from Sid Luft became final and she married Mark Herron.

Within six months they had separated. It happened as though marriage and separation were part of the same act; as if the relationship had been formalized just so it could be broken. As Judy told the story, Herron simply went away without bothering to leave a forwarding address. In her eyes this was just another in a long line of desertions. When she spoke about her marriages, a few months later, in an interview she gave John Gruen for the New York *World-Journal-Tribune*, her attitude toward Herron was somewhat harsh:

Let me tell you, legends are all very well if you've got somebody around who loves you, some man who's not afraid to be in love with Judy Garland.

I mean, I'm not in the munitions business! Why should I always be rejected? All right, so I'm Judy Garland. But I've been Judy Garland forever. Luft always knew this, and Minnelli knew it, and Mark Herron knew it, although Herron married me strictly for business reasons, for purposes of his own. He was not kind to me.

But I bear them no malice, Sid Luft turned out to be a nice man, after all, and Vincente is also very nice.

The slightly hysterical tone of this—"All right, so I'm Judy Garland"—should be taken into account when we consider these remarks. There's no reason to believe her when she says that Herron married her "strictly for business reasons." Rather he seems to have been caught up in a grotesque parody of *The Wizard of Oz,*

in which he was Dorothy snatched up by the whirlwind of Judy's life. If he chose to escape back to his equivalent of Kansas, who could blame him?

The year 1965 was not one of Judy's best, but she was invited to sing at the Academy Awards presentations, which were to be produced by her old friends Arthur Freed and Roger Edens. Another M-G-M alumnus, John Green, was musical director and he expressed grave concern when he saw the extended and elaborate medley Edens had prepared for Judy. He told the producers they were making a mistake, that she could not handle this kind of routine any more. Freed and Edens told Green he was wrong, insisting that Judy was in an upswing and that her voice was in fine shape. With considerable trepidation, Green agreed to hear Judy run through the routine and was agreeably surprised to find that she did indeed seem quite healthy and in good voice. He was still a little worried, however, and prevailed on Edens to shorten the medley somewhat. Even in its abbreviated form, it was a very challenging number and could lead to disaster if Judy was even a trifle unsure of herself.

By the time of the Awards Judy was a total wreck. She could play "I am Judy Garland" for the press and her doting admirers with her eyes closed, but tonight she would be performing for her peers—and she would have to prove to them that she was indeed still Judy Garland. Onstage she was terrible. In the orchestra pit John Green was in tears.

Before long, however, Hollywood decided to take a chance on her again, this time for the film version of *Valley of the Dolls,* based on Jacqueline Susann's novel which featured a character— Neely O'Hara—supposedly modeled on Judy Garland. Judy was too old for

232

that part (it went to Patty Duke), but the producers wanted her for the role of Helen Lawson, a middle-aged Broadway star with the temperament of a Patton tank.

Judy was grateful for this opportunity, yet in a way she resented it. After all, *Valley of the Dolls* did paint a very unflattering picture of a young woman who was supposed to be her own earlier self, and the producers were obviously hoping to capitalize upon the fact that the public associated Judy with the world of pills that was the subject of the picture. She was, in fact, being exploited again.

Her part involved only a few weeks' work, and at first there was no serious problem. The wardrobe tests show her looking well and joking with the crew, but soon the stories began to leak out. People said she would arrive at the studio on time but would stay in her trailer till noon and there were rumors that she was at odds with various members of the company—notably Patty Duke—so it was no real surprise when Fox announced that Judy was no longer in the picture and had been replaced by Susan Hayward.

It seems that the crisis arose largely because Judy did not feel she was being treated with proper respect. Publicly, she claimed that the press had her walking off the set before the set was even built, telling Jerry Tallmer of the *New York Post*:

I didn't give the producers of *Valley of the Dolls* complications. They had lots of complications, in that they were shooting for the foreign market at the same time. It was a political thing—and I always get caught in the switches. *The Wizard of Oz* took a year and a half to shoot—nobody ever brings that out.

I was hired, everybody seemed happy, I showed up every day on time. Nobody knows what happened. I've still got the dressing room key.... I think they were a bit untidy. I think it was Darryl Zanuck's son trying to be like Louis Mayer.

Neither Judy nor the press dwelt on *Valley of the Dolls* because that episode was just one of many disasters. The voice crack-up in Aus-tralia was matched by others in Cincinnati, Toronto and Mexico City. There was litigation involving the management of a Long Island nightclub. There had been a season at the Greek Theater in Los Angeles which saw Judy break her arm after the first performance (the press was told she had fallen over her dog). She threatened to cancel the second concert but was persuaded to appear with the assistance of Mickey Rooney, Martha Raye and Johnny Mathis. A good deal of liquor was consumed backstage, which fanned the bad feelings that were triggered when it was suggested Mathis was hogging the stage. Dizzy from the effect of painkillers, Judy could hardly walk and the concert degenerated into a shambles. Only Rooney's touching solicitude—his evident affection and concern for Judy as he steered her through the performance—saved the evening from ending in a riot.

The rest of the week's engagement was canceled. Fans stoned the box office.

Almost every month some new injury or illness was reported. Pleurisy. Nervous breakdown. Wrist injury. Abdominal pains. Emotional upset. Allergic reaction. If only half the reports were true, it would be difficult to imagine how she could remain alive.

And always there was the pressing need for money. In April, 1967, while in New York, she was told of the foreclosure on her California home, which had been the last symbol of material security in her life. Talking to John Gruen, she said, "In a way I'm glad they've taken the house. It's too big, too impractical. Besides, the man who lived there before didn't love his wife."

For the next couple of years, she would be based chiefly in New York, living in a variety of hotel suites and rented or borrowed apartments. At one point she spent three weeks sleeping on the floor of an apartment belonging to some young friends of Liza.

Later in 1967 Judy was temporarily reconciled with Sid Luft, which led to a series of appearances with Luft acting as her manager once more. In June she performed successfully at the Westbury Music Fair on Long Island, an engagement that was enthusiastically reviewed by John S. Wilson in *The New York Times*:

And then finally she came running down an aisle, behind a flying wedge of burly young men and burst out into the gleaming light of the stage. . . .
Her voice was tight and husky at first. But, as she went along, she seemed to shake it loose by the sheer energy of her singing. She stayed safely within a modest range until she reached the end of "Almost Like Being in Love." Then she reached back for one of her old familiar climaxes—and she found it, all of it.

In August she was booked into the Palace for a four-week run, her act this time featuring spots by Lorna and Joey. She was nervous before the opening (she was living on Dexamils) and at one point locked herself in her hotel room, refusing to let anyone—including her children—see her. Somehow Luft managed to handle the situation and get Judy into reasonable shape in time for her first night.

Judy could create a crisis out of thin air, but Luft was usually more successful than others in protecting her from herself, and in steering her away from obvious dangers. He could not make her drug problem disappear, but he did manage to ration her intake of pills.

The season at the Palace did not receive quite the critical raves of some of her earlier appearances there—there were critics who thought it a trifle hokey for Judy to bring her obviously inexperienced children onstage—but the reception was generally warm and the feeling most commonly expressed was that Judy had pulled off another miracle, rising from the dead yet again.

Once she was back into the routine of nightly performances, Judy began to relax and enjoy herself. During much of her later career she was petrified before she went onstage, and there were times when she was impossible to be with when she came off. After some of her finest performances she would go into tremendous depressions, as if all her vitality had been sapped by her confrontation with the audience. At the Palace, this time around, she managed

to hold back some energy so that, after the show, she could spend time happily with the children or eat a pleasant supper with Bobby Cole, now her conductor, and his wife—Luft taking care to see she did not overtax herself.

After the Palace there was a summer-long tour of major cities, Lorna and Joey traveling and appearing with Judy. At the end of this tour the reconciliation with Sid Luft fell apart and Judy began to go to pieces again. She had contracted to make some appearances at the Garden State Arts Center in New Jersey, and went through with them despite the fact that she was on the point of collapse. The engagement was a disaster, at one concert she appeared to go to sleep onstage.

At this point in her career, audiences had come to expect such things, but still they came to hear her. It's been suggested that Judy's audiences were sick—that they came in the hope of seeing her disintegrate before their eyes. Some people have argued that even the adulation displayed toward her was unhealthy. Undoubtedly there is some truth to this, but ultimately it is too simplistic and cynical to provide a satisfactory explanation of the whole phenomenon. Certainly many people in the audience identified with Judy because of her problems—as I have said, it was precisely her much publicized vulnerability that made her so accessible to her public. It is nonetheless true that they returned to her faithfully because of her ability to rise from the ashes again and again. Everyone knew, after a certain point in her career, that the periodic collapses were inevitable—it was as if they were coded into every atom of her body—but so, it seemed, were the comebacks. Judy had become, it seemed, for her admirers, a unique natural phenomenon, following a cyclic pattern that was as established as the passage of the seasons or the phases of the moon. She had become a symbol of regeneration.

This cycle could not continue forever, though, and now people began to recognize that this was so. Judy must have been aware of it herself.

After the fiasco of the New Jersey appear-

Onstage at the Palace with Lorna, 1967.

ances, Judy was hospitalized for a while and then went to Boston to recuperate. Joey had returned to California with his father, but Lorna was still on the East Coast, and Judy hoped that she would join her. Although remarkably resilient for a fourteen-year-old, Lorna felt she could no longer handle the pressure and instead decided to rejoin her father and brother.

With Sid Luft and his children vanishing from the picture once more, a hole opened up in Judy's life into which the usual collection of hangers-on and parasites began to pour. One of the banes of her existence was that her volatile blend of dynamism and vulnerability had a fatal attraction for a whole multitude of emotional cripples. She would patronize these people, treat them abominably—but often that was exactly what they were looking for and they would worm their way into her life. There were real friends too, of course, like Kay Thompson, and Liza was generally at hand when she was really needed, but they could not be with Judy twenty-four hours a day. Yet if they were not at her every beck and call, she was apt to interpret it as another betrayal. On one occasion she threatened to bill Liza for every penny she had cost since the day she was conceived—a figure which, according to Judy's estimate, amounted to several million dollars. This rage was over as suddenly as it started, and Judy—laughing as usual at her own absurdity—tried to compensate for her explosion by half-drowning her daughter with desperate affection.

Judy would call people at two and three in the morning, demanding immediate attention, pleading and cajoling: "If you love me as much as you say you do, you'll drop everything and come running over when I tell you I need you." She would throw spine-chilling scenes on the phone—sometimes for real, but more often as a kind of demented practical joke, testing a friend's loyalty by seeing if he or she would rush to her aid.

Temper tantrums could be triggered by an innocent remark and Judy began to manufacture grudges. Even her fans—who until now had been virtually sacrosanct—were not al-

Judy's final night at the Palace, 1967.

237

ways certain of a welcome. Told, on one occasion, that a fourteen-year-old had hitchhiked from Chicago just to shake hands with her, Judy expressed complete indifference and refused to see the girl.

Yet there were still days when she was as bright and witty as ever, days when she could light up a room with her humor, whether improvising some piece of instant mythology around the figure of Louis B. Mayer, or describing Robert Goulet as an eight-by-ten glossy. Her memory, at times, was still the startling instrument that had served her so well in her movie days. She could be introduced to someone she had met, briefly, months earlier, and be able to tell him exactly what he had been wearing on that earlier occasion, down to the last detail. Yet at other times her memory was treacherous, distorted by paranoia, and led her to accuse innocent friends of all kinds of imagined crimes against her.

Judy talks with a detective after accusing Tom Green of theft.

Her behavior in this penultimate phase of her life was so erratic that it's easy to believe that her excesses—a particular overdose or perhaps the cumulative effect of many things —may have caused some kind of brain damage. We are no longer talking about someone who is driven to bizarre behavior by the circumstances of her life; we are talking about someone who at times was probably certifiably insane. Only her extraordinary charisma prevented people from admitting that to themselves. At times her madness had a heroic, Shakespearean dimension. At other times it was simply pathetic.

Her paranoia sometimes led to very ugly situations. One notorious incident involved a young man named Tom Green, a publicist with whom Judy had been romantically involved, on and off, since the breakup of her marriage to Mark Herron. She and Green announced their engagement and she had been welcomed by his family in Massachusetts. His relatives had even lent Judy money. Despite these loans, she was always short of cash and—over a considerable period of time—had given Green most of her jewelry with orders to pawn it. (He also either pawned or sold many of his own belongings in an attempt to pay off Judy's debts.) One day, without warning, Judy announced to the world that Tom Green had stolen her jewels and she had him arrested. He spent some time in the Tombs before a friend bailed him out.

This was not the end of the episode. Ordered by his lawyers to stay away from Judy, Green could not escape her telephone calls and eventually, moved by her pleas for forgiveness, sent her a conciliatory note. She called to thank him and said she would be sending something over for him—a present. When the package arrived, Green opened it to discover a toy animal he had once given Judy, mutilated and smeared with blood. A few months later he and Judy were friends once more, though Green did not attempt to put their relationship back on its previous footing.

Judy seems to have forgotten each crisis as soon as it passed—her ferocious day-to-day

238

struggle did not allow for remorse or reflection. She was too busy moving from one mood to the next, indulging each whim as if she sensed there was not much time left. It was not unheard of for her to be discovered, at two in the morning, playing eight-ball in some pool hall on Forty-second Street—dressed in an evening gown and cheerfully oblivious to the drunks asleep in the corner, but agreeably conscious of the stir she was causing. She took a childlike delight in this kind of thing, although sometimes her behavior was more childish than childlike. She loved to disrupt dinner parties by indulging in food fights. In a rented house she once used a valuable painting as a dart board.

During this often unhappy period she visited Mexico where, by chance, she happened to cross the path of her old friend Jackie Cooper. It was not a pleasant reunion. Cooper, vacationing with his wife in Acapulco, was told Judy would be coming into his hotel, but did not see her when she first arrived:

They gave Judy the best and biggest bungalow they had, with the biggest pool.... The next day I got a telephone call at about three o'clock in the morning, from the manager. He said, "Judy is in front of her bungalow, using a lot of bad language and drinking and throwing glasses into her pool and into other people's pools. Would you— can you—do anything?"

I felt badly and said, "Let me try to talk to her on the phone." But she wasn't answering the telephone and finally my wife got them to send somebody up there to tell her I was on the phone. I talked to her for about twenty minutes, and that was the first time I heard a little old lady speaking and saying, "Jackie, we can't be treated like this, after what we've been through and given to this industry...."

Talking to her, he remembers, was like talking to a wall. His wife took over for a while and eventually Judy calmed down to some extent. She thanked them both for their kindness and patience. This state of affairs did not last long, however. Before dawn another call informed

Cooper that Judy had started up again and the manager asked Cooper, as a personal favor, to go into Judy's bungalow and try to quiet her down. (The young man she was traveling with, a hairdresser, had apparently shut himself in his own quarters and was doing his utmost to pretend that nothing was happening.) Cooper and his wife went to Judy's bungalow and sat her down on the bed and talked to her until ten o'clock in the morning, at which time Judy finally fell asleep. By one that afternoon she was awake again and ordering drinks. The manager asked her to leave. She refused. Eventually the management had her bags moved to another hotel.

Judy seems to have taken this in her stride and stayed on in Acapulco for a while longer. The Coopers encountered her there one more time:

About four or five days after that, we saw her in a very nice restaurant, with about five people ... local citizens ... boys ... the oldest couldn't have been more than twenty years old. And she was paying the check and they were ordering lots of food and booze.... And I couldn't bring myself to go over there and do anything.... There wasn't anything to do.

It was the last time Jackie Cooper ever saw Judy Garland.

In 1968 Judy had another brief stay in Peter Bent Brigham hospital (she had come to look on the doctors and nurses there as practically an extension of her family), and then there was an unpleasant, heavily-publicized incident in which she was thrown out of the St. Moritz Hotel in New York, where she had been living. It was reported that she had run up a bill of $1,800, and had left three eight-week-old kittens in a double-locked

239

room filled with costumes and gowns which the hotel refused to surrender until Judy settled with them in full. Sid Luft told columnist Earl Wilson that he had personally paid for Judy's room until the previous week and added that some of the costumes were being held by Tom Green's lawyers, who claimed that Judy owed them money.

Judy was no longer welcome everywhere. Increasingly she confined herself to places where she was sure she would find friendly faces. One favorite spot was Sybil Burton Christopher's fashionable discotheque Arthur, where Judy was always certain of a warm greeting. It was here that she struck up a friendship with a young man named Mickey Deans, a former singer and pianist who had become Arthur's night manager. At a time when Judy was often the butt of rudeness, Deans treated her like a lady. He took her complaints seriously, and he made her laugh. Over a period of close to three years she got to know him well without any real relationship developing. Then, quite without warning, the world was told that Judy and Mickey Deans were to be married. In his book, *Weep No More My Lady,* Deans described the announcement as follows:

There was a party for Merv [Griffin] at Arthur, and [Judy and I] arrived rather late, obviously bursting with a secret.

"Shall we tell them?" Judy asked with a giggle.

Just then Earl Wilson telephoned, and John Springer, Judy's press representative, went to talk to him.

"Why don't you come over, Earl?" He suggested. "I think Judy and Mickey have something to tell you."

John Springer remembers the incident a little differently: Earl Wilson phoned to find out what was happening at the party, and when Springer asked if anyone had any tidbit to pass on, Judy told him to tell Wilson that she was going to marry Deans. Springer laughed and told Wilson Judy said she was going to marry the maître d'. Annoyed, Judy took the phone

Judy and Mickey Deans in London, leaving the Ritz Hotel.

240

and told Wilson that she was not joking, and that he should go ahead and print the story. Springer thought Deans seemed as surprised as anyone there.

Desperately in need of money, Judy had signed for a season in London at the Talk of the Town. She and Deans flew to England, where she was given the usual fanatical welcome. She was also served with papers that claimed that her contract now belonged to a Mr. Howard Harper and a Mr. Leon J. Greenspan. Apparently it had been assigned to them by Sid Luft to secure a loan. Judy had never heard of either Harper or Greenspan and the matter was taken to court. The British judge settled in Judy's favor and she was given the go-ahead to appear at the Talk of the Town.

Her five-week season there was a qualified success. Some nights she was a little lackadaisical, but usually she managed to spark enough life and humor to send the customers away satisfied. There were nights when she was close to her best, and others when she was definitely below par. Only one evening was really bad. She arrived ninety minutes late and when she stepped onstage some patrons responded by throwing bread sticks. This incident drew so much attention from the press, that the impression was given that her entire engagement at the Talk of the Town had been marred by similar episodes.

Judy and Deans had been living at the Ritz. Deciding to stay on in London, they leased a mews cottage on Cadogan Lane and, on March 15, 1969, they were married.

This, at least, was the civil ceremony. Deans' book mentions a secret ceremony conducted in the small hours of the morning, two months previously, by an unnamed priest in "an ancient church":

We had neglected to buy a ring and were in a sudden panic. But the young priest, knowing the circumstances . . . and touched by our needs and love, had brought his grandmother's wedding band. . . .

There at the altar, lit by flickering candles and feeling infinitesimal in this cavernous

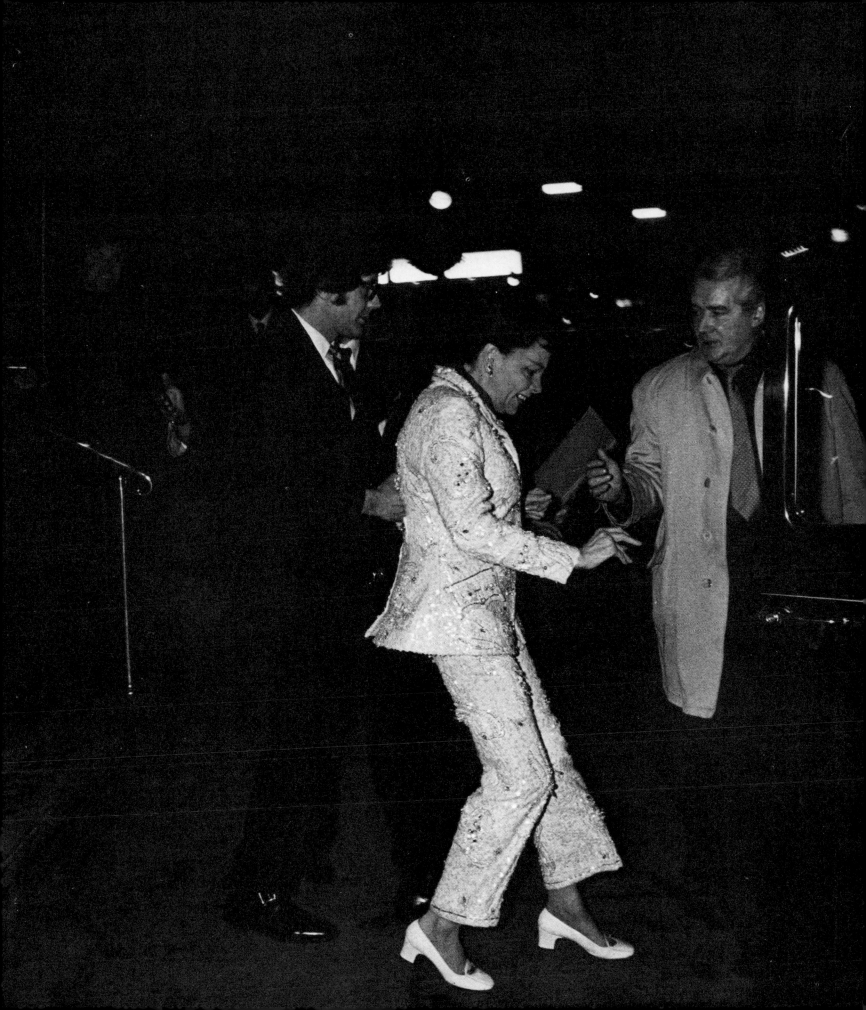

gloom, we were married. We shared a glass of sacramental wine with the priest. . . .

Deans admits there were no witnesses present, so one cannot think this was anything more than a piece of theater designed to set Judy's mind at rest (it recalls a scene in *The Clock* when Judy and Robert Walker enter a church to wash away the memory of the impersonal civil ceremony they have just undergone).

The March 15 marriage was conducted at Chelsea Registry Office with Johnny Ray as best man. Deans had planned a big reception at Quaglino's—a bad miscalculation, as it turned out, since few of Judy's London friends showed up, and everything had been done at such short notice that her American friends did not have time to make arrangements to be there. Even her children were absent.

As usual, Judy put on a brave face but pictures taken that day show her looking rather forlorn and lost in her oddly inappropriate Carnaby Street mod clothes.

A brief honeymoon in Paris was followed by a short Scandinavian tour, with Johnny Ray, and another rash of problems. First, Deans discovered that an attempt was being made to produce a pirate recording of one of the concerts, then an accidental barbiturate overdose led to the cancellation of another performance, and this in turn led to irritating business problems. At the conclusion of this short tour Judy and her husband flew to the south of Spain to continue their honeymoon. While there, she began to hallucinate, probably as a result of amphetamine withdrawal. While abroad, Judy had run out of her usual pills and had not been able to replace them. Deans got her onto a London-bound plane and—with Judy still hallucinating—they returned to England. Back at their mews cottage, a doctor gave her tranquilizers and, after sleeping for several hours, she awoke not remembering anything that had happened.

When Judy recovered from this episode she looked pathetically fragile. She was thinner than she had ever been before, and her skin was beginning to take on a white, transparent look. Her moods were as fluid as ever. One day she would be planning for her future career, announcing that she wanted to do a concert in Paris, and the next she would say that she wanted nothing but the chance to become an English housewife.

When she visited New York that spring some of her old friends had the impression that she had succeeded in this last ambition. They were amused to find Judy Garland boasting about her cleverness at finding various garments for next to nothing on sale. Could this be the Judy Garland who had always spent money so recklessly, even when there was none to spend? The idea of her seeking out bargains at Peter Jones or Selfridges was incredible. But though she went on one extravagant shopping spree while she was in New York—an echo of old times—she did seem to have slowed down.

When she had been sick in the fifties, and looked twice her real age, she always gave the impression that she would somehow pull out of her slump and return to peak form because the energy was still there, just below the surface. And she did it, time and again. But now the energy was running low. Before, with all her problems, she had always been a fighter. Now, except in flashes, her will to fight was gone. Finally, all she asked for was peace and quiet—the very state she'd been running away from all her life.

Back in London, she seemed frailer than ever. She hardly ate. Matthew West, her London press agent, saw her almost every day and remembers that she had to be coaxed into eating. He would try to tempt her by preparing meals that would titillate her visually—arranging a fruit salad into an amusing pattern—but even then she would seldom take more than a few bites. If she was not reminded, she would simply forget to eat. At times, she almost forgot to breathe—suddenly taking a great gulp of air, like someone surfacing from a deep dive.

But there were still gay moments. West tells of an occasion when he and Deans were wait-

242

ing downstairs for Judy, who was dressing for dinner, and they put her Carnegie Hall album on the record player. Descending the stairs a few minutes later, Judy paused dramatically and gasped, "God, who *is* that woman? She is *fantastic*!" (Judy never tired of listening to her own records. Before concerts, she would sometimes play one of her old albums—listening intently, as if she might learn something from it.)

She went out less and less, spending much of her time reading. At around the time of her forty-seventh birthday she was engrossed in the popular study of the Romanoffs, *Nicholas and Alexandra*. With her celebrity's fear of loss of identity, she empathized with the woman who claimed to be the Czar's daughter, Anastasia —"Supposing she really *is* Anastasia and nobody will admit it?" The notion horrified her.

She toyed with the idea of converting to Catholicism. This may have been prompted by the fact that her husband had been brought up in the Catholic Church, but it is also possible that she sensed she was moving toward the end and was looking for some kind of absolution.

On June 20, 1969, Judy was in excellent spirits and seemed to have found some new reserve of energy. She told Matthew West she wanted to go back to work. Looking at her skinny arms, she announced that she would have to put some weight on and build up her strength. With Judy in a very lighthearted mood, the two of them lunched on doughnuts and milk.

That evening she and Deans went to a dinner party celebrating the birthday of their friend Father Peter Delaney. She seemed happy but asked Deans to take her home early and had difficulty sleeping.

The following day, a Saturday, Judy and her husband stayed at home. They were scheduled to go to the theater that evening—Matthew West had tickets for Danny LaRue's closing night—but both felt they were coming down with strep throats and decided to take a rain check. West called them during intermission to tell them what a great show they were miss-

ing and to remind them they were going to the country with him the following morning. Judy liked visiting West's cottage, not far from London, and had been looking forward to the trip.

Phillip Roberge, a London theatrical agent, came over and sat with Deans while Judy excused herself and went to the bedroom. She was still awake when her husband came upstairs. It was, in fact, well before midnight and normally she would have stayed awake for hours but with the illness coming on, she took a large dose of sleeping pills and fell asleep.

Deans slept too and did not wake until early the next morning, when he received a transatlantic telephone call. Judy was not in bed and he found the bathroom door locked. He called out to her, but there was no reply. A little worried now, he climbed out onto the roof and peered in through the bathroom window. Judy was seated on the toilet, her arms folded on her lap, her head cradled in her arms. Deans broke in through the window and tried to lift her. She was dead.

The story did not reach the newsstands until Monday morning, but then it was broadcast in banner headlines. The reports were, for the most part, cautiously worded, but the assumption behind virtually all of them was that Judy had deliberately taken her own life.

Some papers carried an unconnected item which noted that, on the day of her death, a tornado had touched down in Kansas.

"Accidental death by an incautious dose of barbiturates" was the verdict brought in at the inquest. The British pathologist, Dr. Derek Pocock, said that the postmortem showed a high level of barbiturates in her blood—high enough to cause death—but added that there was no evidence she had intended to kill herself. In an addendum he remarked there were no signs of alcoholism or cirrhosis of the liver.

When Marilyn Monroe died, Judy had given friends her own explanation of what she believed had probably happened. It was a scenario that all heavy barbiturate users fear. Judy supposed that Marilyn had taken pills to go to sleep, that they had had only a temporary

effect, and when she woke—or half-woke—she took another batch of pills, forgetting how many she had already taken. The cumulative impact of these doses had been enough to kill her.

The Marilyn Monroe autopsy did not bear this out, but Judy's own death seems to have occurred in just this way. The evidence indicated that her bloodstream was already saturated with barbiturates, and that when she awoke in the night—too exhausted to realize how many she had already taken—she took more pills in an effort to get back to sleep. This time she overtaxed her tolerance and the drugs paralyzed her breathing centers. It was an accident that had almost happened dozens of times before.

Judy's body was brought back to New York and placed in Campbell's Funeral Home on Madison Avenue at Eighty-first Street. Twenty-one thousand people filed past the open casket, many of them more than once, while the crowds on the sidewalk played Judy Garland records on portable phonographs until the family asked them to stop.

Jackie Cooper was in town on business, but could not bring himself to join the crowd at Campbell's, did not want to see her under these conditions. He watched the lines from his hotel window and took note of the names of celebrities who were reported to be paying their last respects:

I looked in the papers . . . to see the people I knew didn't know her a bit getting their pictures taken—and a lot of people being very remorseful, people who didn't have anything good to say about her for many years, and who never tried to do anything for her. Many who had done her a lot of harm—if only by ignoring the warning signs—people who had been in a position to help her.

The funeral service was very simple. James Mason delivered the eulogy, then six young men carried the casket out to the strains of "The Battle Hymn of the Republic."

One of those present at the funeral service

245

was Dr. Marcus Rabwin, the only person there who had known Judy from her birth until the end of her life. For the last several years Judy had had very little contact with her sister Virginia, so Dr. Rabwin was her only link with her real past and with her dead parents: He was a man she sought out when she was in serious trouble, when she was reaching the end of her rope. He was someone she trusted, someone she could speak to without hiding behind the curtain of make-believe. On one of her last stays in California, not long before her death, Judy had asked Rabwin, quite out of the blue, if her father had been a homosexual. It was the first time she had ever mentioned it to him.

This was the Judy Garland who had spent much of her life in the company of homosexuals, who was never so much at ease as in their company, who had loved homosexual men and been loved by them. This was the Judy Garland who had joked that when she died the flags would fly at half-mast on Fire Island. Was it possible that—with all this behind her —she was still not fully able to accept the fact of her father's bisexuality. It's evident that she was troubled by this question to the very end, and looked for certainty where none was to be found. Dr. Rabwin could tell her only that he had heard the stories, but could provide no proof one way or the other. It would seem that this uncertainty had remained one of the central terrors of her existence and lay at the core of her identity crisis.

Once Judy was gone, those who had been close to her were finally free to enjoy the memories, without the fear of what might happen next. In *Rolling Stone* Tom Burke quoted Liza's musings on the day of her mother's death:

We traveled with charisma. . . . There were never less than twenty-six pieces of luggage, and I'm talking about *checkable* luggage. The hand stuff, forget it: shopping bags, food bags, medicine bags. I was always in charge of her personal ice bucket, which she *had* to have. It was her firm belief that there would never be anything, ever, in any hotel in the world that she could just order from room service. But I didn't mind, because mother almost always made it fun. You know? She was *truly* one of the *funniest* people I've ever known! A lot of times we had to sneak out of hotels because she was out of bread, and she would make an incredibly funny game of it. We would put on all the clothes we could, about five layers, and just walk out leaving the rest, laughing. Mama'd say, "Oh, hell, I need a new wardrobe anyway." Descending in the elevator, she would assume her very imperious air, she'd whisper. "No problem, always keep in mind, *I am Judy Garland. . . .*"

We find ourselves returning again and again to that statement: "I *am* Judy Garland." She had to prove to the world, and to herself, that she was somebody—without being sure who that somebody was. Only onstage, or in front of a camera, could she escape the dilemma. Her identity was inexorably bound to her ability to perform. This does not make her gifts any the less remarkable. Judy Garland fascinates us because life surged through her with extraordinary intensity and purity, and the force of the torrent must have terrified her at times.

She *was* Judy Garland—but, underneath it all, she was still Baby Gumm. It was as Baby Gumm that she first developed into a performer, and it was as Baby Gumm that this aspect of her personality began to peel away from the rest. Judy Garland was the name she gave to the performer, and she tried to pretend that her old self no longer existed. But Baby Gumm was always there, waiting for her at four in the morning, and all the pills in the world could not blot her out.

This was why there could be no peace.

Baby Gumm knew the truth about Judy Garland.

246

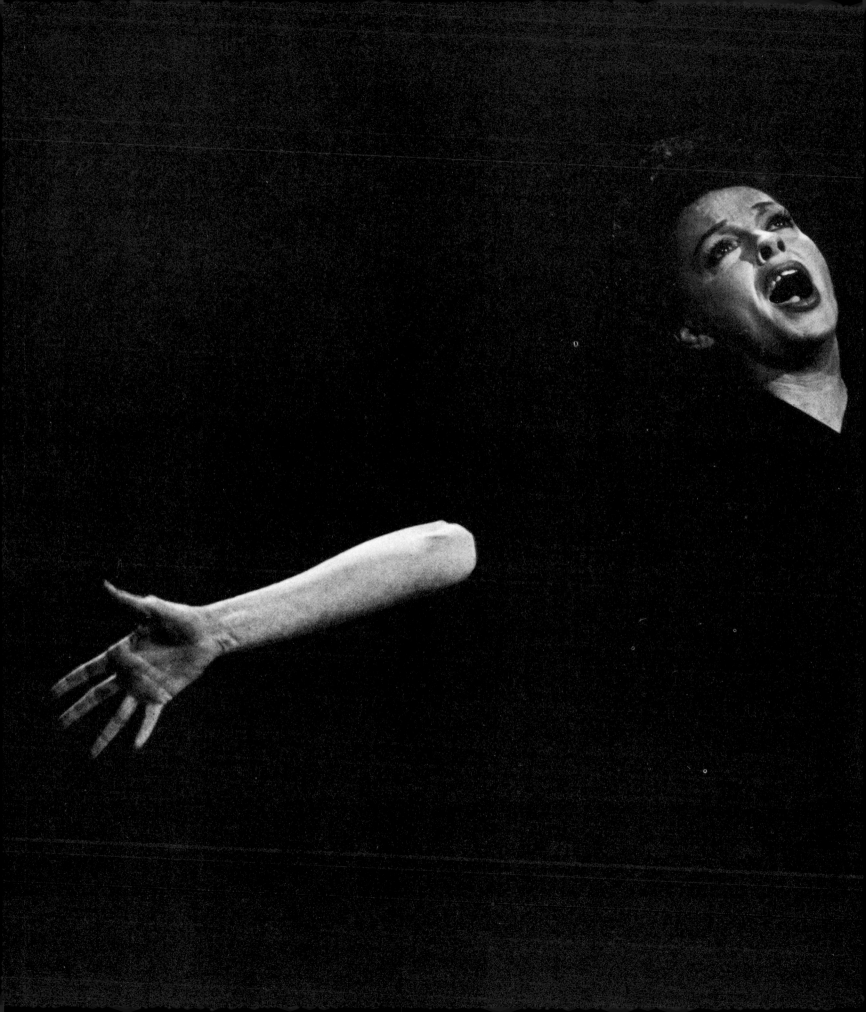

ACKNOWLEDGMENTS

In listings of this kind there is strong precedent for the author to conclude by thanking his wife for her support and patience. I must break with this tradition and begin by thanking my wife, Linda. She gave up several months of her own valuable time to this project—sharing equally in the research, acting as a sounding board for my ideas, and lending her editorial skills and experience to the development of the text that appears here. She suggested the title of the book, and that is indicative of the importance of her contribution to this entire project.

Next, I should like to express special gratitude to Judy's sister, Virginia Thompson, who gave generously of her time and—as is evident, I think—illuminated many previously shadowy corners that have concealed important facts from earlier biographers. She brought to life, for me, events that happened many years ago, and did so with a delicious sense of the absurd, which demonstrated quite clearly that Judy was not the only member of the family who possessed a highly developed sense of humor. My thanks, too, to her husband, John, who added valuable comments of his own, and to his mother, whose hospitality I very much appreciated.

Among others especially close to Judy I should like to single out Vincente Minnelli, Peter Allen, her former son-in-law, and Dr. Marcus Rabwin—a devoted friend and admirer of Judy Garland, and the only person who was close to her from the beginning of her life to the very end.

Thanks are due to a good friend, Tom Jones, now with Walt Disney Productions but formerly at M-G-M, who added to his own valuable reminiscences many introductions and a dozen other kinds of assistance. Thanks, also, to Steve Jeff Harris, whose address book provided other important introductions and whose poolside offered much appreciated opportunities for reflection. The determination of his wife, Judy, to make our months in California as comfortable as possible did a great deal toward easing the problems associated with researching a book of this kind.

Sincere gratitude goes to Bill Chapman who helped in many practical ways, and more importantly, transmitted to me much of his own enthusiasm for Judy Garland, both as a performer and as a person.

Many friends, associates and admirers of Judy, in and around the entertainment industry, took the time to talk with me—some at considerable length—and I should like to thank them here: Jackie Cooper, George Folsey, Gene Kelly, Fred Astaire, Saul Chaplin, Tom Drake, Maurice Kusell, John Green, Joe Pasternak, Jack Cummings, Stanley Kramer, Norman Taurog, Mervyn LeRoy, Buddy Ebsen, Mort Lindsey, George Bassman, Mary Ann Nyberg, Gene Allen, John Springer, Kay Mulvey, Dore Schary, Dore Freeman, Rock

Hudson, Tom Clark, Sally Forrest, Milo Frank, Jack Regas, Bob Schiffer, George Sunga, Jack Elliot, Frank Waldman, Dutch Horton and Matthew West.

Among past and present residents of Grand Rapids, Minnesota, I should like to extend thanks to Marian Latz Kamman, William Kamman, Leo Miller, Mrs. Clifford Miller, Wallace Aiken, Ken Hickman, Kathleen Marok and the staffs of the Grand Rapids Public Library and the Grand Rapids *Herald-Review*.

Residents of Lancaster, California, who assisted me in my research include Harry DuBois, George Taylor, W. M. Redman, Katherine Whittern, Mildred Ward, John Perkins and Doris Vodon. My thanks, too, to W. A. Valentine, George Willey, Suzie Montoya and John Reber of the Antelope Valley *Ledger-Gazette* and to the staff of the Lancaster Public Library.

Others who assisted with information, introductions and in tracing illustrations were Nancy Barr, Bill Gleason, Les Perkins, Peter Hujar, Bob Kushman, Suzanne Weil, Norton Hentz, Jimmy Breem, Wayne Ogle, James Dugdale and Bob and Dorothy Willoughby.

I spent many profitable days at the Doheny Library of the University of California, making use of the extensive movie-related material in the Special Collections, especially the papers left to the library by the late Arthur Freed and the late Roger Edens. Jim Wagner was an extremely helpful and willing guide.

Further research was conducted at the Library of the Academy of Motion Picture Arts and Sciences, at various branches of the Los Angeles and the Santa Monica Public Library systems and at the Lincoln Center Library of the Performing Arts in New York.

It was Margaret L. Kaplan who first suggested that a serious study of Judy Garland would be a worthwhile endeavor, and it was Harry N. Abrams who brought the project to the attention of Harold Roth. Bob Markel has overseen the project in his inimitable way, and Eleanor Potocki, Penny Zug, Lucy Kanson and Susan Kramer have taken care of many important details.

I should like to thank my agent, Betty Anne Clark, for her valuable advice and constant support, and I owe an extraordinary debt of gratitude to Will Hopkins, who has given this book the visual quality and excitement that I had hoped it would have.

Finally, I wish to express special thanks to John Graham who could be described—if this were a more academic field—as a leading Judy Garland scholar. He is a mine of information pertaining to her life and times, and no one has researched her early career as carefully as he. He was generous enough to share much of this research with me and either provided me with or pointed my way to many of the photographs that are reproduced in this volume.

251

PICTURE CREDITS

The publishers are grateful to the following for permission to use the photographs in this book:

Collectors—Bill Chapman, p. 7, p. 51, p. 52, p. 55, p. 58, p. 101, p. 105, pp. 108-109, p. 111, p. 121, p. 147, p. 150, p. 151, pp. 154-55, p. 156, p. 161; Christopher Finch, p. 39, pp. 62-63, p. 102; Lester Glassner, p. 6, p. 10, pp. 18-19, p. 60, p. 71, p. 79, p. 95, p. 100, p. 103, p. 112, pp. 118-19, p. 130, pp. 136-37, p. 153, p. 163 left; Bill Gleason, pp. 2-3, p. 88, p. 89, p. 90, p. 91; John Graham, p. 16, p. 23, p. 25, pp. 30-31, p. 34, p. 43, p. 45, p. 47, p. 48, p. 49, pp. 56-57, p. 59, p. 82, p. 110, p. 124, p. 131, p. 132, p. 134, p. 138, p. 167, p. 247; Leo Miller, p. 22, p. 28, p. 29.

Photographers and Agencies—Burton Berinsky, p. 226, p. 235, pp. 236-37, p. 244; Cornell Capa, Time-Life Picture Agency, copyright Time, Inc., p. 181, p. 183, pp. 184-85; Henri Dauman (Magnum), p. 211; Globe, p. 224, p. 231, p. 241; Tom Hollyman (*St. Louis Post-Dispatch*), pp. 114-15; Maurice Kusell, p. 41; John Loengard, Time-Life Picture Agency, copyright Time, Inc., p. 209, p. 212; Photoworld, Division of Freelance Photographers Guild, Inc., pp. 14-15, p. 172; Sanford Roth (Rapho Guillumette), p. 193; Phil Stern (Globe), p. 202, pp. 204-205, pp. 214-15; United Press International, pp. 8-9, p. 238; John Vachon, p. 187, p. 188, p. 189, pp. 190-91; Wide World Photos, p. 175, p. 229; Leigh Wiener, p. 223, pp. 248-49; Bob Willoughby, pp. 4-5, p. 13, p. 176, p. 195, p. 196, p. 197, pp. 198-99, p. 200, p. 216, pp. 218-19, p. 221.

Metro-Goldwyn-Mayer—Publicity stills and stills from the following copyrighted motion pictures appear through the courtesy of M-G-M: *Andy Hardy Meets Debutante* © 1940 Loew's Incorporated, © renewed 1967 Metro-Goldwyn-Mayer Inc., p. 103; *Annie Get Your Gun* © 1950 Loew's Incorporated, p. 166, p. 167; *Babes in Arms* © 1939 Loew's Incorporated, © renewed 1966 Metro-Goldwyn-Mayer Inc., p. 72, p. 104; *Babes on Broadway* © 1941 Loew's Inc., © renewed 1968 Metro-Goldwyn-Mayer Inc., p. 106 left, pp. 108–109, p. 111; *Broadway Melody of 1938* © 1937 Metro-Goldwyn-Mayer Corporation, © renewed 1964 Metro-Goldwyn-Mayer Inc., pp. 56–57, pp. 76–77; *The Clock* © 1945 Loew's Inc., © renewed 1972 Metro-Goldwyn-Mayer Inc., pp. 144–45; *Easter Parade* © 1948 Loew's Inc., © renewed 1975 Metro-Goldwyn-Mayer Inc., p. 159; *Everybody Sing* © 1938 Loew's Incorporated, © renewed 1965 Metro-Goldwyn-Mayer Inc., p. 78 left; *For Me and My Gal* © 1942 Loew's Inc., © renewed 1969 Metro-Goldwyn-Mayer Inc., p. 116, p. 117; *Girl Crazy* © 1943 Loew's Inc., © renewed 1970 Metro-Goldwyn-Mayer Inc., pp. 118–19, p. 120; *The Harvey Girls* © 1946 Loew's Inc., © renewed 1973 Metro-Goldwyn-Mayer Inc., p. 147; *In the Good Old Summertime* © 1949 Loew's Incorporated, p. 149, p. 163 right, p. 164; *Little Nellie Kelly* © 1940 Loew's Inc., © renewed 1967 Metro-Goldwyn-Mayer Inc., pp. 122–23; *Love Finds Andy Hardy* © 1938 Loew's Incorporated, © renewed 1965 Metro-Goldwyn-Mayer Inc., p. 80; *Meet Me in St. Louis* © 1944 Loew's Inc., © renewed 1974 Metro-Goldwyn-Mayer Inc., p. 130, p. 131, p. 132, p. 133, p. 134, p. 138; *The Pirate* © 1948 Loew's Incorporated, © renewed 1975 Metro-Goldwyn-Mayer Inc., pp. 154–55, p. 156, p. 157; *Presenting Lily Mars* © 1943 Loew's Inc., © renewed 1970 Metro-Goldwyn-Mayer Inc., p. 121; *Summer Stock* © 1950 Loew's Incorporated, p. 169, pp. 170–71; *Thoroughbreds Don't Cry* © 1937 Metro-Goldwyn-Mayer Corporation, © renewed 1964 Metro-Goldwyn-Mayer Inc., p. 78 right; *Till the Clouds Roll By* © 1946 Loew's Incorporated, © renewed 1974 Metro-Goldwyn-Mayer Inc., p. 151, p. 152; *The Wizard of Oz* © 1939 Loew's Incorporated, © renewed 1966 Metro-Goldwyn-Mayer Inc., pp. 2–3, p. 82, pp. 86–87, p. 88, p. 89, p. 90, p. 91, pp. 92–93; *Words and Music* © 1948 Loew's Incorporated, p. 161, p. 162; *Ziegfeld Follies* © 1946 Loew's Inc., © renewed 1973 Metro-Goldwyn-Mayer Inc., p. 139, pp. 140–41; *Ziegfeld Girl* © 1941 Loew's Inc., © renewed 1968 Metro-Goldwyn-Mayer Inc., pp. 106–107.

Metro-Goldwyn-Mayer—Publicity stills on the following pages appear through the courtesy of M-G-M: p. 10, pp. 18–19, p. 67, p. 69, p. 73, pp. 74–75, p. 79, p. 98, p. 101, p. 102, p. 105, p. 110, p. 113 right, p. 142, p. 150.

The photographs on pp. 34 and 48 are from the Garlandia collection of Wayne Martin and are reproduced by special permission.